91
636.1082
005832
92
93
94
96
97
98

RWICKSHIRE COLLEGE

D1587576

WITHDRAWN

Warwickshire College

* 0 0 5 0 0 4 6 8 *

Walers

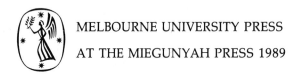
MELBOURNE UNIVERSITY PRESS
AT THE MIEGUNYAH PRESS 1989

Walers

Foreword by Philip Mason, C.I.E., O.B.E.

005832

WARWICKSHIRE COLLEGE
LIBRARY

Class No:
636.1082

Acc No:
00500468

Australian Horses Abroad

A. T. YARWOOD

First published in 1989
Printed in Australia by
Brown Prior Anderson Pty Ltd, Burwood, Victoria, for
Melbourne University Press, Carlton, Victoria 3053
U.S.A. and Canada: International Specialized Book Services, Inc.,
5602 N.E. Hassalo Street, Portland, Oregon 97213-3640
Asia: United Publishers Services Ltd,
Kenkyu-Sha Building, 9 Kanda Surugadai 2-chome, Chiyoda-ku, Tokyo Japan

This book is copyright.
Apart from any fair dealing for the purposes of private study, research, criticism or review,
as permitted under the Copyright Act,
no part may be reproduced by any process without written permission.
Enquiries should be made to the publisher.

© Alexander Turnbull Yarwood 1989

National Library of Australia Cataloguing-in-Publication entry

Yarwood, A. T. (Alexander Turnbull), 1927–   .
  Walers: Australian horses abroad.

  Bibliography.
  Includes index.
  ISBN 0 522 84385 9.

  1. India. Army—Remount service—History. 2. Horse
  trading—Australia—History. 3. Horse trading—India
  —History. 4. Australia—Commerce—India. 5. India—
  Commerce—Australia. I. Title.

382.41610994

This book is number
six
in the Miegunyah Press Series,
the establishment of which was made possible
by bequests under the wills of
Sir Russell and Lady Grimwade

MIEGUNYAH WAS THE HOME OF MAB AND RUSSELL GRIMWADE
FROM THE YEAR 1911

This book is dedicated to Stephen Murray–Smith

Foreword

BEFORE 1914, England was still largely a horse-drawn country. As a small boy, I remember going in a dog-cart with my father on his rounds as a country doctor; I went to children's parties in a horse-drawn cab and used to drive eight miles in a pony-trap with my grandmother when she went to the market in Stanford. When I went to India in 1928, I was transported back in time to those days and beyond. India was still largely horse-drawn but the English in India were horse-oriented to a much greater extent than the England of my boyhood. They talked about horses a great deal; it was assumed that everyone rode; the atmosphere was more that of the mid-Victorian society in which Surtees made Mr Jorrocks say: 'there was no young man wot would not rather have a himputation on his morality than on his 'ossmanship'.

This orientation to the horse was partly because, at least in northern India, the army was so much more in evidence than at home. It was small in relation to the millions of India—about 50 000 British and 150 000 Indian troops to a population of at least 300 million. But it made up a large proportion of the British and the cavalry were still horsed, the guns were horse-drawn and senior infantry officers were mounted. The cavalry to a man played polo, it was an eccentric gunner who did not stick pig, and infantry subalterns and many civilians did as much as they could afford of both. In Calcutta there was paper-chasing; in some places there were hounds or what was called a bobbery-pack; young ladies, commissioners and senior generals alike went for a ride before breakfast every morning. The notice board at the club was covered with advertisements for horses for sale.

Military historians are likely to conclude that the army in India was horse-drawn for far too long. There were two reasons for this, one rational, the other aesthetic. The rational reason was that Delhi was a subordinate government to London and it was agreed that India should maintain at Indian expense forces sufficient for internal security and defence against her immediate neighbours. This was The Minor Danger. For this a horse-drawn army was enough and mechanization was expensive. The Indian government aimed at keeping down taxes. Defence against a Great Power—the Major Danger—was an imperial responsibility and London was not yet prepared to pay for India to be mechanized. That was one reason why India stayed horse-drawn so long. The second—and to a truly military mind the less respectable—was that a great many people in India *liked* horses. The three Commanders-in-Chief before Auchinleck—Birdwood, Chetwode, Cassells—were all cavalry men.

Thus there was a demand for horses in India but it is a bad country for breeding them. There is not much good natural grazing; the plains are intensely cultivated and the plots are unfenced; horses must be hobbled or tethered, (as Yarwood points out). Elephants were used for procession and ceremony, bullocks for ploughing and transport. The native riding breeds—such as the Kathiawari, with his strange ears like the flame of a candle in a draught—are small and wiry and not up to the weight of a British dragoon and his equipment. India has long relied on horses from abroad—Arabs and Persians in particular. In the British period, English Thoroughbreds were imported, 'Capers' from southern Africa, 'Walers' from New South Wales and other parts of Australia. As Yarwood shows, the 'Waler'—which came to mean any Australian horse—gradually established its supremacy for India over all other breeds. In the classical Victorian period, it became the fashionable thing for a prosperous young couple to keep a Waler for the master and one Arab for the lady. British cavalry were mounted almost entirely on Walers; Indian cavalry came to have more and more and gunners relied on them entirely.

All this Yarwood brings out, but also, what was new to me, the difficulties faced by Australian shippers, dealers and breeders, all the teething-troubles of setting up a regular trade. There was much to be learnt at both ends. The young horses came in practically wild, having hardly seen a man, having roamed at will on grass pastures of many thousands of acres. Grass-fed horses must get used to dry fodder before the voyage; there were problems over loading into ships and off again, particularly at Madras. So long as sail was the rule, delays on the voyage were terrible; some horses always died and total loss was not uncommon. Even when steam came in, it was still a long voyage and there were always some losses. Horses usually arrived in poor condition and it was some time before the army authorities in India realized that Walers needed at least six months in a remount depot to grow used to the Indian climate and to regular handling. It was sometimes said that Walers were inclined to be 'nappy'—that is, sulky and self-willed—but that once they had learnt a lesson they never forgot it. The country-bred, used to men from birth, learnt more quickly but needed constant schooling if it was to remember. If this was true, it was probably due to the treatment the Walers received from the first men they encountered.

It is striking to learn that the prices breeders received were so low and varied a great deal. Altogether, it is not surprising that many Australian breeders gave up horses and truned to sheep as more profitable. Reading Yarwood suggests to me that those Australian breeders who continued were influenced by feelings like those of so many people in India—they did it because they liked horses.

The export of horses to India continued though on a diminishing scale until late in the 1930s. Now there is a much smaller luxury trade in racehorses and polo ponies.

Can it be said that association with these beautiful and high-spirited creatures has had any influence on the Australian character, on the ways of thought of the Australian? These are deep waters into which Yarwood is too wise to venture. But his book illuminates one element in Australia's growth and some links with India in the British period, while it provides plenty of material for anyone daring enough to venture into so speculative a field. He has certainly assembled a great deal of information and assessed it with scholarship and detachment. But I am inclined to think that his main reason for writing this book is one we have already seen operating both in India and Australia, that is, that he likes horses.

PHILIP MASON

Contents

Contents

Illustrations

Illustrations

TEXT ILLUSTRATIONS

Illustrations

MAPS

Acknowledgements

NOT FOR THE FIRST TIME, or I hope the last, I am obliged to Don Aitken and the committee of the Australian Research Grants Scheme, which for three years financed my travels around Australia and to the United Kingdom. The venture depended on such help from the beginning. A Johnston Scholarship at the University of Sydney's history department and a fellowship at the Australian National University gave a great start to my work.

Two individuals must be especially thanked. Keith Adam, so well remembered for his *Journey into India* series on the ABC, came up with the idea for this book after a dinner at his home when we agreed that Australian historians have been extraordinarily remiss in omitting to look at the early connections between India and the Australian colonies. Unfortunately, pressure of his work on the Bicentennial Army Tattoo forced him to resign from the project shortly before the actual writing began.

The other man is remembered in the Dedication. He was Dr Stephen Murray-Smith, descendant of three generations of Melbourne horse shippers, who had ideas of writing about the Walers himself, but under stress from other tasks, gladly passed over his material to me and wrote regularly to spur me on. He was a giant of the Australian literary scene.

Jill Bowen and her colleagues in the Stockman's Hall of Fame have been generous in their encouragement. I hope that they and other Australian readers will feel that this book reveals unsuspected and significant dimensions of our pastoral history, for the Waler was bred for export in every part of this country, and the stimulus from the Indian market for military remounts and sporting horses was perhaps critical to the maintenance of equine standards.

If there has been one region I have pictured in my mind from the beginning it is the

Acknowledgements

Upper Hunter and its rich grasses, rolling limestone hills and broken terrain, so ideal to the production of fine horses. The Haydons and the Whites, of Bloomfield and Belltrees, have helped me for five years, not only with information and enthusiasm, but also with nagging questions. Bob Taylor and Helen Rees gave constructive criticism, Alison Powell a more general encouragement, and George Story a quick answer to the question of a title. Stuart McLellan was of great assistance in the preparation of the maps.

Librarians and archivists are well represented in the reference notes. I must mention Penny Pemberton and Michael Saclier of the Archives of Business and Labour at the Australian National University, Elizabeth Imashev and Paul Brunton at the Mitchell Library, Robin South at Battye, Spencer Routh at the University of Queensland Library, Peter Yeend at The King's School Archives, R. J. Bannenburg at the Queensland Parliamentary Library, Robert Longhurst at the Oxley Library, Tony Marshall at the La Trobe Library and Father Eugene Perez of the New Norcia Archives in Western Australia. In England I have special thanks for Richard Bingle and Tony Farrington of the India Office Library and Frances Diamond and Oliver Everett of the Royal Library and Archives at Windsor Castle.

My research has involved a good deal of travelling in Australia and the United Kingdom, making contact with men and women who bred, shipped, or used Walers, and with their descendants. For convenience I have grouped them geographically.

Ex India: my starting point was a visit to Mrs Rachel Lambert, daughter of Brigadier-General Frank Maxwell; on the way to visit her in Devonshire I met Brigadier Nigel Still, who lent fine photographs of Maxwell and his horses. At dinner with Rachel I met Major-General Peter Glover, who put me in touch with Brigadier Thurston Edward-Collins and Lieutenant-Colonel Douglas Gray. The web of contacts continued to expand, including Brigadier John Paley, whose story of the 1986 reunion of Skinner's Horse concludes the book, Lieutenant-Colonel Jeff Alexander, Lieutenant-Colonel P. Massey, and John Cox, son of that great sportsman, Michael Cox of the Central India Horse. In Perth I met Lieutenant-Colonel Alex Walker, who had stories and photographs of the Waziristan campaign. J. C. D. Vanrenen told me of the Renala Stud which his father founded on one of the canal colonies near Lahore before the First World War. It was part of the continuing struggle in India to breed good horses in the face of climatic stress and endemic disease. Also in the United Kingdom I had interviews with Mr Michael Shillabeer of the Royal Mews, and with Dr Stephanie Jones.

In Queensland, the eventual breeding-ground of most modern Walers, I must begin with Charlie Pascoe of Eidsvold, a grand source of stories and photographs of the Indian trade, and Anne Allingham of James Cook University, who took me to see such informants as Harry Creen, John Brabon and Perry Hardy. Also at Townsville, Queensland Trustees kindly gave me access to the J. S. Love Papers. At Mackay, Cosmo Gordon and his son Lance were immensely useful, as was Jack McLean. Hamline Treweeke drew for me the Rarey Strap, used in restraining difficult horses, and Mrs Grace Wallace and Mrs Allan Neville helped with the story of Grosvenor Downs and Rupert, the horse that went to Buckingham Palace in 1906. Mrs Allan Williams was a great help, and in Toowoomba I was assisted by Maurice French, Sandy McPhie and Bill Woods. Bryan Colquhoun had stories of Kidman horses and

Tom Higgins and Mrs Dorrie Champneys made contributions. Peter Gesner of the Queensland Museum was also helpful.

In New South Wales, where the story of the Waler began, my first contact was with the late Jim Haydon and his son Peter of Bloomfield, near Murrurundi; their manuscript collection is reflected in my account of Walers in the Desert Campaign. Peter is still very much involved in the breeding of fine horses, and it is apt to mention that he is now experiencing a term as polo manager for the Prince of Wales. Nancy Gray was again the great facilitator and Judy White was generous with the resources of the Belltrees library. Bob Taylor gave long term encouragement and Professor Marsh Edwards, Dean of the Faculty of Veterinary Science at the University of Sydney, offered the key to a nutritional problem that affected the prospects of Western Australian horses. Good photographs were lent by Mrs Pat Osborne of Currandooley, Tom Waters of Boonderoo, and John Esler and Paul Colquhoun of Albury. Barrie Dyster, Vaughan Evans and Bill Chapman suggested many references and Peter Wright and Elizabeth White spoke of family involvements with Walers. Arch McClellan of Scone showed me his work on pioneers of the Upper Hunter, while Norman Larkin, a Sydney veterinary surgeon, recounted details of inspecting remounts intended for export. My thanks also go to Rosemary Sparkes of Sydney and Peter Stanley of the Australian War Memorial in Canberra.

In Western Australia my outstanding debt is to Charles Staples, who drove me through many of the early horse breeding areas. Father Eugene Perez, archivist of the New Norcia Monastery, was generous in translating the diaries of Bishop Salvado. Professor Frank Broese helped with maritime matters, as did Vaughan Evans of Sydney. Leonard Hamersley told me of his part in present day Waler exports by sea and introduced me to Lyndsay Jameson, who keeps me in touch with the modern polo scene. Help was also given by Keith Bostock, Gordon Butler, W. J. de Burgh, Jenny Golding, June Craig, Cathie Clement and Lise Summers.

In Victoria Donald Vanrenen gave access to the family's manuscript and photographic records of the Waler trade, of which Henry Vanrenen had been a pioneer. Jack Anderson of Geelong lent letters written by an ancestor, John Hirst sent *Argus* references, Professor Doug Blood helped to illuminate African horse sickness, and Des Martin of Wodonga and Heather Ronald gave valuable information. Michael de Burgh Collins Persse also deserves thanks.

From South Australia Paul McCarthy sent files of the *Kapunda Herald* and there were helpful letters from C. M. Baker, J. C. Propsting and Peter Stanley.

In Tasmania, acknowledgement is due to Professor Michael Roe of the University of Tasmania.

From South Africa, an early competitor in the Indian trade, I received the most generous assistance, much of it facilitated by Professor Deryck Schreuder of the University of Sydney. Informative letters and photocopied documents came from Professor Basil le Cordeur of Cape Town and Mrs Doreen Rix of the university library. Professor John Beynon of the University of Natal gave and arranged help and Michael Berning of the Cory Library at Rhodes University sent important material.

It remains for me to thank Philip Mason for his kindness in writing the Foreword, which so beautifully captures the role of the horse, and notably the Waler in Anglo-Indian life. A civil servant in India for almost twenty years, he became the Director of the Institute of Race Relations and quickly achieved a rare blend of readability and

Acknowledgements

academic respectability that enabled him to interpret India in the days of the Raj for millions of readers. His *The Men Who Ruled India* remains the best introduction to the subject and is to my mind the outstanding product of a literary career of unusual variety and distinction.

SANDY YARWOOD
Waverton, September 1989

Conversions

1 hand	10.12 centimetres
1 inch	2.54 centimetres
1 foot	30.5 centimetres
1 yard	0.91 metres
1 mile	1.61 kilometres
1 acre	0.41 hectares
1 square mile	2.59 square kilometres
1 pound	0.45 kilograms
1 stone	6.35 kilograms
1 ton	1.02 tonnes
1 gallon	4.55 litres
32° F	0° C
212° F	100° C
1 shilling = 12d (pence)	$0.10
£1 = 20s (shillings)	$2.00

Horses are measured to their withers in hands.
One hand is four inches; 14.1 hands is 14 hands 1 inch.

Introduction

T HE SCENE IS SYDNEY COVE in mid-1834. A teak three-master named the *City of Edinburgh* tied up in deep water close to the wharf is preparing to load a cargo of colts and geldings intended for the army of the Madras Presidency in India. Convict grooms have begun to lead the horses from a holding paddock to the ship's side, where they will buckle a leather strap around the girth of each animal in turn. With the fastenings secure, the order will be given for the crane operator to hoist away and lift the struggling and frightened horse high into the air, and then lower it into the ship's hold. There another groom waits to lead the horse to an improvised stall, where it will remain until the destination is reached, perhaps eight to ten weeks later.

Captain J. G. Collins, now on leave in New South Wales from his regiment in Madras, the 13th Dragoons, may be imagined supervising every aspect of the tense and noisy operation. It is his own, or at least borrowed, capital that is at risk in this project and as an experienced cavalryman, he can imagine the host of things that can go wrong in moving such excitable beasts as young horses, not just to an adjoining paddock, but half-way across the world. Very likely he waits near the crane itself, seeing the twitching of young ears and the rippling of nervous muscles below glossy coats while his horses are being prepared for the leather strap and the undignified trip to the ship's hold.

No more than two hundred metres south of the wharf lies the entrance to Sydney's first Government House, a picturesque but leaky and draughty building, much altered since Arthur Phillip laid the foundation stone in July 1788. On this Saturday morning of 28 June 1834 it is Sir Richard Bourke who rules in New South Wales, and it is not too fanciful to picture him strolling down to the harbourside to watch the loading of the horses, for he was Irish born, a soldier, and a former acting Governor of

Cape Colony from 1826 to 1828, well aware of the interest of his predecessor, Lord Charles Somerset, in securing to Cape breeders the best possible share of the rich Indian market for military and civilian horses. He knew of Collins's plan to ship remounts to Madras, and as a good proconsul, sympathetic to the interests of his new subjects, he wished Collins success in this and the two shiploads that followed in the next year, making a total of ninety-four horses intended for the Madras army.

Apart from brief reports in the *Sydney Herald*, the colonial press showed no awareness of the history-making activity that was taking place at the dock yard. Admittedly, the cargo consisted of only thirty-two horses and it was not the first time Australian horses had been sent overseas. But it was the firm beginning of an export trade, addressed particularly to the remount needs of the Indian armies, that held great significance for Australian breeders and shippers and Indian users for more than a century.

The trade on which Captain Collins embarked so courageously in 1834 continued on a large scale until the Indian army was mechanized on the eve of the Second World War, though even then Australian horses met the special needs of mountain batteries stationed on the north-west frontier. It was my privilege in December 1984 to meet in Perth Alex Walker, a retired cavalryman who had served as a young subaltern with one of those batteries during the Waziristan campaign of 1940–41. His experiences reflect the diversity of individuals and regions involved in the breeding, shipment and use of Indian remounts. Every Australian colony, territory, or state was at one time concerned in the trade. The people who gave it their skill and enterprise ranged from that extraordinary man of God, Bishop Salvado of New Norcia in Western Australia to the premier Victorian shipper of the late nineteenth century, Henry Vanrenen, and to a representative breeder of the final years of the trade, Cosmo Gordon of Grosvenor Downs, just west of Mackay on the central Queensland coast.

Pukka Indian opinion was by no means easily receptive to horses bred in the Australian colonies, which continued to be labelled as 'Botany Bay' in the India Office. Van Diemen's Land was still receiving Indian convicts in the mid-1840s, in ships that returned to Calcutta with remounts from both Hobart and Sydney, sometimes with the guards making the return journey as grooms. Yet in spite of massive prejudices, felt towards any products of the penal colonies, and more specifically towards the geldings that made up the bulk of Australian horse shipments, the horses soon won a major share of the Indian military market and eventually dominated the private sector through unanswerable successes on Indian race tracks and sporting fields.

Even when the prejudices against Australian horses were perhaps at their height during a time of great military expenditure on imports in the mid-1840s, they were accorded the important distinction of having a new word coined to conveniently describe them. Just as the term 'Arab' had long been used for the foundation stock from which all modern breeding derived, and more recently 'Caper' had become the name for imports from the Cape Colony, so from late in 1846 a horse from New South Wales came to be known almost universally in India as a 'Waler'.

Given the central importance of India in the British Empire and the popularity of Australian horses as vehicles for India's rulers, it should occasion no surprise that the term 'Waler' was applied to these horses almost wherever they were used in imperial wars, at the Sudan, the Boxer Rebellion, the Boer War and above all in the Desert Campaign of the First World War. 'Walers', henceforth without quotation marks, were also exported in large numbers to Japan and the Dutch East Indies, to the Philippines, Singapore and Mauritius, largely for army use. Western Australian breeders enjoyed a significant advantage in approaching some of those markets, and it is a man with the significant name of Leonard Hamersley who has kept up the export by sea of Walers to Southeast Asia in the past twenty years.

My story has as its central theme the export of Walers to India but it would be unimaginable to define the field so narrowly as to exclude such theatres of action as South Africa and Palestine, which employed, and killed, such massive numbers of Australian horses. More important than the scale of the carnage was the contribution made by the Waler to the image of Australians abroad, notably as the gallant Light Horsemen who at Beersheba in 1917 performed one of the last great horse-borne charges of military history.

An expanded subject has the added advantage that it permits a full presentation of one of the classic figures of the Waler trade at the consumer end. I refer to Frank Maxwell, a distinguished Indian Army cavalry officer who fought in the Boer War and won the Victoria Cross on a Waler. A younger son of a Scottish landed family, he epitomized the best qualities of the breed of those who ruled India for so long. What is special about Maxwell is that he kept diaries for twenty years in which he recorded day by day the training and exercising of his wonderful horses, many of them Walers, so illuminating a view of my subject that focuses on the animals as well as on those who rode them.

Narrative history though this is, including accounts of horsey adventures at sea and on three continents, it seeks to contribute to a strangely neglected field of Australian effort. Apart from my friend Dr Malcolm Kennedy, who was recently awarded a Doctorate in Philosophy by the University of Melbourne for an important thesis that looks at the role of bullocks and horses in the development of eastern Australia, there has been complete silence on the part of historians about the remount trade and indeed about the place of horses in Australian history. It has been an extraordinary omission.

Wherever I travelled in Australia, north, south, east and west, I found a complete absence of monographic material on the Waler trade and have therefore needed to construct the entire story from an analysis of primary material collected in all the major Australian libraries, as well as in London at the India Office Library and the National Army Museum. These travels, made with the assistance of the Australian Research Grants Scheme, gave access to people who were involved in the remount trade as breeders, shippers and users, and it is from them that much of the vitality of this story is drawn. One consequence of this dependence on original material has been the appearance of many gaps and deficiencies in my story and I write now only because I know that if I wait for a comprehensive knowledge I shall wait for ever.

1

Walers at the Coronation Durbar

ɪᴛ ᴡᴀs ᴀ ʙʀɪɢʜᴛ, clear winter's morning in the ancient city of Delhi, for hundreds of years the seat of Mogul power in India, soon to become the capital of a new conqueror. For days the people of the countryside had been pouring into the city, anticipating the pageants and celebrations, the fireworks and illuminations, the displays of military power and of princely wealth that would mark India's recognition of the earlier coronation in Westminster Abbey of King George V as Emperor of India.

The day was 7 December 1911. A salute from one hundred and one guns fired from within the Red Fort told the crowd that the King and Queen had arrived at the Selimgarh station beside the fort. It was answered by a *feu de joie* fired from the rifles of troops massed on the plain outside. Soon the King, dressed in the uniform of a field marshal, mounted a fine black charger named Akbar, a gift from the government of Queensland, and joined the procession that was being prepared for the state entry into the city of Delhi.

A moment had come that was full of symbolism for the people of India and the British Empire, which probably instilled in some a false optimism as to the future relations between the British Crown and its Indian subjects. The grandmother of the new emperor was Queen Victoria, who had assumed the title 'Empress of India' in 1876 after the suppression of the great Mutiny, effectively ended when General Nicholson and his troops re-entered the Mogul capital of Delhi and deposed the last of the Mogul emperors, on whom the revolutionary movement had centred.

A durbar (from the Persian and Urdu *darbar* or audience hall) was a public audience or levee held by a native prince, or by a British governor or viceroy in India. The one prepared by the Viceroy, Lord Hardinge, for King George V in 1911, at the King's special initiative, was designed to outdo all previous durbars in magnificence

The state entry to Delhi, 1911

and offer him the opportunity of announcing important boons to the people of India, above all the impending transfer of the seat of government from Calcutta to Delhi.

Some Australian visitors were present in Delhi, notably the Headmaster of The King's School Parramatta and a party of fourteen boys, each of whom contributed to a book about the durbar that was published by the school on their return. Another and more famous Australian present was Sidney Kidman, the 'Cattle King', who occupied with his wife and daughters one of the 40 000 tents in the city of canvas that spread for twenty-five square miles on the plain outside the walls. By 1921, when he was knighted, Kidman was the owner or lessee of 100 000 square miles, grazing more than 500 000 cattle, and so the greatest landholder in the world. What gave him a special interest in the proceedings at the Delhi Durbar was his large contribution to the supply of remounts to the Indian army. By taking his family to India he was in effect 'going round the traps', and he took pleasure in recognizing his brand on hundreds of horses which his sharp gaze lit on during his travels in the sub-continent.[1]

An uncountable number of Walers were stabled in the city as mounts for the regiments of cavalry and mounted artillery that were quartered there for the durbar. The military horse was a potent symbol of the British military power that governed 235 million people in India. Light cavalry and artillery had been essential components in the armies of the conquerors who had held sway in past times, the Moguls, Marathas, Rajputs, and Sikhs. For the British, like the other rulers, the horse was a vital element in governing vast domains with relatively small military forces and that need was much accentuated by the conquest of the Punjab in the 1840s and the assumption of a semblance of control over the fiercely independent tribespeople of the north-west frontier.

Long before the birth of the man who was to greet the people of India as their emperor on 12 December, the Waler, imported in thousands from almost every Australian colony, had been recognized as the prime remount for the Indian army. Walers carried virtually all the dragoons in the British cavalry regiments and many of the Indian irregular troopers. They horsed the gun teams of the horse artillery, served as chargers and polo ponies for British officers of all kinds and carried the colours of the more successful owners who contested the big prizes of the racing calendars of Calcutta, Madras and Bombay.

The King's choice of Akbar, a coal-black Queensland charger which had been selected by Mr Ernest Baynes of Brisbane and sent to India for the King's use, was an apt acknowledgement of the importance of Walers in the government of India, and more particularly of the coming dominance of Queensland in the breeding of Indian remounts. The use of this horse for the state entry into Delhi on 7 December was for the new King a most natural course, for on his previous journey to India in 1906, he had ridden another Queensland horse, a black gelding named Rupert, bred on Grosvenor Downs. The Prince of Wales, as he was then, had liked Rupert so much that he took him back to England and used him for ten years on private and state occasions. One of the most charming little stories associated with the Waler trade comes from the sequel. A photograph taken of the new King George V, mounted on

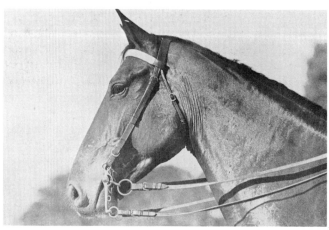

Akbar: a Queensland horse for the King

Rupert in the funeral procession for Edward VII, was published in the *Queenslander* of 2 July 1910. By a trick of light, the brand 2GD/20 was clearly discernible, so that young Alexander Bonar Macdonald was able to recognize, to his delight, that the King was mounted on a horse bred on his father's station.

For his entry into Delhi, the King chose deliberately to ride a horse rather than an elephant, breaking with an old tradition that had been conspicuously followed by Lord Curzon in 1903. It may have been recalled that on an earlier occasion arranged for Lord Lytton in 1877, one of the elephants was said to have startled spectators and horses by breaking wind in the most strident fashion. But the reason given by the official historian of the royal visit to India, John Fortescue, was that the King wanted the people to see him more easily. In the event, as Lord Hardinge later recalled, this did not happen:

> As we passed through the densely crowded streets I noticed that the people did not recognize the King, who after all was a small man, was dressed in a red coat like other Generals and was riding a small horse. He also did not make any kind of demonstration to the people. At the same time as I passed along the people cheered and I could hear them say, 'There is the Lord Sahib, but where is the King?'[2]

Fortescue's description of the procession into Delhi conveys an impression of the colour and power of the spectacle put on by Lord Hardinge. Twenty-eight senior officers of the King's staff led the way, followed by the viceroy's bodyguard, 'gigantic lancers in scarlet and gold', then a party of Life Guards, the Duke of Teck, and the King, with the viceroy and Lord Crewe, the Secretary of State, immediately behind. The Queen was in a carriage drawn by six horses, then came the Imperial Cadet Corps, wearing uniforms of cream-coloured silk with gold finishing designed by Lady Curzon, and a rearguard of Indian lancers.[3]

In the eyes of N. D. Barton, one of the fourteen boys from Australia who saw the state entry to Delhi, the most memorable part (for they too failed to notice the King) was the parade of the ruling princes and chiefs of India. Amongst them was the Maharaja of Gwalior, escorted by a squad of horsemen 'completely clad in chain armour and carrying spears like the knights of old'. The same King's School boy described another ceremony on 11 December in which the King was mounted on Akbar when he presented colours to a number of British and Indian regiments. But he saved his best boyish enthusiasm for the durbar itself on the following day, when the King was to show himself to the people, perhaps 250 000 of them on a circular arena, with 20 000 troops in full review uniform. While he and his friends from Parramatta were waiting for the King and Queen to arrive in their carriage, they were allowed to walk around the pavilion to look at the Indian princes. As young Barton described it:

> and on this day they did indeed 'have 'em all on.' Their long coats of cloth-of-gold, with inlaid jewels in many cases on their breasts; the rings, the necklaces, and the gorgeous crests and brooches, which often had a diamond, a pearl, or a ruby as big as a pigeon's egg in them, all filled us with admiration and envy.[4]

The essence of the durbar was for the King, wearing a heavy new crown that had been made for the occasion at a cost of £60 000 paid for by the people of India, to announce the fact of his earlier coronation and receive the homage of the viceroy and princes of India. He then spoke of the government's intention to undo the partition of Bengal and make Delhi the new capital. A buzz of excitement passed through the huge crowd, the twenty-four trumpeters in crimson and gold blew their last fanfare and galloped out of the arena, the massed bands again played the National Anthem, and the King and Queen left in their carriage while a 101-gun salute was fired.

The detachment from The King's School, wearing the grey and blue uniform that distinguished the oldest cadet corps in the British Empire, stood only fifty yards from the royal pavilion. They received, Barton swore, a special smile from the Queen and a wave from Lady Hardinge, appropriately enough for the sons of some pastoral families which had bred horses for the Indian army for generations.[5]

On the following day, the weather remaining brilliantly sunny, the military aspect that had dominated the durbar celebrations continued. The King again rode his Queensland charger for a review of 50 000 troops, of which the most spectacular moment is described by N. D. Barton:

> After the march past the infantry formed up in line again, while the cavalry and artillery rode past the King at a gallop. The artillery came first, the guns and baggage being dragged or carried by mules instead of horses. There was no mistake about them galloping, either; they came past full tilt, with the gunners holding on for grim death, and the guns bumping and plunging along behind. Next came squadron upon squadron of cavalry and lancers, flashing past with manes, tails and turbans flying in the wind.

John Fortescue, the official historian of the durbar visit, discussing the strongly military and equine aspect of the state entry to Delhi, made a point that takes us close to the significance of the durbar and the place of the horse in its ceremonial:

> it must be remembered that the troops formed the most essential part of the pageant; that indeed there can be no true pageant without disciplined men; that in the last resort everything in India depends upon the British soldier . . . and that in such a huge concourse of soldiers, British and native . . . it was fitting and right that the King should appear in the uniform which distinguished him at once as their chief and as one of themselves.[6]

What was the deeper purpose of the durbar ceremonial? L. D. Wurgraft makes some illuminating suggestions in his book, *The Imperial Imagination*. He argues that the underlying psychological concern of the British community in India was to promote a 'heroic mythology' that referred to British achievements, notably those of the soldiers and administrators who conquered the Punjab at mid-century and later crushed the Mutiny. With a steady increase in the adherence of British officers in the late nineteenth century to conservative ideologies, there was a greater dependence on authoritarian institutions and notions of racial and moral superiority to defend and rationalize their political hegemony.

This aspect of the Edwardian-Georgian Empire is caught nicely by a quotation from Walter Lawrence, private secretary to Lord Curzon:

> Our life in India, our very work more or less, rests on illusion. I had the illusion, wherever I was, that I was infallible and invulnerable in my dealings with Indians . . . [It was an] illusion which is in the very air of India. They expressed something of the idea when they called us the 'Heaven born', and the idea is really make believe—

mutual make believe. They, the millions, made us believe we had a divine mission. We made them believe they were right.[7]

Published accounts of the durbar suggest that the King, himself the author of the durbar proposal, fitted in readily with the Indian tendency to magnify and deify him. Harold Nicolson, his biographer, thought that 'the myriad masses of India see in him the almost magic symbol of a higher justice, the emissary of a Great Protector, omnipotent but unseen'. Yet, drawing on the notes made by him after his visit to India as Prince of Wales in 1905–06, Nicholson creates the impression of a monarch who was concerned to create a softer and more accessible image:

No doubt [the prince had written, summarizing his impressions] the Natives are better treated by us than in the past, but I could not help being struck by the way in which all salutations by the Natives were disregarded by the persons to whom they were given. Evidently we are too much inclined to look upon them as a conquered & down-trodden race & the Native, who is becoming more and more educated, realizes this. I could not help noticing that the general bearing of the European towards the Native was to say the least unsympathetic.[8]

Whatever the intentions of the King and his government, something like deification was a consequence of the durbar. Stacy Waddy quotes the words of an Indian chance acquaintance to whom he spoke on the way back from Delhi to the canvas city. 'The Indians are all King-worshippers. We think that the King is the incarnation of all that is good; and that if he came to the country all good will follow'.[9]

Fortescue wrote of the 'simple, tranquil dignity' with which the King and Queen behaved, creating the feeling that 'they were present as earnest and devout leaders and partakers in a great religious celebration'. After all was over, thousands of people came down to the pavilion where the King and Queen had sat, prostrating themselves and pressing their foreheads against the marble. 'For the East has not yet lost the ancient habit of exalting their Emperor above all human kind . . . So strong is the impulse in men to deify the power which keeps them in discipline and order, and thus brings to them the divine blessing of peace.'

According to Fortescue, even Congress sympathizers were deeply affected by the experience of the durbar. One of them, a Madras Brahman, turned with tears in his eyes to an English friend, and said: 'This is what I have always dreamed the procession of a God must be. If the Bengalis give any more trouble, they will get no support from any other province in India'.[10]

One of the King's deliberate evocations of a Mogul symbol of divine monarchy occurred with his appearance in the afternoon of 13 December on Shah Jahan's balcony in the Red Fort, before a huge throng of people who occupied the plain between the fort and the sacred river Jumna. Yet in spite of all this symbolism and quasi-religious ceremonial the reality of military power as the basis for British rule was never far from the surface.

Not only were there the most impressive manifestations of disciplined power by scores of thousands of cavalry, infantry and horse artillery, there was prior to that the King's arrival in Bombay with a great naval escort. The viceroy's preparations, as described in his reminiscences, also included a pre-emptive strike against potential trouble-makers. On the day before the King's arrival in Delhi he had 'over 300 dangerous characters' arrested and imprisoned during the King's stay, and the same was done before the visit to Calcutta. The general Indian public, he felt sure, 'considered that it was quite the right step for a strong government to have taken'. To guard against assassination attempts during the King's ride on Akbar through the Chandni Chowk, the main street of Delhi, he allowed nobody to stand on the pavement except the British regiments lining the street. Four thousand police were brought up from neighbouring provinces, one of whom was stationed at every window, while the backs of the houses were guarded by Indian troops and the roofs were entirely cleared. No doubt Lord Hardinge wished a year later he had taken similar precautions, for he was the victim of a bomb attack that wounded him severely and killed the umbrella holder at the rear of his howdah, during the course of a procession on elephants down the same street.[11]

Writing of this bomb attack reminds me of another superb Waler that took part in the gallop past the King on 13 December 1911, and whose owner helped to get the wounded viceroy down from his huge elephant in 1912. The story of this horse and of his gallant owner deserves to be told, not because either was typical, but because both expressed the very best qualities to which they could have aspired. What makes it the more desirable to do so is that the horse's gallop at the durbar was his last appearance as a regimental charger. Furthermore, though historians are limited by the range of their evidence,they are bound to make good use of a rich deposit. In this case, a combination of published reminiscences, archival material, and family photographs make possible the telling of a uniquely detailed and colourful story.

Frank Maxwell (1871–1917) was a younger son of Surgeon-Major Thomas Maxwell of the Indian Medical Service, who came from an ancient Scottish landed family. He began his association with the bay Thoroughbred Waler gelding that he bought as a five-year-old for Rs 750 in January 1899, and called him 'English Lord'. Both horse and rider went to southern Africa where Maxwell served in the Indian Staff Corps as a lieutenant attached to Roberts's Light Horse. On 31 March 1900, though not belonging to the horse artillery, Maxwell went out on five separate occasions at Sanna's Post in an effort to save three guns from capture, and in the action both he and English Lord were wounded; indeed, the latter carried a Boer bullet till his death. Lord was invalided back to India, while his master stayed in southern Africa, was awarded the Victoria Cross, and joined the staff of Lord Kitchener, whom he served for many years both there and in India, on one occasion filling in for the commander-in-chief's coachman when he was sick. Maxwell switched uniforms with the man, and was delighted to record in his diary that his chief noticed nothing. The two men had a close, even a tender relationship, and Kitchener stood as godfather for his friend's first daughter when she was born in Sydney in 1910.[12]

Most of Maxwell's career was spent in India, with the 18th Bengal Lancers, though he was on Kitchener's staff and later served as Lord Hardinge's military secretary, keeping the viceroy in touch with the committee which planned the durbar ceremonies of 1911. In the hot weather of 1904 he holidayed at Simla where he met Charlotte Osborne, younger daughter of a pastoral family from Currandooley near Bungendore, who was a pretty and musically talented member of what was known as the 'fishing fleet'. Her grandfather, Henry Osborne of Marshall Mount in the Illawarra, had bred horses for the Indian trade in the 1840s and his descendants were

Frank Maxwell (front, right) as Military Secretary to Viscount Hardinge

active in the Light Horse at the time of the Boer War. The couple married in 1906, lost their only son Patrick to a fever, and went to Australia in 1910, where Maxwell taught cavalry tactics to the Australian Light Horse. More Australian horses were added to his string, and a daughter, Rachel, was born in Sydney, shortly before he accepted Lord Hardinge's offer of the post of military secretary. By 1916, the viceroy acceded to Maxwell's request to go on active service, and he was killed by a sniper's bullet on the western front, having attained the rank of brigadier-general.

Frank Maxwell's diaries at the National Army Museum in London permit a rare picture to be formed of a soldier and sportsman, who possessed courage, modesty, athleticism, and a passionate love for horses. On the one hand, he was awarded and twice recommended for the Victoria Cross, on the other, he won every prize available to an amateur horseman in India except the Kadir Cup, which just eluded him. The diaries record the almost daily round of training the Walers and Arabs that he kept in his stable after returning from South Africa. At the end of each year there was a summary of the horses and their achievements, with English Lord always receiving the first and most detailed notice. Lord accompanied Maxwell almost everywhere, even to England in 1904 for a term at staff college, with a spot of hunting and courting thrown in. One of the most revealing diary entries reads as follows:

> February 23rd (1905) Motored to Farnham as chief witness in case v. Flynn for cruelty in working a lame horse. His driver fined 15s. and costs about 25s. Flynn got off on a quibble; Bench thanked me for running the man in.
> Schooled Haag's ponies.

Another of Maxwell's string was a chestnut Waler mare that he bought for £18 in South Africa in May 1901 from the Australian Remounts and shipped to India. Under the name of 'English Lady' she carried him in the finals of many polo tournaments, including the Delhi Durbar of January 1903 and the Simla Cup of the same year. She was sold in June 1904, when Maxwell was preparing for an English leave, for Rs 1400 (about £116). This price, and the mare's evident capacity, offer interesting testimony on the controversial question of the quality of the Walers that were unlucky enough to be shipped to southern Africa.[13]

From the time of Frank's marriage, though still capable of winning at polo or paper-chasing, Lord was so much the family pet that he often pulled a light buggy on

English Lord (Frank Maxwell in the buggy)

outings and accompanied the Maxwells to Simla for vacations. He was even on hand for the funeral of an infant—an incident that so often punctuated the lives of the Anglo-Indians:

1 Jan 1909. Pat at death's door all day—died midnight 4 Jan 09.
5 Jan 1909. Noon. We took little Pattie out in the buggy with Lord to the old cemetery, instead of burying him in the crowded Delhi cemetery.

Let Charlotte Maxwell tell the last part of Lord's story, as she did in a volume of memoirs that was given to me in England by her grandson, Brigadier Nigel Still.

He went to South Africa with his master and received five bullet wounds, one near the spine which brought on a sort of rheumatism at times when he was growing old, so when we went to Australia in 1910 'Lord' was left in Willy Maxwell's care, with the understanding that if the rheumatism was incurable, an end was to be put to his life, but on no account to tell us. Hearing nothing—good or bad—when we returned in November, we presumed that the old horse had been destroyed.
In 1911 King George and Queen Mary came to India. At the Review in Delhi, I happened to be sitting next to Sir John Fortescue (later historian of the 1914–18 War). He was watching with intense interest. When the 'Gallops past' began, he said with some sadness, 'They aren't coming *fast* enough, they aren't coming FAST enough. Oh! now this Regiment really IS,' and what was my joy to see 'English Lord' at the head of it —Willy Maxwell was the Colonel—old 'Lord' fairly galloping with all the vigour and pace of his youth.[14]

Frank Maxwell's horse summary at the end of 1913 recorded that Lord's rheumatism had made him very lame, so he was sent out to pasture on a grass farm in the Punjab owned by Malik Hayat of the Tiwana Lancers.

The great durbar was held at the height of the British Raj and the Waler's prominence is shown by quoting again from Stacy Waddy. A second class honours graduate from Balliol, and an essayist of no mean ability, it was he who had had the idea of taking the party from The King's School to India for a colourful lesson in life and history. Waddy discusses the contrast between Indian and English ideas of ceremonial, and throws a different light, perhaps, on the choice of a horse rather than an elephant as the mount for King George V.

To the Eastern the idea is richness in detail and mass; and to the Western all would be spoilt if rich details were set incongruously side by side with much that is poor and unworthy. The horse is the typical animal of the one—fit to show to the last hair; of the other, the elephant—decorative in mass, but, as Dickens says, he 'employs the worst tailor in the world,' and must not be looked at from behind, where his breeches are baggy.[15]

For the fourteen durbaris from The King's School the experience of the durbar, with its rich expression of imperial power and solidarity, was highly formative. Peter Yeend, the school's archivist, gives details of the boys and their later careers. All of them served during the war that began three years later, nine or ten in the Light Horse, and four lost their lives. Most were country boys, long familiar with the stock from which the Walers were bred. The Nathaniel Barton who wrote the chapter on the durbar ceremonials came from a station called Namina, situated on a hill outside Wellington. At twenty-one years of age he became the youngest major in the Australian army and saw the surrender of Jerusalem. In the 1930s he was active in the revival of the Light Horse and went to London to act as second in command of the sovereign's mounted escort at the coronation of King George VI. There is a nice circularity to be seen in Colonel Barton's presence at this further ceremony.[16]

2

Origins: India and Australia

WE SHOULD BEGIN by defining what we mean by the term 'Waler'. It was coined in Calcutta in 1846 to describe conveniently the horses imported from New South Wales as army remounts, hacks and racehorses, used chiefly by the army and well-to-do civilians. Within a short time the word was being used throughout India for horses bred in any part of Australia. Walers appeared increasingly under that appellation in Indian racing programmes and they were soon put under a handicap, like imported English Thoroughbreds, to bring them back to the field with Arabs and country-breds. The name appeared in official notifications issued by the government of India to advise approved shippers of their allocations for the coming buying season in the Indian cool weather of November to March. We find the term 'Waler' in the published and unpublished reminiscences of Indian military and sporting life, a fact that becomes more apparent by the end of the nineteenth century, when the Australian horse's dominance of both fields was complete.

Walers were later taken to Durban by the Indian regiments that fought in the Boer War—among them, Frank Maxwell and his famous gelding, English Lord. The influence of these British officers reinforced, if need be, the well-established habit for Australian journalists and equine writers to think of Australian horses overseas as Walers. A. B. Paterson used the term in his despatches from the front to the *Sydney Morning Herald*, and no doubt thought of them in the same way when he acted as a senior remount officer with the Light Horse in Palestine.[1]

There is no question as to the currency of the term 'Waler' to describe the scores of thousands of Australian-bred horses in the remount and regimental lines of Egypt and Palestine. It was probably applied as well to many of the New Zealand horses in the Middle East, for they had begun appearing as Indian army remounts from the 1890s. The literature of the time is full of the Waler, and one example comes from

H. S. Gullett's description of the Light Horseman's ability to live off the land, both for himself and his horse, commandeering fodder when need arose. 'He dismissed such incidents from his mind with the scornful thought that a General Staff which could not settle trifling affairs of that sort with the natives was not fit for its job, and rode on happy because the bulging nosebag ensured an evening meal for his beloved waler'.[2]

In essence, the Waler was an Australian horse abroad, working chiefly in the countries washed by the Indian Ocean, though also in the Middle East and Asia. Initially, it was a horse bred in New South Wales and imported to India for military, sporting or domestic purposes, and the term remained current there for nearly a century, applying soon to all Australian horses. The word later had unquestioned currency in both southern Africa and the Middle East, and was used, if less frequently, to describe Australian horses that were imported from the early days of the horse trade to Ceylon, Mauritius and Singapore, and later to Java, Siam, the Philippines, China and Japan. Writing in 1923, H. S. Gullett referred to: 'Australia's walers, already famous for their work in India and in the South African and Russo–Japanese Wars', so lending his considerable authority to a broad use of the term. I would not apply it to the thousands of Australian horses that followed Samuel Marsden's first shipment to New Zealand in December 1814. That trade was begun long before the word 'Waler' was invented and the green pastures of New Zealand are insufficiently remote or foreign to convey the sense of transplantation that the term always implied.[3]

Australia had no horses until they were brought in by the First Fleet in 1788 and in subsequent importations. In this as in all areas of animal husbandry in Australia, breeders enjoyed the advantages of a clean sheet, uncluttered by the mistakes of past generations and, above all, free from established equine disease. It was a freedom guarded by the great oceans that surround Australia, ensuring that diseases would be incubated long before ships arrived from suspect ports and protected later by strict quarantine regulations.

The foundation stock was largely drawn from Cape Colony, including two entires and five females landed from the *Sirius*. Another four came from India in 1793 and there was an influx of thirty-three from the Cape, out of a total bought there of forty-one and carried in the *Britannia* in 1795. This stock was of the Arab breed, popular in both the Cape and India, so that by 1799, when the Thoroughbred Rockingham was brought in from the Cape, Australian blood lines were predominantly Arab.

With the setting up by the military and civil officers in New South Wales of pastoral estates based on convict labour and often financed by a combination of government salaries and lucrative commerce, the way was open for the growth of a class of land users who would own and breed fine horses. They aspired to this partly because of the prestige implied by the possession of pure-bred Arabs and Thoroughbreds, but also from a recognition of the potential rewards from horse breeding in a country where pastures and climate, and the needs imposed by great distances, favoured the rapid growth of horse numbers.

Equine quality controls were effectively maintained in Australia by the high cost of transporting stock from the principal sources in the Cape, India and, increasingly, in Britain. Northumberland, the Thoroughbred stallion sent out to Major George Johnston in 1803 by his old commander, would have eaten no more feed than a cart horse. So only high quality stock were chosen for the voyage, which in itself had the effect of weeding out the less fit, through a mortality rate estimated by Malcolm Kennedy at 20 per cent of the eighty-eight horses imported in the twelve years to 1800.[4]

The early Waler shipments to India, as Malcolm Kennedy points out, reflected the dominance of Arab blood that traced back to the Australian horse's origins in the Cape horse, but from mid-century the blood line was increasingly Thoroughbred, especially in the sires. Like the Man From Snowy River's horse, a Waler was typically 'three parts thoroughbred at least', with the origin of the fourth element depending on its intended field of service. Because of this variation, it is not easy to offer a single satisfying physical description, though if pressed, one might quote the specifications given to Captain J. G. Collins by the Madras remount authorities in August 1833. They remained broadly applicable for a century, apart from the reluctant abandonment in the 1850s of the ancient preference for stallions: 'All horses to be entire, and at least half bred [half Thoroughbred], sound in wind and limb, compact, active, and capable of carrying 17 stone, not under 3 nor above 7 years old, nor under 14 hands high. Horses above 15 hands are neither desired, nor prohibitable'.[5]

Walers were bred in the well-watered, limestone-rich valleys of the coastal rivers of New South Wales, including the Clarence, Richmond, Hunter and Shoalhaven. These areas abound in different types of grass, which give a highly nutritious diet to grazing stock, while the limestone ensures the production of good bone, perhaps the first quality looked for in a military horse. The horses grew to perfection in the high country of the Upper Murray in pastures of surpassing beauty on stations like Khancoban and Bringenbrong, which are still famous for the production of racing stock, but they were also bred successfully on the western slopes and western flowing rivers between Bathurst and Cootamundra. The Campbells of Duntroon near Canberra were important to the trade, as were the Osbornes of Currandooley to the east of Lake George, where they followed the lead set by Henry Osborne at Marshall Mount in the Illawarra district. He was constantly pressed by Captain Robert Towns to contribute to speculative cargoes in the 1840s, as was his near neighbour, David Berry, whose property was situated on the spectacular river flats of Coolangatta at the mouth of the Shoalhaven.

Some of the best Walers grew up in broken, hilly country littered with fallen timber and stones, and scarred by watercourses that prepared them for the deep *nalas* of India. Foals rapidly learned in such terrain to lift up their feet, for a sharp rap on the ankle was the sure consequence of carelessness. It was a perfect start for a polo horse and equally for a mount that might have had the prospect of carrying a heavy rider in the brisk confusion of a cavalry charge.

The contrasting experiences of Indian and Australian foals and their effects on action and agility are illustrated by the comments of two men who knew them well. Veterinary Colonel J. H. B. Hallen made the following remarks in 1889 in the light of his time in charge of horse breeding operations in India:

in a country whose fields are unfenced, and where horse stealing is (in some regions) common, the natives could not give their young stock the degree of liberty necessary for their full development. The practice of closely hobbling, or even chaining and padlocking the fore-legs together, was universal, and its natural result was deformity of limb, narrowness of chest, and ruined action.[6]

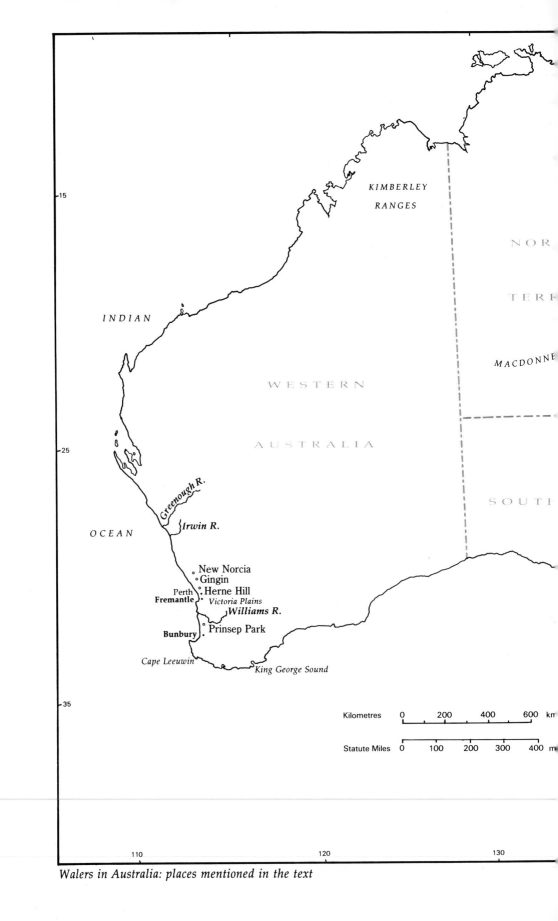

Walers in Australia: places mentioned in the text

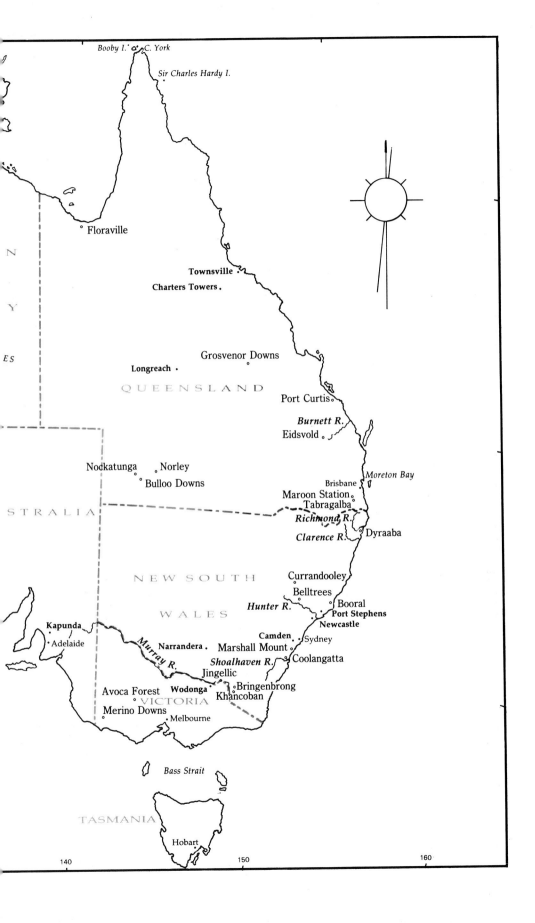

Booby I. ⚬ C. York

Sir Charles Hardy I.

N

Y

E S

Floraville ⚬

Townsville .

Charters Towers .

Grosvenor Downs ⚬

Longreach .

QUEENSLAND

Port Curtis ⚬

Burnett R.

Eidsvold ⚬

Nockatunga ⚬   ⚬ Norley

Bulloo Downs ⚬

Moreton Bay

Brisbane ⚬

Maroon Station ⚬

Tabragalba ⚬

STRALIA

Richmond R.

Clarence R.   ⚬ Dyraaba

NEW SOUTH

Currandooley ⚬

Belltrees ⚬

WALES

Hunter R.   ⚬ Booral

Port Stephens

Newcastle

Kapunda .

Camden .

Adelaide .

Narrandera .   Marshall Mount .   . Sydney

Murray R.

Shoalhaven R.   ⚬ Coolangatta

Jingellic .

Avoca Forest   Wodonga .   ⚬ Bringenbrong

Merino Downs ⚬   VICTORIA   Khancoban .

. Melbourne

Bass Strait

TASMANIA

Hobart .

140   150   160

Currandooley in the 1890s: the terrain in which Walers grew up

Sir William Denison went in January 1861 from the Governor-Generalship of the Australian colonies to the Governorship of Madras, where he was an enthusiastic supporter of the claims of Australian breeders to supply the remount needs of the subcontinent, largely because of his awareness of the nutritional advantages enjoyed by colonial-bred foals. Writing from Calcutta on this subject on 4 January 1864, he considered the features of foals bred in India and Australia, from Arab sires and Australian dams:

> Their legs are always clean, they never throw a splint; and though, now and then, if bred in India, they show a tendency to the shuffling walk of the Arab, which brings him down on his nose occasionally when walking, yet this was the exception, not the rule: they generally bent their knees and pasterns well, after the pattern of their Australian parent, whose first hint of the propriety of this is given a few days after its birth by a hard rap on the shins against a log in the bush.[7]

This environmental influence, combined with the breeding that has produced what we now know as the Australian Stock Horse, made the Waler a naturally adept cavalry mount or polo pony: the durable truth of the proposition is demonstrated by the continuing export by air of highly priced polo ponies to join the stables of rich players in Southeast Asia and the United States. Much of this is equally true for the Waler breeding regions of the whole of eastern Australia, though the greater susceptibility of Queensland pastures to protracted drought depleted the quality of foals, as at the end of the nineteenth century.

What is also generally true of the Waler's breeding is that it could only be accomplished by people who owned roomy, well-bred mares and had access to good

Thoroughbred stallions. After criticisms of the Queensland horses sent to southern Africa late last century, the point most often made was that a majority of the state's little breeders paid no more than a few shillings in servicing their mares, when the charge for a good sire was £5 5s. On the big stations which became the typical units of production in the twentieth century, owners had their own top Thoroughbred and draught stallions and, like the Macarthurs and the Scotts in the formative years of the 1820s and 1830s, maintained careful records.[8]

The prime advantages of Australia as a potential supplier of horses to India were the low costs of land and labour in the early years of the remount trade. Assigned convict labour was comparatively cheap and much of the land, including that grazed by such pioneering breeders as the Macarthurs, Lawsons, Coxes, Johnstons and Marsdens, was granted by the Crown in recognition of services rendered, or held under squatting licences that cost only ten pounds for twenty square miles each year. This was notably true of the Australian Agricultural Company (henceforth the A.A. Company), which in 1824 had received a grant of a million acres from the Crown to encourage its investment in the colony. As was appropriate for such an imperially conceived company with a head office in London, it aspired early to take advantage of the Indian market and when Captain J. G. Collins came from Madras in 1834, it was the A.A. Company Commissioner, Colonel Henry Dumaresq, who seemed best able to respond to the opportunity.

Let me underline this economic argument about the importance of cheap land as a basis for the remount trade by noticing the trend away from the higher priced pastures of New South Wales and Victoria, and the dominant position of Queensland breeders by the second decade of the twentieth century. In those years when the trade was at its height, characterized by economies of scale at every point, it was a central Queensland property of a thousand square miles, with perhaps a thousand

Young Kentyre, a Clydesdale stallion used on Grosvenor Downs

well-bred dams, and some expensive Thoroughbred and Clydesdale stallions, that was the typical Waler breeding ground. Also typical of this era were the big British India steamships, which carried six to eight hundred horses apiece through Torres Strait, taking three weeks in the trip to Calcutta and rarely losing more than one or two per cent of their stock. The economies enjoyed by Australian suppliers by virtue of cheap land and grazing were indispensable to offset the terrifying risks associated with the long journeys to India, especially in the days of small cargoes in sailing ships. They faced buffeting by head winds as they beat west across the Bight or the risk of uncharted rocks in Torres Strait. In the middle passage they were often becalmed and saw the supplies of water and food sink lower every day. In the Bay of Bengal cyclones hit them with devastating power, almost wiping out entire consignments when the hatches were battened down, as happened to Henry Vanrenen in the *Udston* in October 1874. Even in the Hooghly River on the last leg of the journey to Calcutta, shifting shoals and strong currents had to be negotiated, as Henry Prinsep found in 1870, when he lost most of a cargo of horses and timber, but fortunately his young wife and baby survived.

The final point to be made is the high degree of compatibility between a horse's life on an Australian station and that on regimental duty or polo playing in India. Australian pastures in summer were so dry and hard as to develop a like quality in the hooves of horses, preparing them for the flinty ground on which they would do much of their campaigning and play all of their polo.

No better summary could be given of the character of the horses that went to India than E. M. Curr's description in his 1863 classic, *Pure Saddle-Horses*, based not only on pioneering experiences as a squatter in Victoria, New South Wales and Queensland, but also on extensive travels by horseback in Europe and the Middle East.

Red Duke, one of the Grosvenor Downs Thoroughbred stallions

Remnants of an Army, *oil painting by Lady Butler: the terrain in which Walers were used*

On the first importation of horses into New South Wales, the animal was too valuable to be neglected, and the demand being limited held out no inducement to owners to sacrifice quality to quantity by too early breeding. As the animal increased in numbers, a degree of stoutness and capacity for work quite unknown in England began to manifest itself in the colonial-bred horses, and the English emigrant was surprised to find that the horse he had bred in the country of his adoption was remarkable for a vigorous health and freedom from sickness and disease, and would endure fatigues and perform journeys on grass-feed alone, which would have overtaxed the parent stock in England on the best stable keep. This robust health he still possesses in a remarkable degree. His stoutness was still further increased by the importation of thoroughbred stallions, who, be their pedigree what it might, have had no equals as foal-getters amongst those since introduced. The racing and Arab blood of Whisker and Satellite seemed at their meeting to flow with fresh vigour in the land of the South. As our horses increased in number they still continued not only to uphold, but even to add to their early reputation, thus substantiating their first testimony as to the fitness of the Australian pasture and climate for their full development and perfection. The gentry now, both in town and the bush, rode horses of rare stamp, whose performance surpassed even what their figures promised. The Mounted Police and Border Police, heavy men frequently, with heavy accoutrements, bestrode chargers such as no horse-regiment in England could or can turn out, and have been frequently known, as I have been informed by credible persons, to do their 70 miles for four or five consecutive days without difficulty. Of course I mean on grass-feed alone, without hay or corn. (pp. 143–4)

The Australian saddle horse's ability to endure the stress of prolonged journeys through dry country on grass feed was another factor in its suitability for India's remount needs, which brought the Waler into being as a fact of military life from the mid-1840s. Just a few years earlier, during the First Afghan War from 1838 to 1842, a great invading army made up of divisions from Bengal and Bombay suffered terrible losses of horses and baggage animals on the roundabout route to Kandahar, which for the Bengal detachments involved a march of 1005 miles. In 1839 the Bengal Field Force lost 46 per cent of its cavalry horses and from Bombay 28 per cent were lost, chiefly from the want of food and water in terrain that consisted largely of 'waterless desert and desolate mountain'. Then, after a series of political blunders, came the retreat from Kabul in January 1842, from which only one man, Dr Brydon, stumbled into Jalalabad on a commandeered horse to tell the awful story. Two squadrons of the 5th Bengal Light Cavalry and about 700 irregulars were annihilated and, as Churchill wrote of the disaster, 'The repute of European arms was deeply smitten and the massacre resounded throughout the peninsula'.[9]

One effect of these losses was to create a favourable market for speculative cargoes of Australian horses that were sent to India in response to the collapse of local stock prices in the depression of 1842 to 1846. A more durable result was to impress on the minds of Indian cavalry buyers the importance of securing remounts that had a character for endurance. Though it was to be some years before the Walers were so perceived in India, General Sir James Outram had noticed the superior performance in the campaign of Arab and Persian horses and, more significantly, of recent imports from Cape Colony, which had contributed to the better showing of the Bombay Army.[10]

Although the core of this story is the remount trade between Australia and India, a trade that began with Captain J. G. Collins's three cargoes which left Sydney for Madras in 1834–35, the broader story had an earlier start. The *Sydney Gazette* of 30 November 1816 carried the following advertisement:

> *Horses Wanted* Wanted to purchase immediately, a pair of dark Bay, Brown, or Black Geldings, of about 14½ hands—also a Brown Gelding of 14 hands. They must be of good figure and temper, free from vice or blemish, and have long tails, being required for a Gentleman in India. A liberal price will be given. Apply to Mr Riley at Sydney.

Alexander Riley's initiative of November 1816 was a characteristically individual response to the Asian and Southeast Asian demand for horses suited to domestic and sporting markets. Though an overwhelming proportion of Walers consisted of military horses, intended for service in India, East and Southeast Asia, southern Africa and the Middle East, their export began, as it ended, with the satisfaction of private buyers, mostly sportsmen. This part of the trade came to be seen by Australian horse shippers as no more than the icing on their cake, for it was the military horses, the powerful 'gunners' for the horse artillery, the largely Thoroughbred officers' chargers, and the less handsome 'bounders' intended for other ranks, which filled the stalls in the horse ships that plied the remount trade for more than a century. Before the story gets under way, however, brief answers should be given to two questions. Why did India, and especially its armies, have such a long felt need to import horses, and why was that need so readily satisfied by Australian breeders?

India's rulers, from the Hindus, Moguls and Marathas to the Sikhs and British, imported large numbers of horses for military, domestic and sporting uses because of deficiencies in the scale and quality of the local supply. Horse breeding in India came under stress from the ravages of endemic disease, from severity of climate, which ranged from the awful cold of the north-west frontier to the baking heat of the plains, and from the poverty of most native pastures. In combination, these factors caused horses to be hand fed rather than free ranging and to be stabled and cossetted, and often ill exercised, during their formative years. Only in exceptional cases did these conditions permit the production of strong, agile animals suited to the rigours of military life. Even when the military studs or private breeders succeeded in respect of quality, they necessarily failed in point of cost. It was an economic question, related to the cost per unit of a stud-bred animal, that largely determined the Troup Committee's decision in 1867 to abolish the studs and in effect to depend on Walers.

The use of cavalry as an arm of the Honourable East India Company's military forces began in October 1782 with the arrival in Madras of the 23rd Light Dragoons. In Robert Clive's campaigns that had conquered much of Bengal, horsed units had played an insignificant part, consisting as they did of some mounted civilians and a few native irregulars. It was the initiative of Sir Eyre Coote, the Commander-in-Chief, that brought out the 23rd, soon to be renamed the 19th, for in fighting Hyder Ali in Mysore he had felt the absence of a cavalry force to counter the activities of the Mysorean light horse. As Fortescue wrote in his *History of the British Army*, 'they hung about their enemy like rooks about a heron, hustling, threatening, swooping, always too far away to receive injury, always near enough to inflict it'. In the peace that followed, Colonel John Floyd used the officers and men of the 19th as the nuclei for disciplined, well trained units in Madras, Bengal and Bombay, thus founding the first regular native cavalry in India.[11]

Here two general points need to be made. In its expansionist campaigns of the first half of the nineteenth century, the Company's armies fought opponents, notably the Marathas and Sikhs, who numbered their cavalry in tens of thousands. Horse casualties were high, and there was a direct relationship between the losses suffered in the Sikh Wars in 1843 and the decision of the Governor-General, Lord Ellenborough, to despatch a horse-buying mission to Australia in 1844.

An army comprising a European nucleus and a native majority looked tiny against the 160 millions, at mid-century, of the subcontinent and therefore, even when British territorial expansion ended, there was a continuing need for well-horsed cavalry and artillery to maintain control. Both were indispensable on the north-west frontier, where speedy reprisals were needed to respond to the border raids across an ill-defined line by mounted tribesmen, who descended on remote Indian villages and carried off booty and nubile women. For much of the century, secretaries of state in London and commanders in India went to bed of nights bedevilled by the thought of Russian influence in Afghanistan and fearing a descent upon the northern plains. To counter such possibilities, and more generally to exercise a police role throughout India, large mounted forces were maintained.

Until the reorganization that followed the Mutiny in 1858, there were separate armies in each of the three presidencies, of Bengal, Madras and Bombay, though brought together, as in the First Afghan War, under the commander-in-chief. Philip Mason explains that 'By the time of the Third Maratha War [of 1817–19], the army in

India was an army in being, a professional army, consisting of cavalry, artillery, engineers and infantry, with doctors, a veterinary branch, and Government agencies for procuring bullocks, horses and grain'.[12] Although the East India Company footed the bill for the whole, there was a division between the King's service and the Company's, with the royal regiments taking clear precedence.

A succession of British regiments came to India for terms of duty that might last for twenty years, with reinforcements from home and drafts of time-expired men departing. At the end of the term of duty, men had the chance of transferring to the Company's service or going into civilian employment. Within the Company's service there were both European and Indian troops, with the former alone able to rise to the command of anything more than a company. In each of the Presidency armies until the Mutiny were two battalions of the Company's Europeans; both here and in the native regiments it was Europeans who occupied all the ranks above that of lieutenant.[13]

Some elements of the Indian army—the cavalry and the horse artillery—also needed remounts to provide for the wastage of horses by combat, disease and old age. The cavalry consisted of three types, the royal regiments made up entirely of Europeans, which might be drafted to India for a tour of duty, and two types of native regiments with white officers. The latter were either irregular or regular, or to use the Hindustani and Marathi names, *silladar* and *non-silladar*. The irregular or *silladari* cavalryman, like the English yeoman, supplied his own horse and accoutrements, his stabling, attendants, forage, camp equipment, clothing, swords and lances, though not firearms, ammunition and medical stores. In return for this outlay he received, through most of the nineteenth century, about twenty to thirty rupees a month, or about two to three pounds sterling. The idea of the *silladar* trooper was drawn from Mysorean and Maratha models, in which the most valued riders were those who provided their own horses and served under leaders who had been commissioned by princes.

British practice in India modified the local tradition for *silladari* regiments in ways described by the great modern historian of the British cavalry, the Marquess of Anglesey.

> A recruit, instead of bringing a horse and kit, brought their value in money. On discharge he returned the horse and kit with which he had been issued to the regiment and received back their market value in cash. The replacement of horses and equipment was covered by a 'horse fund' in every troop, to which each man subscribed from his pay and horse allowance. In the course of the years, and in the different regiments, many variations of these two 'provident funds' grew up, but in whatever shape they operated they were designed to ensure that troopers were not left destitute or in debt at the end of their service. Equally important was the proprietary pride in the regiment which his share in its economy gave each man.[14]

It may seem something of a puzzle that cavalry should have taken so long to gain recognized places in the three Presidency armies. Mason suggests 'a shade of reluctance on the part of men mainly of middle-class origin to introduce into the society of Madras the essentially aristocratic figure of the cavalry officer who might despise them as traders'. From the viewpoint of the troopers themselves, and more particularly their officers, there was the difficulty, which continued to be felt until the coming of the Waler, in finding horses in India that approximated in power and speed to the type of mount which had evolved in the latter part of the eighteenth century in response to the demands of the sport of fox-hunting. And the true excellence of the army of British and sepoy troops which conquered Bengal lay in its infantry, whose muskets and bayonets had prevailed so uniformly against 'hordes of undisciplined horsemen'. Yet with the arrival of the British cavalry regiments after 1782 and the parallel development of native cavalry regiments, these mounted forces contributed to an impressive series of victories.[15]

After the battle of Sitabaldi in November 1817 any lingering doubts were removed by the dramatic part played by four troops, chiefly of the 6th Bengal Cavalry, in an engagement between a British force of 1500 men and a Maratha force of 20 000. At a moment when the Marathas had broken through the British defenders on the crown of a hill and seemed about to destroy them utterly, Captain Fitzgerald launched his four troops direct at the enemy's principal mass of cavalry, scattered it 'like a whirlwind' and captured the guns. This 'devoted and generous disobedience' gave Scot the opportunity to summon his infantry to a supreme effort; 'animated by this glorious example', they poured in a volley, charged with the bayonet, cleared the hill and remained 'masters of the plain'.[16] It is worth noticing that apart from British officers and a few gunners, only Indian troops took part in this signal victory.

From an early stage in their importation to India, Australian horses were recognized as being ideal for the horse artillery and in the final quarter of the nineteenth century that vital arm of the Indian army was almost exclusively horsed by Walers. Eighteenth-century battalions had been equipped with bullock-drawn field pieces, six-pounders and twelve-pounders, with the men on foot. The difficulty of keeping up even with infantry and the desirability of combining light artillery with cavalry made for important changes. First came the introduction of 'galloper guns', two of which served with each cavalry regiment, worked by mounted crews. An Experimental Brigade was formed in 1800 from foot soldiers trained in the use of three- and six-pounder guns, which they had to gallop across country, with ammunition wagons, then pull up, swing round, unlimber, and start firing at a range of half a kilometre, then limber up and gallop on again. So marked were their efforts during the Second Maratha War that in 1809 the brigade was developed into three troops of horse artillery.

One feature of the artillery was that it always had a higher proportion of European troops than native and when the horse artillery's composition settled down in the 1820s it had always a predominance of European units. This was a precaution, as Philip Mason points out, that reflected the Company's belief in the decisive nature of this arm of the forces and its reluctance to trust large numbers of Indians with such a powerful weapon. In the others, of course, the native regiments were predominant.[17]

So much for the horsed units of the Indian armies, at least by way of introduction. What of the horses themselves, and the problems associated with their supply?

Aptly enough, for a nobleman whose ancestors included many distinguished cavalrymen, the Marquess of Anglesey begins his discussion of this question by remarking: 'It is generally agreed that the finest horses in the world for cavalry, and much else, are the English Thoroughbreds'. The breed was developed during the seventeenth century from superb imported Arab stallions, which descended from a pure desert breed known in Arabia as Kehilans. With judicious selection and further importations during the reign of William III, a larger and faster horse grew on the kinder northern pastures which happily inherited the staying power of the Arab, its beauty and 'kindness of disposition'.[18]

The hunter that was developed in the late eighteenth century was substantially Thoroughbred and it became the standard cavalry mount, growing in size from an average height of 14 hands 3 inches in 1800 to 15 hands 2½ inches a hundred years on. Seen as a potential remount for India, it had three disadvantages: a sensitivity to extreme climatic changes, a dependence on ample forage and a cost, landed in India, that was beyond the pockets of many officers.[19]

In 1794, less than eight years after the coming of the first British cavalry regiment, each of the three Indian Presidencies had set up horse studs in which to breed its remounts. Veterinary science was then barely in its infancy and in England itself there were only two qualified veterinarians, graduates of the famous French school at Lyons. Dependent on farriers as horse doctors and equipped with little understanding of genetics, the studs were at first a grotesque failure. Those at Bombay and Madras were closed and the one at Bengal was about to follow when the Company engaged the services of one of the most brilliant and adventurous men to appear on the Indian scene.

William Moorcroft, former joint head of what is now the Royal College of Veterinary Surgeons, was brought in by the Company in 1808 to superintend horse breeding in Bengal. At Pusa in Bihar he produced remounts far superior to those of his predecessors and made significant progress in dealing with the contagious equine diseases that ravaged India. Yet his horses were not cheap, and the Pusa-bred remounts cost the officers who were permitted to buy them 800 rupees or £50 at the official rate of 1s 3d that prevailed for the first half of the century. The impact of such a price may be measured by noticing that the basic pay of European subalterns was £273 a year at mid-century, while that of Indian cavalrymen ranged from twenty rupees a month for a *sowar* or trooper to 300 rupees for a *Resaldar* first class, the highest rank then available to native officers.[20]

Moorcroft's final essay in this field was a series of attempts, beginning in 1812, to find in Central Asia a breed of horses that would make more suitable sires than the Arab or Thoroughbred. It was the Turkoman breed of Central Asia that gave most promise, he thought, and at one point he made a treaty with the government of Ladakh that sought to open up a trade route through which horses might be supplied to India. (The constant refrain of the Indian remount authorities at least from the 1830s was the desire to find a source of horses, bred if possible in India itself, or in countries from which a steady flow might be expected, free from the vagaries of diplomacy and military action. Remembering this, we might see a degree of inevitability in the relationship that was built up with Australian suppliers.)

Upon the death of Moorcroft 'beyond Bokhara' in 1825, the studs reverted, as General Sir Frederick Smith put it in 1891, to 'the control of their original incompetent superintendents . . . The product was the laughing-stock of the army and the despair of the East India Company. From first to last the Studs cost millions; the mismanagement was staggering and unbelievable'.[21]

While the Indian studs were pursuing equine excellence with such disappointing results, a parallel operation got under way that produced lasting satisfaction for all the interested parties. This came to be known as the Indian Remount Department, which was an agency of the army charged with the task of buying suitable animals for the Indian cavalry and horse artillery in whatever market, domestic or foreign, it thought most appropriate.

The Presidency of Madras raised the first four regiments of Indian cavalry in 1785, so it is appropriate that it should also have appointed the first remount officer, in the person of Lieutenant-Colonel D. Campbell, who opened up lines of supply from Hyderabad and the Deccan in the same year. He travelled widely, 3000 kilometres in 30 months, and bought 1675 horses. In the same year, Colonel Floyd was buying for the newly arrived 19th Light Dragoons, securing ponies of 14 hands 2 inches, some of them Arabs from Travancore, for double the price paid by Campbell for Native Cavalry remounts.[22] It was the shape of things to come, both in relation to the price differential and to the start of an interest in Arab remounts.

A Madras remount officer's life was not an easy one. Many of the Kutch remounts bought by native agents in the provinces near Kathiawar were shipped to Mangalore, on the south-eastern coast of the peninsula. One difficulty was the risk of losing cargoes to the pirates who were then so active on the coast, and who had ready markets in the stables of Indian princes. A more durable problem, which was not solved until the end of the nineteenth century, was the absence of natural deep water harbours within the Madras region. In one of the few studies of the early remount trade, Major R. A. Addington explained that the Arab dhows bringing the horses could not cross the bar at Mangalore, so country boats were sent out to meet them. The horses were swung out into the boats, which took about six at a time, and they were then taken into shallow water, where the boats were capsized and the horses forced to leap out and flounder ashore.[23]

In spite of the primitiveness of this arrangement the numbers of remounts coming through Mangalore increased to nearly 1000 per annum in 1804, when it was decided that the stud at Ganjam was unsatisfactory. Major Patrick Walker was brought back as remount officer and in 1809 built a pier and crane at which the country boats could be more safely unloaded. Because his experience had shown the susceptibility of the horses to the north-west winds after landing from the stuffy atmosphere of the ship, he also built stalls to accomodate 102 horses near the pier, at a total cost of Pagodas 2500, or Rs 8750. His masters were well pleased.[24]

Astonishingly, even at Madras itself the same perilous and cumbersome system prevailed, until an artificial harbour was completed in 1904 by Sir Francis Spring, after efforts that had begun in 1877 with the construction of breakwaters, which were almost wiped out by the cyclone of 1881.[25] The situation confronting the first Australian horses to land in Madras in 1834 would have been much the same as that encountered by a Western Australian shipper, as described in the *Perth Gazette* of 22 November 1867. It will be clear from a perusal of this extract why Madras was quickly left behind by Calcutta in the remount trade. The writer had accompanied a consignment of horses which included a batch from Edmund Brockman, one of the pioneering breeders of remounts in the west. The vessel, perhaps four weeks out of Fremantle, has anchored in the roads two kilometres from the coast, and the horses must be landed by flat-bottomed *masullah* boats of about four metres in length and half as broad, built from planks of wood laced together, and possessing the flexibility which alone permitted their survival.[26]

> Thin, weak, and with sores, their trials should end here but for the barbarous custom of landing them on the beach through the rollers. A boat of thin planks . . . manned by fifteen to twelve coolies brings one horse ashore, which is landed after this fashion:—
> The rollers thump her up high and dry knocking the horse down or against the sides several times; the boat is then turned over on its side seaward and the horse tumbles out as best he can. The rolling surf intimidates the poor thing, and if he will not budge after brutally applying sticks he is dragged out by the halter. Frequently the boat is let go when the animal is but half out, and thus balanced on the gunwale has to drag its hind legs out over the side, grazing them sorely.

By the end of 1810, Major Tylden writes, the remounting of India's armies progressed significantly with the establishment of what became known as the Remount Department, under William Moorcroft as its first *de facto* Director of Remount and Veterinary Services. In the same year the first moves were made to import military horses from abroad, with the despatch of Lieutenant St J. Blacker, 1st Madras Light Cavalry, to the Persian Gulf to buy Arabs, described as '14.2 high, short limbed, boney, full chested, broad across the loins, round sided and deep barrelled'. From 1811 to May 1813 Blacker supplied a total of 584 horses at an average price of Rs 542.5, of which 412 were selected for the cavalry. (That was a high success rate.) The board that passed them judged them to be 'infinitely better calculated for the service than the generality of those procured from Cutch . . . and better adapted for heavy weight and to endure fatigue'.[27] The Gulf of Kutch in north-western India remained until 1818 the chief source of Madras remounts, which included indigenous breeds such as the Goelwar, the Gondel and some from as far away as Kabul, Kandahar and Khorassan. A severe famine in the region in 1811 accentuated the move to buy Arabs, and the Kathiawari horses began a climb in popularity, based on the stamina and speed bred into them for centuries by their owners, raiders from time immemorial, whose lives depended on the quality of their horseflesh—not unlike Australian bushrangers.[28]

Amongst the first imports to India under the new programme were the remounts from Cape Colony, often known as Capes or Capers, which for forty years enjoyed an almost unrivalled prestige. Descended from Arab horses that had been imported by the Dutch from Java in 1652, the Cape horse was a result of crossing with the English Thoroughbred, with a hardiness that came from generations of adaptation to the poor pasture and harsh climate of the veld.[29] Writing of 'the Cape Horse in India' H. A. Wyndham referred to the breed's great powers of endurance and quoted the opinion of a Bengali in 1847,

> A Caper, after he appears to be beat, has only to be treated to an offsaddle, a kick on his nether end, and a roll or two on the bare ground to make him as fresh as when he started . . . A roll is as good as provender to a tired Cape horse.[30]

Cape horses were ideal for the forced marches and rough fare of sustained campaigns, as they proved soon after Lieutenant-Colonel Havelock bought sixty-five of them for £25 each in 1837, intended for the 4th Light Dragoon Guards. 'They were considered the best horses in the Regiment and worth twice the sum given for them, as they stood the march to Cabul better than horses of any other description.'[31] Can it be wondered that in the campaigns in southern Africa at the end of the century, this horse should have defeated all comers, including the Thoroughbred and the Waler?

The breed's career in India began with a shipment of remounts that sailed from Table Bay in December 1769 in the *Duke of Kingston*.[32] No progress seems to have been made in the trade till Cape horses began to race on the Indian turf in 1812. The first venture was unsuccessful but after 1815 when Captain Christopher brought in the well-performed roan horse Escape, there was a smart succession of Capers doing well at Calcutta meetings.

As was also to be true of Walers in India in the mid-1840s, the despatch of race-horses coincided with shipments of remounts, a trade strongly associated with the initiative of that controversial sportsman, Lord Charles Somerset, Governor of Cape Colony from 1814 to 1826. By introducing Thoroughbreds from England, crossing them in some cases with the best Cape horses, selling the progeny to local farmers and promoting exports to India and Mauritius, Somerset made a huge contribution to the colony's pastoral prospects. In a despatch of 1817 he claimed to have founded an export trade that would be worth £25 000 per annum.[33] Profits from horse breeding balanced the losses some farmers sustained in other areas and Martinus Melk told the Commissioners of Inquiry in June 1824 that his exports to India had brought good profits. One name cropping up at the Inquiry was that of Mr D. van Reenen, a sub-stantial landowner and horse breeder whose descendants became famous both in the Australian remount trade of the nineteenth century and in the breeding of military horses at Lahore in the twentieth.[34]

Significantly, Melk was asked by the Commissioners if his breeding estates at the Berg River and St Helena Bay were subject to 'Horse Sickness'. In my reading of Cape documents, this is the first mention of the epizootic disease that laid waste the horse breeding provinces of southern Africa, killing 64 850 horses in 1854–55 (a monetary loss of £525 000 sterling), though in his report of 1894 the Director of the Colonial Bacteriological Institute explained that the known history of the disease went back to 1780–81. It was this disease, more than any other factor, which prevented the Cape horses from realizing their potential in India. At the same time, it gave Australian breeders and shippers an opportunity which they grasped eagerly.

3

A Great Trade Begins

A S MAY BE SAID of any trade that aspires to stability and continuity, the early and long term success of Waler exports depended on a conjunction of interest between producers and consumers. The great initial task of demonstrating that conjunction fell to the lot of a small number of entrepreneurs, people with the vision to identify real possibilities and possessing the capital, courage and tenacity to pursue their chances even in the face of disappointment. The conjunction that gave rise to the Waler trade depended at the Indian end on that country's inability to breed quality horses at acceptable prices; at the Australian end it was a matter of having an exportable surplus of such stock, which could be made available to Indian buyers.

What seems remarkable is the speed with which breeders, merchants, and ship owners in New South Wales recognized the prospects in Asia and moved, tentatively at first, then decisively, to take advantage of that market. When Alexander Riley inserted in the *Sydney Gazette* the advertisement given in the previous chapter, seeking three good horses for a private gentleman in India, the Australian colonies were less than 29 years old and their equine population stood at about 3450, chiefly saddle and light harness horses with Arab blood. In July 1834 when the remount trade had its true start with Captain Collins's three cargoes for the Madras army, total horse numbers were perhaps 14 000, hardly a reservoir on which exports might be based. Indeed, this soon proved to be a false start. Within a year or so, the local demand for saddle horses that was generated by Australia's first pastoral boom made domestic prices climb so strongly as to remove any interest in speculative exports.[1]

Alexander Riley's contribution to the incipient horse export trade did not stop short with the small consignments to India of 1816. With his partner Richard Jones he shipped twenty-five young horses in the *Fame* to Batavia in May 1817, so making the first substantial export of livestock from the Australasian region, to a market that remained modestly profitable until well on in the twentieth century.[2]

Although Riley returned to London at the end of 1817, to make his name as the pioneer exporter of Saxon Merino sheep to New South Wales, he has a special significance in the horse trade, not only because of his role as an initiator, but from his being so typical of its founders. In addition, he had an Indian connection in the shape of his younger brother, Edward, who was almost certainly the 'Gentleman in India' to whom the 1816 export was consigned.[3] In this he reflected the intimacy of the links between India and Australia until the Second World War. Cargoes of Indian food, clothing, livestock and rum had sustained the colonists from the earliest times. Sydney's first free merchant, Robert Campbell, was a partner in a Calcutta firm. Our soldiers, governors, lawyers, farmers and traders frequently came to the colonies after experiences in India which shaped their attitudes and gave them ideas about trading opportunities. The impulse to send horse cargoes to India was fed, in turn, by the need of colonial shipowners like Robert Towns to find back lading for ships which all too often sailed in ballast to India where they would seek cargoes for England.

Another colonist who made a brief contribution to the horse trade was that much loved figure of Sydney society, the naval officer, John Piper. Amongst his papers at the Mitchell Library is a letter sent to him by John Richard O'Connor, a Calcutta merchant, dated 28 August 1820, enclosing a Bill of Lading for a nine-year-old grey Arab stallion named Scotchman. The animal had raced successfully in India as a four-year-old and, as O'Connor pointed out to Riley, his male progeny would sell well if exported to India. His cost including freight and insurance was Rs 2156 (or about £144). It was suggested that this be met by Riley's despatching six large wethers, a cow in calf and four pairs of horses, 'no rips—for there are as good judges here, as any part of the world'. They could be sent on the return voyage to Calcutta in the brig *Haldane*, with the same groom to look after them.[4]

Soon after, the name of John Macarthur made its first appearance in the manuscripts that record the beginnings of the horse trade. This man, a long time friend of John Piper and the leading prophet of the export to England of fine Merino wool, had built up at his Camden estates an extensive horse stud based on Thoroughbred, Arab and Cleveland Bay stallions and mares. On 1 July 1822 his friend Captain George Gambier wrote from Barrackpore near Calcutta to describe the happy outcome of a mission he had carried out for Macarthur, transporting a young stallion to India, intended as a present for the Governor-General, the Marquess of Wellesley, to show him 'a specimen of what is doing' in New South Wales.[5]

Such attentions to the great and powerful were part of Macarthur's *modus operandi*, as he had shown in making available to Commissioner John Bigge, during his stay in the colony, a high-bred Arab stallion. Our interest in this present to Lord Wellesley lies in its demonstration of Macarthur's belief in the potential value India held as a market for Australian horses.

Gambier's letter gives the first account of an Australian horse making the long voyage to India. When they arrived at Calcutta on 23 June, which must have been immensely trying at the height of an Indian summer, the horse was in 'excellent health and spirits', as he had proved a good sailor, soon settling into a routine and maintaining a 'voracious appetite'. Gambier was able to give the horse far more attention and space than was allowed to the poor beasts that followed. On the way north from Sydney before reaching Torres Strait, Gambier put the horse in a sling to help him deal with the ship's rolling, a practice that was not without its later critics. Later, he was given a thick coir mat to assist his footing, and every day he managed to roll several times, stretching out to sleep at full length both in daytime siestas and at night. John Macarthur did not live to see Collins's first cargoes of remounts leave for India in 1834, but his sons James and William were in the vanguard of the trade when it took off in 1843.

While Macarthur was preparing to send his present to Lord Wellesley, Thomas Henty, a farmer and banker of Sussex in England was beginning to contemplate a relocation to the Australian colonies, impelled by the poor state of agriculture in England and by hopes of ample horizons in the Antipodes. A letter of January 1822 was sent to John Street in New South Wales, inquiring about agricultural prospects there and in Van Diemen's Land, and asking particularly about the chance of finding in India a market for the 'best blood horses'. When the Hentys arrived at the Swan River in 1829 to take up their huge but almost worthless grant, the stock they carried out in the *Caroline* included the Thoroughbred stallion Sir John. Yet, writing to his brother William soon after arrival, James Henty expressed doubts at the chance of breaking into the Indian market, since the trade from the Cape of Good Hope had taken such strong root through the efforts of Lord Charles Somerset. It was not until the Hentys went to Port Phillip that they were able to realize those early hopes.[6]

The potent name of John Macarthur reappears in the annals of the horse trade with the founding in 1824 of the A.A. Company, incorporated by Act of Parliament, with a capital of £1 million and a land grant of a million acres at Port Stephens. For Macarthur this was the culmination of a twenty-year-old dream, and there were Macarthurs both on the London board and in the colonial committee of management. Though concerned primarily with the satisfaction of the English demand for fine wool, the company soon built up the largest horse stud in the colony, importing large numbers of blood stock and also buying in the colony itself, from 1825 to 1827, a total of 108 horses, comprising 2 entires, 54 mares, 25 geldings, 9 colts and 18 fillies, at a cost of £4692. A statement of horse imports by the company to July 1829 showed a total landed at Port Stephens of 2 blood stallions and 5 mares (which I take to be Thoroughbred), 3 Cleveland stallions and 11 mares, and 2 Welsh pony stallions and 9 mares. As early as 26 May 1828, John Macarthur was able to write to the directors from Port Stephens after a visit of inspection that the horses were in 'a progressive state of improvement . . . and will soon become valuable as a supply for the colony, and I should hope, an export to India'.[7]

What helped to give reality to these expectations was the relocation of much of the A.A. Company's huge grant from the infertile and damp area near Port Stephens to the far superior grazing land of the Liverpool Plains. Soon after this was done, Colonel Henry Dumaresq was appointed as Commissioner to replace Sir Edward Parry. In addition to holding runs near what became the town of Armidale, Dumaresq had the model property of St Heliers, which Edward Eyre described in 1833 as 'the best-ordered, best-managed station on the Hunter'. Here, in a river valley that was to become the first cradle of horse breeding in Australia, the Colonel in his declining years made great contributions to the development of Thoroughbred and Cleveland Bay stock. His reputation as a horseman and desire to promote the export of remounts would soon find expression, with the arrival of Captain Collins from Madras.[8]

One further point needs to be made about the colonial situation in order to explain the favourable response that was briefly accorded to Collins. By the time of the annual count of the Company's horse stock on 30 April 1831, the total had risen to 277, comprising 77 Thoroughbred and Cleveland, 143 'colonial' (largely Arab-descended) and 57 Welsh and Timor ponies. In the 8th Annual Report that published this information, the significant observation was made: 'With horses of good breed the Colony of New South Wales had latterly become abundantly stocked, so as to close, in some degree, the prospect of a profitable demand in the home market for animals of any but the finest kind'.

To put the matter of market strength in perspective, there is an illuminating summary of the Company's horse sales during a ten year period from 1831, enclosed by P. P. King in a despatch to the directors of 30 April 1842.[9] Three horses had been sold in 1831 at an average price of £78, and fifteen in 1832 at an average of nearly £24, which represented at that time an annual wage for a pastoral worker. From 1833 to 1835, larger numbers had been sold, for depressed prices ranging from £5 to £14. After this period of slump, the demand was stimulated by a pastoral boom that is conveyed by the title of Stephen Roberts's classic, *The Squatting Age in Australia*, and horse prices climbed from £22 in 1836 to a high point of £54 in 1840.

In the light of these figures, which show the Company realizing the lowest horse prices in the decade in three successive years from 1833 to 1835, it can be understood that when Captain Collins came looking for remounts in the very middle of the downturn, he had the advantage of colonial breeders and more particularly of the Company, which was under pressure to improve its performance after management crises in the late 1820s.

We return now to a more detailed examination of the circumstances that prompted the Indian armies to seek remounts in Australia.

William Moorcroft's career in India from 1808 to 1825 is the apt starting point, because it was regarded for much of the nineteenth century as the high point of the Bengal Stud, with successes that gave later superintendents a measure of their own failures. More useful to us than this idealized perception of the Moorcroft era is the way in which it dramatized the basic problems of breeding horses on a large scale in India. Reduced to essentials there were two almost intractable difficulties: the procurement of suitable foundation stock and the overcoming of severe environmental hazards, relating to climate, disease and food supply. The summary that follows draws heavily on Garry Alder's pathbreaking biography, *Beyond Bokhara The Life of William Moorcroft Asian Explorer and Pioneer Veterinary Surgeon 1767–1825*.

As a young convert from human to animal medicine, who founded the practice of veterinary science in Britain, Moorcroft was taught by Lord Heathfield the prime importance of size and bone in cavalry horses. It was an understanding that lay at the centre of his work in India. While engaged in a most lucrative London practice that included King George III and the Prince Regent as clients, he was commissioned by his friend Edward Parry in 1800 to select breeding stock for despatch to the East India

Company's new studs in Bengal and Madras. Three years later he was appointed superintendent of the company's small stud at Padnalls, near London, which was set up to breed foundation stock for the Indian studs.

As we have seen, the campaign fought by Lord Cornwallis against Mysore in 1790–92, and the growth of princely armies modelled on European patterns with cavalry and artillery had forced an urgent development of the company's mounted forces. For European dragoons, riding at a weight of 18 stone (or 115 kilograms), neither the country-bred mounts nor the Arab imports were sufficiently powerful. As Garry Alder explains, anticipating the situation that confronted Moorcroft at Pusa after 1808:

> Unfortunately almost no horses suitable for cavalry were bred in the company's territories at all. The military purchasing agents were forced to range further and further to the north in pursuit of a dwindling supply, as political upheavals in Afghanistan and elsewhere continued to erode the once-great northern horse trade. Even more serious, supplies from this source were liable to be cut off at a moment's notice by the Maratha powers across whose territories they came, just when they might be needed most. (p. 50)

In the days before the shortening of the route to India by the construction of the Suez Canal in 1867, it was not possible for the company to contemplate the despatch to India of hunter-type remounts. During the Napoleonic wars the problem of supply was exacerbated by the risks of action by French privateers at many points of the long oceanic route, making the transportation of even the much smaller numbers of breeding stock a hazardous and often uneconomic venture. In January 1807, just before retiring as Commander-in-Chief, Lord Lake had recommended abolition of the Bengal Stud on the ground of its inefficiency and the purchase of remounts on the open market. Lake had been appalled by the discovery that after ten years effort and the expenditure of a million rupees, only 47 horses had been produced of a quality acceptable to the cavalry, giving a unit cost of staggering proportions. But the Board of Directors refused to disband, and decided to reinvigorate the stud by sending out to Pusa an outstanding veterinarian. Moorcroft was to be tempted away from London by the offer of Rs 30 000 p.a. (£ 2000), a salary exceeded in India by those of only a few officials, such as the Governor-General, the Commander-in-Chief and the Chief Justice, and by the opportunity of service and adventure, as it proved, on an unlimited stage.

On the way to Pusa, which lay 300 miles upstream from Calcutta, Moorcroft experienced the perils of the *masullah* boats in the Madras surf, before crossing the Bay of Bengal and entering the Hooghly. That crossing began on 16 October 1808, the very day, as Garry Alder points out, on which insurances on ships in the area ended for three months, with the break up of the south-west monsoon and the start of the cyclone season. At first light on 27 September the pilot came aboard to navigate the *Indus* for 100 miles through the ever-changing shoals of the Hooghly River, giving Moorcroft a sample of what Australian horse shippers would encounter for nearly a century.

Sailing ships proceeded with the incoming tide under reduced rig, aided in the contest with the shoals by native rowing boats. On the change of tide they would tie up for six hours, visited by day by boatmen from Kedgeree hawking welcome fruit

Dalhousie Square, Calcutta

and vegetables, and at night by clouds of mosquitoes, while on shore could be heard the sounds of the tiger-infested jungle. Consider Alder's description of the final leg of the journey:

> In those days, the river at this point hid the city almost till the last moment, although the scattering of splendid white houses on the river bank, with their wide porticoes and green shutters must have been a welcome reassurance of approaching civilization. And yet next morning, if Moorcroft were up in the first light of dawn, and he probably was, he could have feasted his eyes on what many at the time believed to be the finest city landscape in the world. For they were anchored in Garden Reach, Calcutta. The river at this point was about twice as wide as the Thames in London, with fine gardens running down to the water's edge. Behind, facing the water in an irregular line and bright in the clear air, were the recently built, magnificent villas and palaces of the well-to-do and, a few hundred yards upstream, the ivory splendour of the new Government House. The crowded native town with its tangle of mat and thatch huts and narrow lanes—the real India—was out of sight just to the north. (p. 80)

The central feature of the Bengal Stud was an estate of 5000 acres (2023 ha.) on the banks of the Burhi Gandak River, a tributary of the Ganges, 300 miles north of Calcutta. There, in highly fertile and well-watered pastures Major William Frazer, the previous superintendent, had set up the Home Branch of the stud, which had the task of breeding the stallions and mares that were supplied to Indian farmers who contracted to breed horses in association with the stud, spread over an area comparable in size with southern England.

When Moorcroft completed his first inspection of this vast operation he 'knew in his heart that the apparently startling decision in 1807 to abolish the stud was really the sound one'.[10] Not one of the three branches of the stud was in good shape. The Home Branch had been undermined by Frazer's excessive attachment to Arab stallions, which for all their beauty and stamina lacked the size and bone that Moorcroft saw as essential. Badly drained with much of the pasture spoiled by great *jheels* or shallow marshes of stagnant water, and subject to insect-borne infections, which in 1810 killed many of the English stallions, this land was but slowly improved by the new superintendent's drainage and irrigation schemes. For many years he believed the Pusa site was a critical problem, causing the high incidence of *bursati* (a skin eruption that was rapidly spread by flies), strangles (an infectious febrile disease caused by bacteria), and a weakness in the horses' backs and loins called *kumri*. The stables were poorly ventilated and overcrowded, with some 1300 horses and as many workers, even before the arrival of a further 360 horses from the disbanded Madras stud.

The Zamindari Branch was based on the loan of stud stallions to selected local breeders spread over a wide area, with 50 mares a year being covered and the best progeny being bought by the superintendent and kept at Pusa until the colts could be drafted to regiments and the fillies to another branch of the stud. Moorcroft was staggered by the mismanagement of this branch. The stallions were so poor that he proposed immediately to geld more than half; at the same time he found only 20 per cent of the mares were of the standard cavalry height and of these, many were old, neglected and diseased, with 'their forelegs diverging from each other like a half opened pair of compasses'.[11] When Moorcroft's first committee of cavalry officers inspected a batch of 133 young horses purchased from the *zamindars* (or landholders) by Frazer in his last year they found not one suitable for drafting to a regiment. Moorcroft began reforms, improving the quality of the stallions and using a system of incentives and rewards to encourage a more faithful performance. But better results were not attained until his final years.

Major Frazer's chief effort had been with the Nisfi Branch of the stud, which farmed stud mares out to local breeders who were paid a rupee per month for their keep and required to put them to a stud stallion at Pusa once a year. The progeny had a guaranteed sale to the stud as yearlings, with half (*nisf* in Arabic) going to stud and breeder alike. Perhaps the basic flaw was that the scheme appealed only to poor men who starved the mares and fed their children instead. During seven years operation only 162 horses of adequate size were produced by 2000 mares.[12]

Moorcroft embarked on an immediate programme of agricultural improvement at Pusa, which had the effect by the end of his term of reducing casualties from disease by 90 per cent, largely from the effects of his planting of extensive crops of oats, lucerne and potatoes. He believed that the traditional grass feeds, with their high concentration of sodium carbonate, contributed to the outbreaks of *kumri* and *bursati*.[13] But he remained convinced that the existing stud operation was fundamentally wrong, both in the character of the Pusa site and the quality of the breeding stock, so in January 1811 he set out on the first of his great journeys in search of some alternatives.

By the time of his return to Pusa in August, Moorcroft was satisfied that he must look beyond the equine resources of the entire Ganges valley in order to satisfy the need for suitable breeding stock. Going through the once flourishing breeding areas of Rohilkhand and to the famous fair at Hardwar far to the north of Delhi he received a general account of decline, both in the efforts of breeders and the resources of the traditional channels of the horse trade. Even the Maratha horses were a disappointment, though he met an ancient Rampur dealer named Ahmad Ali Khan who told him much of the old routes used by Afghan merchants going to the fabled city of Bokhara, north of the River Oxus in Central Asia, and bringing back to Kanpur and Lucknow strings of fine Persian and Turki horses. 'But that was before war and anarchy in Afghanistan and northern India disrupted the traffic'.[14]

The story of Moorcroft's remaining years, at least on the face of it, is of a constant effort to find foundation stock of sufficient size and bone to revitalize the Bengal Stud. His biographer thinks that 'an even stronger imperative than new breeding-stock may have been his own persistent inner drive to escape from the confines of routine and orthodoxy'.[15] Moorcroft took three major journeys, first in 1811 to the north-west, then in 1812 into Tibet and Nepal, and, from 1819 to 1825, the epic journey to Bokhara, where he died in mysterious circumstances, failing not only in the immediate mission to buy better horses but also in the crucial subsidiary plan to open up a secure trade route by which future purchases might be made. Though struck by the suitability of Bokharan horse management and of the desert lands along the Oxus as a place for breeding 'the finest horses in the world', Moorcroft could see that five years of constant warfare had taken a toll of the horse stock, spoiling the teeming bazaars of Bokhara and disrupting the ancient channels of the horse trade with the south. When he died of a fever at Andkhoi on 27 August 1825 most of the forty or so 'moderately good horses' he had managed to buy were lost, as were the lives of many friends and servants who accompanied him.

Before leaving on that tragic journey, Moorcroft had fought for six years against a now hostile board at Calcutta to preserve the breeding operation at Pusa, defeated in the short term by the legacy of his predecessor, which kept the stud's production of colts to less than a hundred a year, or an eighth of the cavalry's needs. The board criticized the frequency of Moorcroft's recourse to gelding, taking the view that the operation 'injures the figure and courage of the animal'.[16] It also distrusted his use of cross-breeding to obtain size and bone, and felt understandably nervous at the long absences of their superintendent. Yet his agricultural, medical and breeding measures were at length successful.

In his last year at the stud Moorcroft had the pleasure of seeing significant achievement, both in the dramatic success of his oats crop at Pusa at a time of general famine and in the quality of drafts from the new Circle System which he had planned in 1814 as a modification and extension of the Zamindari Branch. From Patna to Hardwar, Pusa mares as well as stallions would be made available to local breeders under closer supervision, with the government able to buy yearlings at prices determined by quality. Garry Alder sums up the results, though unfortunately without giving details:

Entirely new were the solid statistics of falling unit costs and the startling rises in the quality and quantity of the cavalry admissions from 1819 onwards. For a little while the Bengal breeding-studs came close to realizing the high hopes held out for them from the very beginning. Indeed Moorcroft's period at the stud was later looked back on by his baffled and disappointed successors as an unattainable golden age and the credit was always given to him. (p. 207)

Madras Landing, *aquatint by C. Hunt after J. B. East, London 1856*

It was not from Bengal but from the Presidency of Madras that the initiative came to seek remounts in Australia. One obvious reason was that Madras, since the abolition of its stud in 1808, needed to go further afield in seeking remounts. From the end of the Third Maratha War in 1819 India experienced a period of virtual peace for twenty years and therefore lacked the most urgent stimulus to recruit fresh horses. Yet deficiencies had been remarked in the Madras native cavalry, with a military letter of 28 January 1831 transmitting a complaint by Lord Dalhousie about the 'inefficient state of H.M.'s 13th Light Dragoons' with regard to its horses.[17] Problems continued in 1832, and in a draft despatch of 2 October 1833, disappointment was expressed at the bad condition of the horses of the Light Cavalry, as a result, it was said, of the extent to which officers, including even the former commander-in-chief, had taken chargers from the Remount Department for their own private use. The directors hoped that 'prompt and effectual measures' would be taken to restore the native cavalry to its former character.

On 1 June 1833, Brevet Captain J. G. Collins of the 13th Light Dragoons wrote to Henry Chamier, Chief Secretary of Madras, submitting a novel and comprehensive scheme, the essence of which was speedily carried out. Collins suggested that he be given eighteen months leave and half pay in advance with a view to his visiting New South Wales and Van Diemen's Land, where he would buy horses for the Madras artillery and dragoons, with a contract ensuring their purchase at ruling prices, subject to approval by the remount committee. Linked with this central proposal was the imaginative idea that a depot be set up at King George Sound in Western Australia, staffed by retired or convalescent Indian army people, where remounts could be collected from the eastern Australian colonies for eventual despatch to Madras.

Collins's military life had occupied nineteen years, including seventeen in the 21st and 13th Dragoon Regiments. He had travelled in Europe on half pay for two years, studying the supply and management of military horses. In support of the retirement idea he quoted the views of Lieutenant-Colonel Hanson about the salubriousness of the climate in King George Sound and Perth. As to the quality of eastern Australian horses, he depended at first on the pronouncements of Robert Dawson, the former agent of the A.A. Company, and of Charles Frazer, the colonial botanist. He reminded the chief secretary of the degree to which British rule in India depended on the efficiency of its mounted forces. Their maintenance with an adequate supply of remounts was too often frustrated by hostile seasons, plague, famine and the capricious action of foreign powers, which led to the suspension of supply. Madras itself drew most of its horses from the Persian Gulf but that supply, he said, had recently been dislocated by 'famine and the sword'.[18]

This proposal was favourably received and Collins wrote again in early August 1833, citing the opinion of Captain Forbes of the 39th Regiment, who had commanded the mounted police in Sydney and believed that the colony would be an apt source for powerful horses, since the average height of the 144 horses under his command had been just under 15 hands. Collins argued, rather optimistically, that whereas the usual remount lasted less than eight years, the colonial horses, 'from their superior size, strength, and blood will be found equal to double the length of service of the present troop horses'.[19]

The Madras government moved now with breath-taking speed, and we find an official letter being written on 9 August to the New South Wales Colonial Secretary to introduce the Collins mission. As horses fit for cavalry were thought to be available there in considerable numbers at a moderate price, the government requested the issue of a proclamation stating that Madras was ready to take 200 horses immediately, and for the three following years, at an average rate of Madras Rs 590, for each horse delivered and passed by a committee as meeting their basic requirements in respect of breeding, age, height and conformation, as detailed in the previous chapter.[20]

Collins sailed from Madras on 23 September via Mauritius and Van Diemen's Land. A month earlier he had written privately to the Colonial Secretary in Sydney anticipating some of the problems facing the project, not least the feeling of jealousy on the part of commissariat officers, formerly supreme in their influence on remount purchasing in Madras, at the invasion of their domain. That feeling was likely to produce many unfair rejections and consequent hardship to the colonial breeders who took the risk of despatching horses subject to committee approval after landing. He planned therefore to offer a fair price to the breeders on the spot, hoping to encourage them to 'evince a becoming liberality in endeavouring to promote a project now in its infancy which if it succeeds must be in time a Source of Wealth and Prosperity to them'.[21] An important concession made to Collins by the Madras government before his departure was that, in spite of their doubts about the suitability of geldings in the service, they would be prepared to accept as many as fifty in the first year's importation.[22]

Soon after arriving in Sydney the captain took a seven years lease on land at Petersham on the western outskirts of the city where horses were to be collected for shipment. From here he wrote on 12 February 1834 to the Colonial Secretary, Alexander McLeay, explaining his intention of offering breeders a choice between selling to him in the colony or despatching horses to Madras at their own risks. In this letter we see the first breakdown that was ever attempted of the costs of horse shipments to India[23] and a remarkably astute appreciation of the likely importance for the horse trade of exchange rates between India and Australia. Collins pointed out that Madras rupees had a current value in the colony at the depreciated rate of one shilling and eight pence, so cutting the Madras price of Rs 590 down to an effective £44 in Sydney. (His arithmetic was defective: £49 3s 4d is correct.) If Collins were to act as shipper, however, he would arrange by a process of barter to receive the rupee at two shillings, so getting the full £59 for each horse and making a profit of nearly £10 a head. As he told McLeay, 'by this alone can the plan succeed'. (See Appendix 1.)

Sir Richard Bourke brought to the governorship of New South Wales a love of horses and recent experience at Cape Colony, which had already exported racehorses and remounts to India for more than a decade. Though his name does not appear in the surviving papers relating to the Collins project, it can be imagined that he was highly favourable to the venture. As well as issuing a proclamation in the terms desired by the Madras government, Secretary McLeay sent circulars to the colony's magistrates in May 1834, asking them to confer with horse breeders and report on the number of horses in each district and on the interest of the proprietors in the plan to export remounts.

The magistrates' replies showed a general disinclination by breeders to ship on the terms offered by the Indian government. Police Magistrate Reed wrote from Newcastle to say, on the basis of eight years service in Madras, that only a very rich man could take the risks of sending horses on such voyages to have them landed through the surf at Madras. No one at this stage would contemplate the further hurdle of possible rejection by a committee in Madras, and we see the first of many demands for the appointment of agents who could purchase in Australia. The emphasis on entires was most awkward, for colonial breeders gelded all but a tiny proportion of their colts, because of the expenses associated with keeping them entire. More secure fences were needed, and the penalties imposed by recent legislation on the owners of straying stallions made gelding unavoidable. Colonel Henry Dumaresq, Commissioner of the A.A. Company, was one of the few breeders who indicated a readiness to keep colts entire so as to meet the Indian preference. Until this was modified the trade was bound to remain a small one.[24]

Collins toured the colony's chief horse breeding areas with Veterinary Surgeon Lindesay, who had joined him in Sydney after deciding, apparently, that Van Diemen's Land was not yet ready to export. Collins told the outgoing A.A. Company Commissioner, Sir Edward Parry, that he had 'never seen anything in the Colony, to compare with the Company's Stud', and at once bought twenty horses: ten yearling colts at £8 each, seven two-year-old colts at £14 and three geldings of three years at £20.[25] A few of those horses were amongst the cargo of thirty-two that left Sydney for Madras on 2 July 1834 in the *City of Edinburgh*, a ship of 366 tons under the command of Captain Baker.[26]

A fortnight earlier, Collins had sent a circular letter to the proprietors of colonial studs seeking to line them up for the supply of entires to India. Referring grandly to the 'cargo of magnificent horses' that awaited a ship to Madras, he had offered an arrangement that would compensate them for the expense of keeping colts entire by taking two-thirds of each crop at £8, £14 and £20 each, as yearlings, two-year-olds and three-year-olds respectively. The list of breeders is of interest in showing the dominant position of the A.A. Company amongst the respondents, with 128 brood-mares, followed by Samuel Terry with 70 and William Lawson with 50. Also significant is the composition of the A.A. Company stud: in addition to the 128 mares, there were 101 fillies ranging from one- to three-year-olds, 42 entires, including 30 of the current crop, and 80 geldings of one to four years.

Two further cargoes were sent by Collins to Madras, 30 in the *Henry Tanner* of 388 tons on 2 January 1835 and 32 in the *Duchess of Northumberland* of 451 tons on 12 June 1835.[27] Collins then sailed to London, attempting to negotiate with the Secretary of State, Lord Glenelg, for the most favourable terms of leasing land on which his young colts could be brought to maturity before shipment to India. The block he had chosen was at Kangaroo Valley just inland from the Illawarra coast, a naturally secure site with steep hills that would contain his stock. What he wanted was a long lease, rather than the colonial limit of one year, to justify the heavy capital outlay. In the letter of 13 February 1836 to Glenelg, Collins let fall the surprising information that the Madras government no longer felt it needed horses from New South Wales, because it was assured of a sufficient supply from the Bengal Stud. However, Collins was confident of being able to undersell Bengal, provided that he received the desired lease. He quoted the cost of Bengal horses at a total of Madras Rs 721, including a first cost of Rs 456 and transportation Rs 255, and compared it with the Rs 590 that his remounts had cost landed in Madras. The colonial horses had the further advantage of being better bred and stronger, largely because of the purity of the atmosphere and freedom from such diseases as strangles, hydrophobia and glanders. Indeed, he informed the Secretary of State, if he were granted the lease, and effected the promised savings and improvements in quality, the Bengal government might itself follow suit and rely on colonial remounts.

How very right and prescient. But of course, Glenelg stuck to the rules and left the matter of the lease to the local government's decision. Collins still persisted, and wrote again to Glenelg on 10 June 1836 seeking a chance to buy ten sections of land in the Kangaroo Valley at ruling prices, payable over 15 years. Again, official obduracy.

When Collins finally left Portsmouth in the Hope in January 1837, he planned to take up a lease in Kangaroo Valley. On the ship with him was 'a splendid Thoroughbred horse of great muscular Powers and perfect symmetry', by Sultan out of Fila da Puta, and further such importations were planned. His confidence had been restored, apparently, by the receipt at India House of favourable reports from regiments of artillery, dragoons and cavalry in the Madras army after a year's trial of his horses. In summary, he wrote to Glenelg,

These reports all concur in stating that the Australian Horses possess good constitutions and tempers, are good feeders, and tractable, docile, and steady in their work. Some of the Reports describe them as being far superior and of more value and likely to be more serviceable than the general Remount Horses that have been hitherto furnished.[28]

What was the outcome of the Collins experiment in Australia and India?

By May 1835, when Colonel Dumaresq wrote to his directors, Captain Collins had received 'very satisfactory Reports' of the horses received in Madras from the July 1834 shipment. Though the A.A. Company Archives do not permit an exact description of the stock sold to Collins, the statement of sales to June 1834 shows that all the horses, whether gelding or entire, were mixtures of different strains, mostly Cleveland Bay and colonial, and Thoroughbred and colonial.[29] In September 1834, Dumaresq wrote to London to apologize for the low prices received from Collins (i.e. £8, £14 and £20 for one-, two- and three-year-old colts), but assured the Board that they 'fully represent the present value of Horses in this Colony', and he added, 'if we can obtain a *Certain Market*, even at the above rates, an Expensive branch of our rural system, will become one of considerable profit'.[30] The sales encouraged him to open up a separate station for the young stallions on the Avon River near Gloucester, with the brood-mares left on their old run at Alderley and fillies and geldings transferred to the Liverpool Plains.[31]

Yet conditions in the colonial pastoral industry did not favour the continuance of horse exports for much longer. Migrants were again flooding in by the mid-1830s, both those with capital and assisted migrants; new banks and pastoral companies injected large funds, and there was a breathless eagerness to take up land beyond the limits of location. All this resulted in the pushing up of the prices of horses along with other stock.

Small wonder that when Captain Collins returned to Sydney in mid-1837 he was unable to continue operations. A most revealing despatch of 30 June by Henry Dumaresq passed on to his board the assurance which the colonel had just made to Collins, that 'it is of much importance the Indian Market be kept open for the Horses of this country'. It did not escape Dumaresq that the company could export directly to India without using an agent, but he concluded: 'At present, there is a great demand for Horse Stock, in the Colonial Markets—and my hopes for establishing more desirable sales abroad, are not such, as to induce me to forgo immediate advantages, in favour of problematic success elsewhere'.[32]

In so admitting a preference for a bird in the hand, Colonel Dumaresq spoke for all colonial breeders and the situation did not change until the collapse of prices for wool and stock of all kinds in the protracted and severe pastoral depression which began in 1842. It was then that the Indian market for remounts and sporting horses took on an appeal that lasted for nearly a century.

What did the Madras army users think of the Collins horses? Surprisingly enough, the captain's summary of January 1837 for Lord Glenelg was not far from the mark. A report on five Australian horses received by the 2nd Regiment of Light Cavalry on 7 March 1835 was strongly favourable. A black entire was described as 'A strong active horse in excellt condn good tempered in every respect fit for the service', while a chestnut gelding was seen as 'in every respect fit for cavalry purposes'. Very significantly, several artillery officers remarked on the suitability of Australian horses for this branch of the service, so anticipating what was soon to become their area of special renown.[33]

Rather hostile reports came from Collins's own colleagues in the 13th Light Dragoons. Colonel Richard Brunton commented on the horses' 'want of blood and muscle', which indicated to him that they were 'never likely to stand the work of this country if called into active service'. The regimental veterinary surgeon considered them inferior to Arabs, and the riding master, though seeing them as tractable, thought them unsuitable. But six months later, on 1 April 1836, Brunton seemed almost converted to an acceptance of the horses from Botany Bay.

Amongst the most approving were Captain Kerr of the Bodyguard, who saw the horses as strong and serviceable and 'perfectly steady in the ranks', and Lieutenant-Colonel William Burton commanding the horse artillery at St Thomas's Mount, who wrote on 14 October 1835 of seven Australians recently posted to the troops that they were 'perfectly quiet, and good movers'. He expected them to turn out 'far superior to and more serviceable than the generality of remount horses'. Reinforcing this impression is the high acceptance rate indicated by a Madras letter of 6 July 1836, which referred to forty-one New South Wales horses being passed by the remount committee from a consignment of fifty-two received from Collins, probably the survivors from two cargoes of a total sixty-two embarked at Sydney, for which an average of Rs 590 was paid to Collins's agent.[34]

Putting these remarks in context we should recall that the three Collins shipments marked the very beginning of the Australian remount trade with India and that the horses received, as a consequence, none of the advantages that would come with experience at every point from breeding and shipment to sale and posting. They spent, probably, from seven to ten weeks on the water, standing all the way, only to be dumped in the surf at Madras. They were met by a well-formed anti-convict prejudice that was expressed by the entry in the India Office Index 'BOTANY BAY alias NEW SOUTH WALES', not to mention the tenacious preference for the Arab. And it seems likely that the horses were far from being the best available in the colony at the time Collins was buying, judging by a remark dropped by Phillip Parker King when writing to his directors in April 1842 of the past decade of the A.A. Company's horse sales. As he put it, 'In the years 1834, 5, and 6 Horses were very cheap, and your Stud was culled by Captain Collins for the Indian Market'.[35]

In 1838 the Indian armies embarked on the First Afghan War, so ending a long period of peace, and the Bengal Stud soon proved incapable of meeting demands from other presidencies. One effect is to be seen in the East India Company's approval in April 1840 for an arrangement made by the Madras government with Collins in New South Wales to supply one hundred horses annually at Rs 590. Yet the board concluded by returning to a basic principle, 'that you will not relax in your endeavours to obtain remounts from sources under your own control or under that of the Government of India'. But the situation in the colony was no longer propitious. With the dramatic rise in local prices, Collins was unable to land his horses at less than Rs 700, so that the government decided to cancel his authority to buy. With that, the new trade came temporarily to a halt.[36]

4

Depression, War and Trade 1843–1850

I N MARCH 1843 Josiah Betts, a landholder at Wilmington and prosperous son-in-law of the Reverend Samuel Marsden, remarked in his diary on the contrast between the smiling face of his pastures, recently blessed by late summer rains, and the depression suffered by merchants and agriculturalists in the colony of New South Wales.

> Stock looking remarkably well—abundance of every necessary article of subsistence; but monetary distress unprecedented in the colony—Horses scarcely saleable at any price. Fat stock very, very low—Agricultural produce selling for next to nothing . . . Wages have undergone nothing like a proportionate deduction, and the prospect of the most stable and wealthy of the settlers is anything but satisfactory.

In April, Betts was even more gloomy, in spite of further rain:

> Nothing can exceed the luxuriance of the vegetable world . . . and yet such a scarcity of money was never remembered. The daily increasing number of Insolvencies & Sherriff's Sales have so reduced the price of stock, that the solvent stockholder has no Chance of disposing of anything at a remunerating price.[1]

Agriculture and commerce in eastern Australia remained in the grip of an acute and comprehensive depression from late 1842 till the end of the decade. Not for the last time in the country's history, it was gold that finally turned the economy around for some long-term sufferers, as late as 1851. For years before the crash, prices had been forced up by reckless gambling in land and pastoral stock of all kinds, stimulated by a flow of British investment and by the colonial government's expenditure on bounty immigration. Events preceding the crash included the fatal combination of falling London wool prices, local drought and loss of confidence, with the government contributing by raising the price of Crown land and reducing its commissariat spending in consequence of the abolition of convict transportation.

Stephen Roberts wrote of the months from February to December 1843 as an 'economic nightmare'. In the Legislative Council W. C. Wentworth spoke of the issue of six thousand insolvency writs, while 'merchants were without custom, traders without business, and mechanics and artisans were pining for want in the streets'. Several banks failed, including the Bank of Australia with its aristocratic clientele, and by the end of 1843 there were 1243 unemployed mechanics or labourers in a Sydney population of about 37 000.[2]

From the viewpoint of the incipient horse trade the vital signs were those that told of a general rural depression and a desperate search by colonial shipmasters for outward cargoes. From December 1841 to January 1843, beef and mutton prices fell from 5 pence to 2½ pence a pound and by the end of 1843 to less than 2 pence. Wheat prices had halved, as had wool, the colonial staple. Fat cattle, working bullocks and horses fell in price by more than a half. In effect, as Josiah Betts had remarked, horses were scarcely saleable 'at any price'. For the colonial horse breeders, including the A.A. Company, which had increased their studs and imported bloodstock with a view to profiting from the apparently limitless surge of pastoral expansion, there was the distinctly unpleasant prospect of horses eating their heads off, and grooms and labourers needing to be paid, while the animals themselves constituted an embarrassment of ever-growing proportions.[3]

Linked firmly with this new problem of surplus and locally unsaleable stock was one of much greater antiquity. Shipowners, both British and colonial, had always experienced difficulties because of the preponderance of inwards over outwards trade. The commercial pages of the *Sydney Herald* and later of the *Shipping Gazette* from 1833 to 1843 tell a consistently depressing story of ships leaving Hobart and Sydney in ballast, looking for cargoes in China, India and Southeast Asia, so as to avoid the costly embarrassment of sailing back to England with empty holds. One of the colonial shipmasters was Robert Towns (1794–1873), who had settled at Sydney in 1843 after ten years in command of a ship that had sailed annually to the colony. Married to a half-sister of W. C. Wentworth, Towns represented the London firm of Robert Brooks & Co. and built up his own fleet of whaling ships and general traders, one of which, the *Royal Saxon*, was to contribute regularly to the remount trade. In the vast collection of Robert Towns's commercial correspondence at the Mitchell Library is the evidence of one man's undeviating persistence in drumming up support from colonial breeders so as to fill up his ship with horses intended for India. Without exaggeration, we might call it the Towns factor in the setting up of the horse trade.

The final element to be mentioned here is the scale of the remount problem facing the Indian armies during the ten years that followed the beginning of the First Afghan War in 1838. After four years of campaigning that were significantly destructive of horseflesh, the armies were engaged in the conquest of Sind and the Gwalior campaign in 1843, and from 1845 to 1849, the First and Second Sikh Wars, with an interval from 1846 to 1848. In each case the British and irregular units of cavalry and horse artillery had vital functions, for their adversaries were able to field huge mounted forces—50 000 in the Sikh army alone. Losses of the scale involved in this sort of warfare were beyond the resources of the Bengal Stud, even with supplementation from the efforts of remount officers in the three Presidencies, drawing on the horses made available by horse breeders in the region. The Company's military rivals were themselves competing in the South Asian horse markets, and they made the fairs of Central Asia inaccessible to British buyers. Lord Ellenborough, the Governor-General, had no alternative but to seek remounts outside the region. As he wrote to the commander-in-chief on 28 May 1844, 'We are cruelly in want of horses & must get them wherever we can. I think we shall send Agents to Sydney'.[4] A new and substantial phase of the remount trade was about to begin.

There were other reasons for going beyond the Bengal Central Stud in seeking horses. Aside from the basic obstacles to horse breeding relating to climate, disease and inadequate fodder, the Bengal Stud had suffered a number of political crises in its fifty-year life that had put in doubt its continued existence. William Moorcroft's appointment in 1808 had been an alternative to the abandonment of the Stud and even during his distinguished superintendency there had been a major challenge from the board to which he was responsible. No studies have been published of the Stud's performance in Moorcroft's final years, or of the period that followed. However, amongst the India Office Library papers for the mid-1840s is a letter from Major C. Thynne Thomas, late superintendent of the Stud, which throws light on the recent history of that controversial institution.

Writing from retirement in Guernsey in January 1845, Thomas attributed the latest failures of the Stud to a decision made in 1833 by Governor-General Lord William Bentinck. At a time, he said, when the Central Stud had been in its most flourishing state, beginning to pay off the large debt which had accumulated since the early years, Bentinck had made changes that effectively broke it up by undermining the relationship between the stud and its widely spread breeders. Prior to the new order, breeders who used stud mares had been bound under a heavy surety to keep the mares and their produce in good condition and sell the colts and fillies to the superintendent at a price ranging from Rs 90 to Rs 140. With Bentinck's order that contract was unilaterally broken and the price of fillies was reduced to Rs 70. The result was that the fillies were so neglected that many grew up 'flat sided, leggy and unthrifty', so badly affected that no after care could remedy the defects. (It will later be seen what a huge impact on the economics of remount breeding would be made by a change of policy that virtually abolished entire horses and threw the ranks open for the first time to geldings and mares.) At the same time as the price for fillies was reduced, the stud stallions were withdrawn from the *zamindari* breeders, so that the confidence formerly subsisting between the Stud and both classes of breeders was rapidly destroyed.

As a further explanation for the deficiency of Indian-bred horses, Major Thomas argued that the loss by many Indian princes of their independence had removed a basic motive for horse breeding, since they no longer maintained private armies of any size. The large horse fairs of the north and north-west had been deserted for years and some of the most famous breeds had become virtually extinct.[5]

So much in explanation for the Indian government's going overseas for horses. But why send to Sydney, rather than to the Cape, which had sent small numbers to Calcutta for some years, perhaps six in 1840–41, twenty in 1841–42, but none in 1842–43? The small scale of the trade suggests a sufficient answer, in view of the dimension of the 1844 crisis. The Cape itself was also militarily disturbed and therefore in doubt as a source of remounts. Again and again in the decades that followed the government of India showed a prime concern with the certainty, as much as with the quality, of the remount supplies.[6]

It is possible that the Governor-General had taken advice from officers who had seen something of the Australian horses imported by Captain Collins in 1834 and 1835, though the more likely influence was the favourable reception accorded to a speculative cargo of twenty-three well-bred horses which left Sydney for Madras in the *Duchess of Kent* on 15 April 1843. Amongst them were thirteen colts bred by Robert and Helenus Scott at Glendon on the Upper Hunter, sired by some of the best Thoroughbreds that had raced in the colony, including Dover, Trumpet and Toss. At the time of sailing, Dover was still winning races at Page's River, though by this time he carried the colours of a new owner, Thomas Haydon, whose descendants still breed fine stock horses and polo ponies on Bloomfield, near Murrurundi. To put this reference to racehorses in context, it should be remembered that for the colonial turf the stress was still on stamina rather than speed and the custom was for horses to take part in heats before engaging in the finals. As reported in the *Sydney Morning Herald* of 13 April 1843, Dover, a chestnut entire, won the final in a canter, landing a purse of fifty sovereigns for Mr Haydon.[7]

Before pursuing the subject of the *Duchess of Kent*'s cargo and its likely contribution to the standing of Australian horses in India we should notice the pedigrees of the Scott brothers themselves. As was so often true of the founders of the remount trade, they had strong links with India, having been born in Bombay, sons of Helenus Scott who had given, in Nancy Gray's words, 'thirty years of outstanding medical service in India'. Though Dr Scott had died on the way to New South Wales in 1821, his sons had settled on the Hunter River at Glendon, near Singleton, and had imported Arab and Thoroughbred stallions that, on the dispersal of the stud in the 1840s depression, contributed to the formation of worthy successor studs. It was entirely appropriate that the first cargo of horses to leave the colony for India in the 1840s should have come from the Scotts of Glendon.[8]

The eleven Scott horses that survived the trip to Madras sold for a total of Rs 8117, making an average of Rs 737.9, or about £62. On 1 May 1844 the Herald published a letter written from Madras on February, describing the warm reception given to cargoes by the *Duchess of Kent* and a similar consignment by the *Stratheden* which sailed on 27 July 1843, and printing an extract from a Madras newspaper of 26 December 1843 that must have given heart to the struggling horse breeders of New South Wales. It reported that horses from the two cargoes had sold for between six and seven hundred rupees apiece, and estimated an average profit for the consignors of more than Rs 300, assuming a purchase price in the colony of £10 each. Dubious as these estimates are, the remarks that followed were full of promise:

> [The Australian horses] are considered unexceptionable as draught cattle, and if good for anything under saddle, must answer very well for our Cavalry. If therefore it would be cheaper to purchase them for our mounted service, we do not see why we should not encourage the Australian horse dealer in preference to the Arab and Mogul merchants. Sydney being a colony offering many facilities for the retreat of our worn-out officers, we should rejoice to see a regular steady trade growing up between it and India, and as bearing upon the national interests of both the countries, it is desirable

the Government should give the subject of obtaining a periodical supply of horses for our Cavalry from Sydney its favourable consideration, provided the cattle are un-exceptionable, and the supply could be always calculated upon for every emergency of the service.

The emergency to which Lord Ellenborough responded on 28 May 1844, by sending remount buyers to Sydney, was outlined in a report of 21 April by Major-General I. R. Lumby, the Adjutant-General, summarizing the shortfall of remounts available to the mounted branches of the army. Heavy losses had been sustained in the wars against Sind and Gwalior in 1843 and—to look only at the eleven regiments of light cavalry, each with an establishment of 420 *sowars* or troopers—there was a total deficiency of 657 horses, or an average of nearly 60 per regiment. Those units, stationed at Muttra, Firozpur, Ambala, Nussurabad, Sind, Nowgong, Ludhiana, Meerut and Kanpur had apparently lost most severely in the fighting. Over the whole army the deficiency came to a total of 903, which it was thought the Bengal Stud could not supply.[9]

Some illustration of the actions which had given rise to the casualties is useful here. The modern historian of the British cavalry is the Marquess of Anglesey, who explained the aim of cavalry in these terms:

To be able, with speed, to manoeuvre a number of horsemen into a well-dressed line; to throw that line at a wavering enemy with shattering rapidity; thus, in an instant, to smash all opposition, imposing irreversible disintegration, and, finally, to pursue with relentless vigour: these, in the thinking of the majority of British cavalrymen, whether heavy or light, were the chief objects of all training. Preparation for the great and glorious moment of truth was virtually everything.[10]

Major-General Sir Charles Napier wrote in his journal before the campaign in Sind the frank and alarming words 'We have no right to seize Scinde, yet we shall do so, and a very advantageous, useful, humane piece of rascality it will be'. One of his outstanding officers, commandant of the Scinde Irregular Horse, was Lieutenant-Colonel John Jacob, whose regiment played a decisive part in the battle of Miani in which a substantially sepoy army of about 3000 faced tribesmen seven times more numerous. Jacob's description has special value for the impression it gives of the country in which the action occurred.

[I] went left and pushed my horsemen into the most awfully difficult ground you can imagine. We had so many falls that more than fifty horses were on their heads at once, and at the same time the fire from the village not sixty yards distant was tremendous, every nullah also was lined with matchlock men concealed in and firing through the thorns. A great number of our men and horses were shot there. My horse, a first-rate hunter, was mortally wounded through the belly and lungs, other balls struck my sword scabbard, etc. . . . We charged right through the enemy's camp, slew more than a hundred of them and took Nusseer Khan's standard . . . Our charge decided the battle (the General told me so on the ground).[11]

At the final battle of the Sind campaign in March 1843, which involved two of the regiments mentioned in the summary above—the 3rd and 9th Bengal Light Cavalry

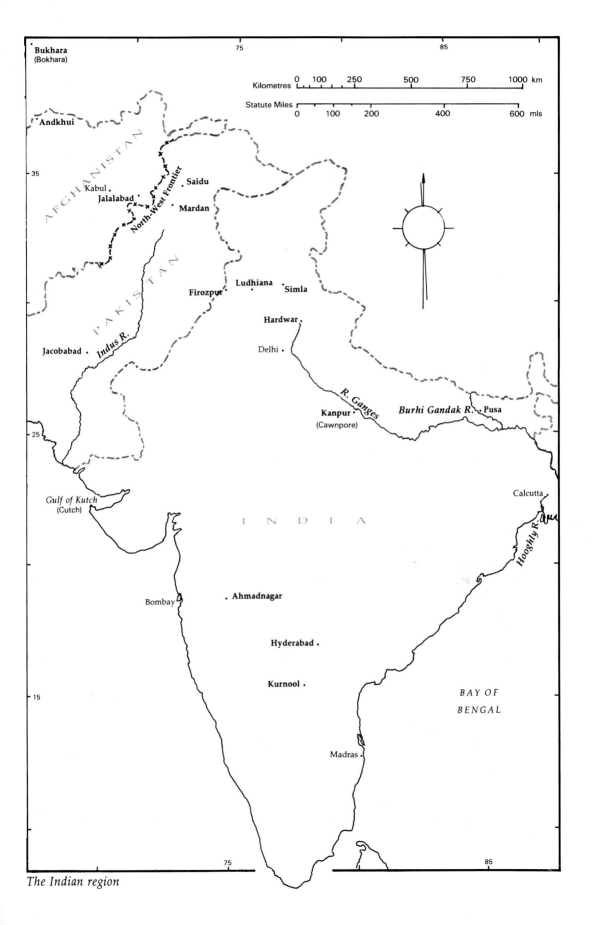

The Indian region

—a shattering charge was made against the Baluchi forces of the last Emir who remained opposed to the British conquest of the province, which is described by William Napier:

> the whole body of cavalry at full speed . . . the spurs deep in the horses' sides, the riders pealing their different war cries, and whirling their swords in gleaming circles—there . . . the gorgeous troopers of the 3rd Cavalry, there . . . the wild Scindian horsemen, their red turbans streaming amid the smoke and dust of the splendid turmoil.[12]

This demonstrates the need for strong, agile horses—and helps explain why remounts were in such demand. To return to Lord Ellenborough and the despatch of buyers to Sydney—the crucial letter is to the commander-in-chief on 28 May 1844:

> We are cruelly in want of horses & must get them wherever we can. I think we shall send Agents to Sydney. There we shall be able to procure 800 or 1000 firm large strong Horses, but they will not be in use before the Autumn of 1845.
> I have requested General Gilbert to take over the Stables here. There are 1500 to 2000 Horses in them, but they are principally Arabs or so called & high priced. If we can get any at an average of 550 Rs it will be worth while to do so. A large batch of Horses is coming from the Cape; but these will be dear.
> The Sydney Horses lately imported sold high & gave a good Profit. They were much thought of. It is only in Sydney that we can properly mount European Dragoons. Cost what it may we must have a well mounted Cavalry and a well Horsed Artillery.[13]

As may be imagined, this viceregal announcement came not from thin air but from a decision of the Governor-General in Council, which had been communicated to the Military Board on 10 May by the military secretary. Colonel Stuart explained the decision in terms of the 'very reasonable prices at which horses of a good description are procurable in that colony'. The other circumstance which was seen as favouring the scheme was the low rate of freight between New South Wales and Calcutta, a product of the paucity of outward cargoes from the colony.[14]

In the correspondence that followed between Ellenborough and Gough the latter said he would be glad to get Australian horses, which, with the Cape horses, he saw as best for European dragoons and the artillery. One possible element in the situation was the recent decision to replace six-pounders with nine-pounders in the horse artillery, a move prompted perhaps by the heavy calibre of the Sikh batteries, which were soon to be confronted by the British forces.

Writing again on 14 June 1844, Ellenborough mentioned a subject that would recur many times in the ninety years that followed: what was the best time at which colonial horses should arrive in India? He discounted the idea that the New South Wales horses would not stand the rigours of the Indian climate, arguing that since they 'have more blood than the generality of English Horses brought to India', they would do just as well. The last Australian horses, he said, had come with winter coats to face an Indian summer, which was a 'severe trial'. An effort should be made in future to bring them to Calcutta in about October, to give a time for gentler acclimatization. This fitted in well with the climatic demands of the north-about route along the Queensland coast and through Torres Strait, which was open from May to September inclusive, when the prevailing winds were the south-east monsoons. But it put ships and cargoes at great jeopardy for the timing of their journey across the Bay of Bengal, which saw the beginning of the cyclone season on 15 October. It was on that day in 1874 Henry Vanrenen lost almost his entire cargo on the *Udston*. The dilemma was nearly insoluble and in the last resort it was a matter of balancing one imperative against another.[15]

This brief discussion of the supply route for Australian horses recalls a question which had been at least in the background of Indian army thinking since the days of William Moorcroft. At his death in 1825, after spending ten years in trying to tap the great horse fairs of Central Asia for breeding stock and remounts, he was utterly defeated by warfare in the breeding areas themselves and by instability along the route to Bengal. Naturally the possibility was canvassed again at the time of the 1844 emergency, when the obstacles to the proposal were put strongly in a military letter from Fort William to the Governor-General in Council:

> Supposing the communication to be effectually made, yet other important questions arise. Can the forbearance of the intermediate governments be safely reckoned upon? Is not the political animosity of some, and the unbalanced power of all, likely to be exhibited in a manner which will repress all enterprise amongst horse dealers, whose expectations of profit might be completely disappointed by exactions in the route. Such exactions being rigidly and systematically enforced, merely because the horses are destined for the British government in India.[16]

As no real alternative had been found, the government of India appointed three officers as agents to sail to Van Diemen's Land and New South Wales to buy a total of 1000 horses, for which an average sum of Rs 550 was to be paid including purchase price, freight and all costs up to delivery in Calcutta. The officers were Captain Arbuthnot Dallas, former assistant secretary of the military board, Captain W. W. Apperley, son of 'Nimrod', the famous English equestrian writer, and a veterinary surgeon, Mr Parry.

During the early discussion of this mission it was suggested by the Indian government that Dallas carry with him a case of 15 000 sovereigns to facilitate his purchases in Sydney. The most fertile imagination must draw back from an attempt to visualize the effect of such a treasure on the minds of the citizens of New South Wales, starved as they had been for some years of bonanzas of any kind. But the India Office, though not famous for levity, commented that since Dallas had been authorized to draw bills on the treasuries of Hong Kong, Mauritius, and all the Indian Presidencies as well as the British government, 'we cannot apprehend that he will experience any pecuniary difficulty in buying horses in New South Wales'.[17]

Dallas, the senior member of the mission, arrived in Sydney via Manila on New Year's Day 1845 and found a governor and community eagerly awaiting him. Apperley came via Van Diemen's Land, where he looked briefly at the island's horses and commented in his first report of 19 January on the depressed state of the colonial economies and the consequent decline of horse breeding, which had resulted in few brood-mares being put to stallions. But he added, 'Our arrival has put them up in their stirrups again and I hope they will have the good sense to be satisfied with moderate prices'.

In his instructions from the military board Dallas was told of what to expect in the colonial horse markets. Animals 'quite equal to the Government of India's purposes' were quoted at £12–£15, but it was thought that £20–£30 would be 'a very fair price', especially in view of the high cost of stud horses, which had not been less than Rs 587 (about £49) in the past six years. He was to buy horses aged from three to seven years, in a height range from 14 hands 2 inches to 15 hands 2 inches, paying the best attention to their constitutions and soundness. The further and vital point was made to Captain Apperley that because of the colonial practice of castrating the vast majority of male horses, he would have to buy geldings. For large consignments, shipping space should be available, it was thought, for £20 a head (not including fodder), with a quarter to be paid in Sydney and the balance in Calcutta. The Indian government expected to be able to purchase annually from New South Wales on contract, subject to approval from remount committees, but a beginning had to be made 'by actual purchase'.[18]

Much of the board's information had come from the breeders' agent and the superintendent groom who had accompanied a cargo of horses that left Sydney on 26 January 1844 and arrived in Calcutta on 3 April. Missions had to be prepared to travel within a distance of 120 miles from Sydney, and use the ample stabling in the city before cargoes were despatched, when horses should be accustomed to dry feed, as many casualties occurred when they were embarked straight from the grass. Ships of 500 to 600 tons should be sought, which would carry eighty horses in the main decks and hold without crowding. One groom should be provided for every ten horses, with the head groom receiving £1 for each horse landed in India.

The East India Company's mission remained in Australia until April 1847, buying about a thousand horses in New South Wales, though apparently none in Van Diemen's Land. They offered pastoralists a most welcome chance of sales and the colony a valued access to outside currencies in the shape of rupees and sterling. For colonial horse breeders it was, as some appreciated at the time, a much needed encouragement to lift their game to satisfy a large-scale demand for sound, well-bred horses that had the power and stamina required by military buyers. Beyond the immediate economic advantage was the long-term benefit from the growth of prosperous studs that were able to import high quality Arabs and Thoroughbreds and so establish what Malcolm Kennedy describes as a genetic pool on which sound developments could be based.[19] It would be difficult to exaggerate the importance of this genetic base as a preparation for the demands that would be made upon Australia's equine resources during the decades of hectic growth that were ushered in by the gold discoveries of 1851.

One of the colonists who appreciated the Dallas mission was George Leslie, who had followed his pioneering elder brother Patrick, the 'Prince of Bushmen', into the management of Canning Downs in the newly opened Moreton Bay district. The brothers were soon married, respectively, to Emmeline and Catherine Macarthur, daughters of Hannibal Macarthur and therefore welcome to Camden Park, giving them an intimate awareness of the prospects of colonial horse breeding. George Leslie took one of the best stallions to Canning Downs and by 1847 was sending highly bred horses to India, for which he hoped to make profits of £50 to £60 a head, selling them presumably as officers' chargers or racehorses.[20]

George Leslie's letter 'home' in March 1847 gives an impression of how the Indian mission was received. Captain Dallas had been introduced to the Leslies by brother William, and Apperley was something of a lion as the son of 'Nimrod', writer for the *Sporting Magazine*. He described the three officers as 'very gentlemanlike nice people' who were 'much liked' in the colony. They had leased a fine mansion, Bungarribee, on the Doonside Road near Blacktown, built in 1825 by John Campbell, a brother of General Sir Colin Campbell of Indian Mutiny fame. Bungarribee had a dramatic and unusual central portion of two storeys, circular in shape, and was known amongst the colonial gentry as a centre for hospitality, festooned in summer with roses and other fragrant flowers. Since the two previous owners, Henry Kater and Charles Smith, had been leading horse breeders before the crash, the outbuildings, barns and fencing arrangements were well suited to the officers' needs. Up to 160 horses were kept and stabled there, accustomed to hay and corn and then shipped off to Calcutta. Leslie's understanding was that the officers hoped to make their agency permanent, so permitting the abolition of the Central Stud in Bengal. But the remount crisis had been brought under control by the end of 1846 and, when George Leslie wrote his hopeful letter in March 1847 from Canning Downs, the officers were negotiating with Captain Towns for passages on the *Royal Saxon* to Calcutta.[21]

Dallas and Apperley, and their masters in India, appear to have envisaged the mission to New South Wales as having a fairly durable character. That was the clear understanding of the delighted colonists, and the impression is strengthened by the establishment at Bungarribee, and even more by the fact that the officers were accompanied by their wives and children. That the mission did not turn out to be permanent was due largely to the Indian government's discovery that the shortfall in supplies from the Bengal Stud was not so great as expected. An India Office despatch of 22 October 1845 which took account of remount returns in November 1844 seized on this point and asserted that a permanent agency was not after all required in New South Wales. 'We are anxious', it continued, 'that the demands of the service should be met if practicable, and without detriment to the efficiency of the service, from the resources of our own territories'.[22]

A possible factor in the decision to withdraw the mission was that the officers did not sufficiently like the standard of the horses available in the price range in which they were purchasing. James Macarthur wrote to a business friend in Tahiti on 25 November 1845, saying that the officers complained 'of the want of Blood in the colonial stock which they say is indispensable. They have given generally for unbroken colts made quiet to lead from £13 to £18 or £20. A few they have purchased at higher rates but only a few superior horses I believe'. But the more compelling reason was the government's realization that it did not need to take on the risk and expense of buying in New South Wales and shipping on its own account when so many colonists were prepared to do it for them.[23]

The risks involved in shipping horses from Australia were dramatized by the fate of the very first consignment. There were twelve of the Company's horses on board the *Hydrabad* when it missed the entrance to the Cumberland Passage and struck a sunken rock about 100 miles east-nor'-east of Cape York. Though no human lives were lost, all 118 horses were drowned. From the sailing of the *Hydrabad* on 26 April 1845 to the despatch of the *Emily Jane* on 12 September 1846, the mission sent a total of thirteen identified cargoes to Calcutta, with an embarked complement of about a thousand horses. A further twelve horses were attributed to Captain Apperley in the cargo of the *Royal Saxon* when it left Sydney on 10 April 1847, carrying away the three officers and their families and so disappointing the hopes of colonial horse breeders. Though an attempt was made to find a horse cargo in Hobart for the big new ship *Sir George Seymour* of 850 tons, it sailed in ballast in late April 1845 and eventually left Sydney on 28 June with 130 Company horses for Calcutta. This disappointment may have been a consequence of the comparatively high prices then current in Van Diemen's Land, a product of smaller numbers and of the demand for stock in South Australia. Yet the island's farmers contributed substantially to the remount trade, then and later, by supplying much of the hay and corn that was used in the horse ships, with the surplus being landed in Calcutta to provide a healthy diet for the animals until they were assigned to their regiments.[24]

Private horse shipments to India began with the *Duchess of Kent*'s cargo in April 1843, of which the Scotts' well-bred horses realized an average of £70 apiece for the eleven survivors. They continued in 1844 with further consignments to Madras but from the time of the *Blundell*'s departure for Calcutta at the end of August that port remained the prime destination for Australian horses until the trade came to an end. Even while Dallas and Apperley were putting together their thirteen cargoes of remounts in the middling price range, the leading breeders such as Macarthur, Osborne, Johnston, Lawson, Dangar, Icely and Campbell were despatching a smaller volume of horses for private sale, consigned to agents in Calcutta. The trade continued for several years at a diminishing rate after the East India Company's agents departed in April 1847. Though the demand for remounts fluctuated wildly for decades, according to the levels of military activity and the effectiveness of Indian breeding programmes, there remained a steady flow to India from Australia of racehorses, hacks and carriage pairs, with polo ponies added to the list when that game swept the regimental playing grounds of British India in the last quarter of the century.

It was fortunate for the early image of Australian horses in India that the first consignment in the 1840s was of the high standard set by the Scotts of Glendon in 1843. In the following year they reached the apex of the trade with sales at Calcutta of three geldings, intended presumably for racing, which brought sums of £550, £600 and £940, giving total nett proceeds of £964. Equally important, because longer continued, was the contribution of James and William Macarthur of Camden Park. They had twenty-five horses, only two of them Thoroughbreds according to Patrick Leslie, on the *Blundell* when it left for Calcutta under the charge of George Alexander Plaistowe, together with consignments from the Johnston brothers of Annandale, Campbell & Company, Thomas Icely, and other gentlemen. A total of seventy-three horses, described later by the *Shipping Gazette* as the 'finest lot . . . ever exported from the colony', landed in Calcutta on 29 November 1844 after a passage of thirteen weeks. Plaistowe reported that though the ship had been free from storms, the heat had been dreadful. Two of the Macarthurs' twenty-five had died—one from inflammation of the lungs, the other from inflammation of the bowels—but the survivors remained in 'excellent health and condition'. Sold at auction by Cockerell & Company on 16 and 21 December, at the height of the Calcutta sporting and social season, they cleared, after auction charges had been deducted, an average of Rs 1028.5 per head, or about £80 each. What an encouraging and well deserved start this was for the enterprising Macarthurs! As William Macarthur wrote to his friend J. C. Bidwill from the comfort of the Australian Club, their nett proceeds came to £1560. The price

Showing horses to non-military buyers

was not only a reflection of breeding and management skills but also, as George Plaistowe remarked, a tribute to the good sense of the consignors in embarking only well-broken horses in top condition. He contrasted this experience with that of the *William Mitcalfe*, which had landed its horses 'in most wretched condition' after a much shorter voyage of nine weeks.[25]

The uncatalogued manuscripts of Captain Robert Towns, held at the Mitchell Library, give a strong picture of a sailor turned owner who set up his merchant's shingle at Miller's Point in 1843 at the beginning of a prolonged depression, and worked 'as regular as the platipus', as he put it, in an effort to find cargoes for his ships. One of them was the *Royal Saxon*, which he had skippered in 1838 when Captain Chauvel came out from India to become a pastoralist. In due course his grandson, Harry Chauvel, commanded the Australian Light Horse in Palestine. Towns wrote letters to horse breeders all over the colony, holding out to them the prospects of the Indian remount market as a ray of economic hope, and puffing the claims of his beloved *Royal Saxon* as a roomy and well-managed ship of 510 tons, apt for the carriage of horses. Dallas and Apperley must have agreed, for they twice used the ship, on the second occasion embarking their families together with some horses intended for resale in India, when their mission was terminated in April 1847.[26]

Towns usually charged £25 a head for carrying horses to Calcutta, the price covering freight, food and water, and payable only when the horse was landed 'safe from the tackles'. For large consignments, such as those from the remount buyers, there was sometimes a discount and he used a variety of schemes to attract custom. Breeders with quality stock for sale were encouraged by arrangements of the kind he made with James and William Macarthur on 26 August 1848. They provided the horses,

Towns the freight and all expenses except insurance, and the nett proceeds were to be equally divided. For favoured customers such as the Macarthurs there were silk scarves and dress materials brought back from India for the ladies. And again, for the Squire of Camden, there was the offer on 2 April 1849 of a 'splendid English horse, for exchange, if you need a change of blood'. This reminds us of one of the important long-term consequences of the horse trade with India, since Towns and other ship-masters took the opportunity of importing Arab and Thoroughbred stallions as speculative return cargoes, so contributing to the genetic pool on which breeders would draw in the decades of pastoral expansion that accompanied the gold rushes.[27]

Another mark of Towns's inventiveness was his use of a ship to convey horses from Sydney to Calcutta, and then to return with a human cargo. That happened twice with convicts being conveyed from Calcutta to Hobart, in 1845 and 1849, and the idea led him into one of the most disastrous ventures of his career. On 1 September 1845 he wrote to his Captain Finley, master of the clipper *Orwell*, giving detailed orders for the care of thirty horses sailing to Calcutta via Torres Strait, and for the purchase of a return cargo of a hundred Indian indentured labourers that were to be brought back between decks as an investment shared with William Charles Wentworth and Robert Campbell. His Calcutta agents, Allen Duffill & Company, were to assist in arrangements for the labourers, whom the captain was cautioned to treat with 'every kindness & protection' as the Indian authorities 'look with great jealousy on the removal of these people from their native country'. Finley's perform-ance, Towns warned, would help to decide 'the fate of a question of great importance to this Colony'. He was referring to the desire he shared with other large scale non-resident pastoralists of importing contracted labourers who would replace the sorely missed convicts, notably in point of cheapness and in their being tied for years to hard labour on remote stations. The limit to his concern for their welfare was shown by his drawing the captain's attention to the Indian regulation calling for the ship-ment of women with them in the proportion of fifteen per hundred, a mute but potent statistical indictment of the whole Indian indentured labour system—and its exploitation by colonial employers.

The *Orwell* venture turned out in every respect a 'most ruinous & vexatious affair', with the head groom, Mason, proving to be an incompetent drunkard, and Towns's captain and agents letting him down badly with the choice of the labourers, 'the most disgraceful decrepit set that can be imagined', he angrily wrote to Allen Duffill on 3 April 1846. Worse still, the *Orwell*'s arrival had coincided with that of the *Theresa*, which carried a larger and classier cargo of horses and so depressed the market. Nemesis had a further card to play, for the *Theresa* returned at the same time as the *Orwell* with a competing cargo of rice and sugar, and it was then discovered that by a defect in their contracts, the labourers could not be held to their engagements. Towns had no option but to send them back to India. Yet he told his new agents that he would persevere.[28]

Towns's provisioning of his horse ships is detailed in his letter of 8 June 1846 to Captain Dallas offering accommodation for thirty horses on the *Royal Saxon* at an all up cost of £25 a head payable in Calcutta. Ninety days provender was to be put on board at the daily scale of 10 pounds of hay, 5 of bran, 2 of corn, with 6 gallons of water per horse, and grooms in the proportion of one to every eight horses. He was not exclusively committed to Calcutta, which he considered a tediously expensive port, not least from the frequent need to engage a steam-powered pilot for the navigation of the Hooghly's hundred miles of shoals and currents. So, when writing to Henry Osborne of Marshall Mount in the Illawarra on 23 July 1846 about a shared horse venture to Calcutta in the *Eagle*, he suggested that they join in a similar one to Madras in the *Eleanor Lancaster*.

The files of the *Shipping Gazette* in the 1840s reveal the rapid development by the men involved in the horse trade of skills and techniques which contributed to the survival of their charges and to their own success in a physically dangerous and financially hazardous business. Whereas an entrepreneurial shipowner like Towns would appoint his own superintendent and head groom, a number of breeders, like the Scotts, Macarthurs, Johnstons and Campbells, would often charter a ship and appoint their own trusted managers. George Plaistowe, who sailed for the Macarthurs with the marvellous cargo in the *Blundell* in 1844 and with the *Theresa* in 1845, was such a man. Robert B. Dawson, son of the one-time agent of the A.A. Company, was another who sailed several times, while Henry Ximenes, a former ensign in the Indian Army who went on the *Eagle* in 1846, was yet another. One of their chief contributions was to pass on their dearly bought knowledge by writing reports and detailed letters that brought together the latest market information or ideas on horse management at sea.

Consider Henry Ximenes' letter published on 17 April 1847:

> In the first place, none but well broken in cattle [horses], averaging from four to six years old, should ever be sent, and they only in the month of August, so as to arrive at the commencement of the cold season, when the indigo planters, gentlemen from England, and officers on leave ... visit Calcutta to make purchases for the year ensuing.

He gave an example of horses that sold badly in the hot weather but resold in the cold for another 250 per cent. The better-bred horses gave least trouble but the coarser Clydesdale types were constantly falling down and blemishing themselves. It was essential to ship horses in good condition, for 'it is easy', he said, 'to keep a horse up to its mark, whereas I never found a poor horse thrive on the passage'. Finally he cautioned against the custom of stopping to replenish water at Kupang (then Copang). Four days after doing so in the *Eagle* four previously healthy horses had died in one day with the gripes, which he attributed to brackish water.

One anonymous superintendent wrote a set of 'Hints to the exporters of horses to India' which occupied nearly a page of the *Shipping Gazette* of 10 April 1846. His chief complaint was with the false economy that crowded the maximum number of horses and fodder onto one ship, producing, he said, a recognized mortality rate of nearly one in three. A big roomy ship with good ventilation and wind sails reduced the danger from inflammation of the lungs but even so the air below was terribly stale and offensive. In addition, the temperature below deck in areas such as Kupang could be as much as ten degrees higher than the on-deck temperature of 80°F, even at seven o'clock in the evening. He was the first to describe the phenomenon of the runaway Australian horse on arrival in India: 'I myself saw three flying away over the country, and several are reported as having galloped themselves to death'. In the latter years of the trade sophisticated techniques were used to deal with this problem

The view between decks, 1875

but little was done about one of the root causes—the shipping of wild, unbroken horses.

It was R. B. Dawson who had the honour of bringing to the attention of his fellow colonists the use of the term 'Waler' in India to describe horses from New South Wales. Writing from Maitland on 28 December 1846 he quoted from a Calcutta resident's recent letter: 'From what I see and hear, it is my impression that the walers, as they are called, are growing into favour. In the recent sale, any horse showing good shape and breeding brought from 600 to 800 rs'. Even before this, Australian horses had made their appearance on Indian tracks. Lara and Young Muleyson were the first to run at Calcutta and at the 1844–45 meeting they won two races, as a consequence of which the Waler was put on the same handicap as the Caper, carrying a penalty of fourteen pounds against Arabs. At the same time both received an allowance of fourteen pounds from the English Thoroughbred, reflecting the difference of six months in the estimation of their birthdates. By the time of the Calcutta meeting of 1849–50, Walers had established a pre-eminence in India that lasted for a century, winning fourteen races compared with six for Arabs, six for country-breds and three for Thoroughbreds.[29]

In September 1847 the *Shipping Gazette* took pleasure in telling its readers that Mr Parry, the veterinary surgeon attached to the Dallas mission, had revised his formerly low opinion of Australian horses. Writing to his friend Dobie after returning to India, he now fell into line with the opinion of Captain Apperley, who had consistently thought well of them for the turf and for general purposes. ' "The Walers", so our horses are called, "are looking up; indeed they are in great demand".' He had sold a colt of Dobie's for a clear profit of Rs 2000 (or £167), and racehorses sent over recently by James Macarthur and Stuart Donaldson had been highly successful under the names of Paris and Jumper. Another import to Calcutta was Selim, by Vagabond, who had been winning all his races. A price of £1000 had been offered for him but refused. Parry reiterated the need for shippers to protect the reputation of the Waler by sending only sound, well-broken horses, remarking that it cost just as much to feed a bad horse as a good one.[30]

What of the A.A. Company during this seed time of the horse trade with India? The Court of Directors in London remained almost perversely opposed to the sort of speculation that was earning such rewards for the Scotts, Macarthurs and Wyndhams. As commissioner, Phillip King repeatedly urged such ventures on the principle that, since no sales were possible locally, it was necessary to resort to exports in order to get rid of the surplus and pay for the expenses of the stud, which by this time stocked 930 head. A mere six horses were sold by King to James Macarthur for £20 each to make up his consignment by the *Theresa*. But when at last King received permission for speculative exports in November 1845, he found himself in the absurd position of having only twenty-five horses that were deemed suitable for the Indian market. Two main sources of damage to the stud may be identified. Parry, the veterinary surgeon accompanying the mission, was most critical of what he called the A.A. Company's 'mistaken partiality' for Cleveland Bays, which had imparted undue height and coarseness of head, characteristics much disliked in India where Arab grace and beauty were the touchstones of equine form. It was with the hope of rectifying this that King bought from Alexander Berry in June 1846 the imported Arab stallion Sir Henry but the unwanted features persisted. In June 1851 the company's deputy governor, Archibald Blane, then resident at Port Stephens, wrote to the Court describing 'a coarseness of Head and forehead as a prevailing feature' amongst their stock. Once again a handsome Arab was purchased —the stallion Glenmore—renowned for victories on the turf at Madras, Delhi, Meerut and Calcutta from 1845 to 1847. A potent if apparently minor difficulty was the company's practice of docking the tails of its horses, rendering them quite unsuitable for India, if not for Australia. The company's second great problem was the run down in the stud that followed the cessation of sales in 1843, bringing to an end the healthy stimulus of culling and rigorous attention to quality.[31]

If the A.A. Company found it frustrating to be rendered impotent in the face of the Indian remount bonanza, much worse was to follow after February 1850 when permission was again received for speculative exports to be made to India. In this final phase of the company's interest in the horse trade, ships were engaged to pick up the horses at Carrington on Port Stephens, when consignments ranging in size from twelve to fifty-eight head were punted out from the shore and hoisted aboard. Local breeders, such as Major Innes at Port Macquarie, thought it desirable to take advantage of a nearby port but without wharves and cranes the process was so slow as to impose perhaps decisive initial problems. Loading the fifty-eight horses on the *Dudbrook* took five days, contributing to the strains of what was to prove for many a fatal voyage. These cargoes went principally to Madras rather than Calcutta, largely because of the friendship struck up with the Port Stephens people by the visiting East India Company officer, Mr Hagger, who was soon to become involved also with a scheme to bring horses to India from Western Australia. In the despatches relating to these transactions we see evidence of the difficulty experienced by Australian horse shippers for decades from being unable to insure horse cargoes except against total loss.[32]

And the losses were indeed heavy. A despatch from Archibald Blane of 14 November 1851 describes the fearful casualties on the *Tartar*, which had lost fifteen horses from a cargo of fifty, thirteen within the first fortnight and two more after landing through the surf in such an emaciated condition that they had to be carried to the yards. The experience made Blane wonder whether, without a home market, 'it is expedient to extend the breeding of Horses beyond the wants of the Establishment'.[33]

Any remaining doubts were removed by the company's loss of all but ten from a cargo of thirty-five shipped to Madras on the *Dudbrook* in September 1851. Although the reasons for this mortality remain something of a mystery because of conflicts in the surviving testimony, a number of facts are undisputed. Captain Smith provided only five grooms to look after a total of seventy-one horses, not much better than half the accepted proportion to cover the emergency of storms, which necessitated constant handling to get horses back on their feet after being knocked over when the ships rolled in heavy seas. He diverted the ship to Timor and delayed for nine days while he improperly traded a batch of dogs for a private cargo of Timor ponies, during which time three of the company's horses died in the extreme heat. A further twelve died in the Bay of Bengal, according to the superintending groom's final testimony, because they were cut down to less than half the ration of food and water. This case of deliberate neglect helps to explain, incidentally, why horse shippers commonly bought and handled their own fodder on the run to India. Captain Smith must have been a fool as well as a knave, since he earned no freight on the horses that died. Landed in Calcutta after three months and a day at sea, the company's ten survivors were sold in miserable condition at an average price of Rs 300. It comes as no surprise to see Arch Blane's relief, expressed in a despatch of 7 August 1852, at the 'great improvement in our Home Market' for horses, in consequence of the gold discoveries, which would 'obviate the necessity of seeking one in India'.[34]

These unhappy experiences on the horse export trail were matched for the A.A. Company by a calamitous decline in the quality of the stock, notably after the appointment of Captain Marcus Brownrigg as General Superintendent in June 1852. James White, a former stock superintendent, submitted a damning report in November 1854 of the dilapidation of the horse yards, the running down of the stallions and the general neglect of horse breeding (no doubt under pressure from the desperate labour shortage) at a time when the company might have expected to profit from the enhanced local demand. A committee reported to the Court of Directors that:

> Your horse stock, which at one time stood so high in the estimation of the Colonists . . . and which has mainly contributed to give to the present Australian breed of horses that excellence which they are known to possess—your horse stock is now reported by your present superintendent, Mr. Hodgson, to have so deteriorated in breed as to be, comparatively speaking, worthless.

In the company's 36th Annual Report it was announced that the stud had been disposed of, 840 head selling for an average of £3 17s 6d and it was then 'distinctly understood that the breeding of Horses, even on a limited scale, will not be sanctioned'.[35]

It remains to conclude this account of the first ten years of sustained horse exporting from New South Wales to India by glancing at the beginnings of trading from other Australian colonies and to other Indian Ocean and Southeast Asian destinations. No claim is made for comprehensiveness nor is an accurate statistical summary aimed at because of the huge volume of additional research that would have been involved, for extremely modest results.

First, a snippet from the *Shipping Gazette* for 13 May 1848, which recorded what was almost certainly the first shipment of horses from the Port Phillip District, soon to become the Colony of Victoria and in time the very hub of the Indian trade. The breeder referred to was Henry Nicholas Loughnan, who was appointed a magistrate for Gippsland in February 1852:

> *Horses for India* Another attempt is just about to be made again to open up this branch of lucrative traffic with India. Mr Loughnan intends to ship a number from his own stud at Gipps' Land, where he has for some time been breeding expressly for the purpose. A few will go from New South Wales to make up the cargo, in the charge of Mr Knight, the Veterinary Surgeon, who intends going to India to practise.

Horse exporting from Western Australia to India had been viewed from the start of the Swan River Settlement as a likely first fruit of colonization, given its relative proximity to the intended market. In fact, the colony experienced twenty years of desperate poverty, in which no energies or finances were available for breeding and shipping horses of appropriate quality. Even when the economy received a lift from the infusion of labour and government funds that accompanied the flow of British convicts after 1850, there were substantial problems to overcome. Most crippling of all was the absence of a deep water port accessible to the pastoral districts, and that was an obvious deterrent to any shipmaster interested in the Indian trade. They found it galling in the extreme to lie out at Gage's Roads waiting for the weather to permit the winching aboard of fractious young horses brought to the ship's side by lighters. Less obvious, though perhaps finally decisive, was the unsuspected absence of trace elements in the colony's pastures, which were necessary for the best development of bone and muscle.

Yet the tug of geography soon overcame these obstacles, if to a very limited extent. The splendid manuscript record of Arrivals and Departures for the Port of Fremantle, kept in the Battye Library, shows a trickle of horse exports on small ships, bound initially for Indian Ocean destinations. It started with the 93-ton *Emma Shenat*, Jas Harding master, which had sailed in with sugar from Port Louis on 2 July 1845 and left on 21 August with a cargo of horses, cattle, sheep and potatoes to return to Mauritius. An even smaller ship, the *Vixen*, of 43 tons, left for Colombo on 4 January 1846 with four horses, some sandalwood, and salt fish. That combination of timber and horses was to run through the Fremantle records for forty years. January 1849 saw the start of horse shipments to Singapore with the sailing of the *Rance* of 190 tons, with three horses and sandalwood, and the *John Bagshaw* a fortnight later with a similar cargo. With the rare exception of a moderately sized ship, this was to be the shape of the horse trade out of Fremantle. Very simply, the masters of bigger ships rarely felt they could afford to risk the delays involved in a sojourn at Fremantle. So, when the Indian horse trade became more and more specialized, with big ships aiming at the economies of scale, they seldom thought of Western Australia, which became linked with the markets in Singapore, Batavia, Port Louis and Manila for smaller numbers of horses below the remount standard.

The first of those exceptions was the sailing of the *Royal Saxon* of 510 tons for Calcutta on 20 February 1851, after six days in Fremantle, adding from ten to fifteen horses to its Sydney batch of seventy-two. Robert Towns had been considering such a move for some years in conjunction with D. C. Mackay & Company of Calcutta, perhaps buying a small ship for the trade with Swan River, South Australia and Port Phillip. Part of the inducement for the *Royal Saxon* voyage west in February 1851 was that the Torres Strait route was then closed, and the south-about route via Cape Leeuwin and then due north across the Indian Ocean was open, at least for good ships that could battle west against the 'Roaring Forties'. In the correspondence leading to this venture, Towns offered to drop his charges from £25 to £22 10s when ten or more horses were shipped. Times were again hard.[36]

Not until the emergency of the Indian Mutiny of 1857–58 were there any departures from Western Australia of large cargoes of locally bred horses, though some smaller consignments did go to Madras. The first of these was the *Mermaid* of 472 tons which sailed on 26 June 1851, followed by the *Minden*, a ship of 917 tons which had brought convicts from London and sailed for Madras on 14 October, no doubt seeking there a back lading to Britain. Interest in Madras had been stimulated by the plan of Thomas Hagger, a Madras veterinary surgeon, to set up in Western Australia a horse breeding company financed by his military colleagues, using Arab stallions imported from India. Hagger's letter to George Leake was published with a flourish in the Perth *Inquirer* of 17 October 1849, with a superbly confident editorial which predicted that 'in after-years Western Australia will be established as the principal (may we say only?) market for the supply of horses for the Indian Presidencies'. Under the plan, which was based on a Bengal model, the stallions' services would be provided free to contracted breeders who engaged to sell their colts at guaranteed prices to the local remount agent, keeping the fillies as a bonus.

Hagger arrived in March 1851 with news of four Arab stallions to follow, and proceeded to visit the horse breeding districts. It is not clear how far the company proceeded with its plans. Some cargoes did sail to Madras but the trade did not achieve the dimensions or the regularity that was hoped for so earnestly in 1849, when Hagger and his friends were talking of a progressive reduction in the Madras Presidency's dependence on the local Ossoor Stud, until the army was remounted entirely from the produce of Western Australia. The reasons for that disappointment will be considered in a later chapter.

5

India and the Great Remount Debate 1846–1873

A T THE END OF the first volume of his *History of the British Cavalry*, the Marquess of Anglesey sums up the main lessons of the period from 1815 to 1850. For the cavalry as a whole, the time since Waterloo had been marked by extreme conservatism, so that neither tactics nor training methods underwent any material change. Though Britain remained at peace, the armies of the Honourable East India Company fought nine campaigns, six of them between 1838 and 1849, beginning with the First Afghan War and ending with the Second Sikh War. Anglesey concludes that, notwithstanding this experience, the military thinking which informed the minds of the British commanders remained unchanged from that of the Napoleonic Wars. He goes on: 'Indian campaigns, it was for ever being made clear, required a larger proportion of highly mobile troops, particularly cavalry, organised for preference into permanent flying columns. Yet when the suppression of the Mutiny in 1857 and 1858 demanded as never before just such bodies, they did not exist'.

Another lesson that was belatedly learned from the terrible shock of the Mutiny was that the native *silladari* cavalry was in many ways superior to the native regular. In the irregular units the typical recruit was a landowner or farmer who had a stake in the country and who, by bringing into the regiment a contribution so valuable as his own horse, experienced a feeling of proprietory pride from having a share in its economy. That feeling was expressed within the Bengal army in 1857 by the comparative steadfastness of the eighteen *silladari* regiments, whereas all ten of the regular native cavalry had to be disbanded for varying degrees of disloyalty. As early as 1835, Lord William Bentinck had appreciated this:

> The Irregular Cavalry [he wrote] . . . is the favourite arm of the native. It attaches him

to our Service by the strong ties of interest and affection. It prevents their being engaged against us, and if the system were sufficiently extended it would, at a trifling expense, afford us all the advantages, moral and military, which the Russians have derived from the Cossacks.[1]

This was recognized after the Mutiny by the abolition of the regular or *non-silladar* system, except in the Madras Presidency, where it alone had been used in the native cavalry.

Yet, more than a decade before the Mutiny, changes were being discussed, and made, in the operation of the remount services, which reflected the stresses of the almost continuous warfare of the 1840s, and the needs imposed on the army by the huge annexations of territory that had taken place.

The conquest of the Sikh kingdom had the effect of moving the East India Company's border far to the west, through the five rivers of the Punjab, from the Sutlej to beyond the Indus. Vast as was the increase in the area to be administered and controlled, an even greater task came with the Company's inheriting from the Sikhs their thousand-mile border with Afghanistan, for centuries one of the most turbulent regions in the world.

Sir Henry Lawrence, who was placed at the head of the new government, applied ten regiments to the defence of the trans-Indus frontier, five infantry and five cavalry, which experienced a continuity of active military service that was exceptional within the British Empire.

Part of the reason for this was the character of the Muslim state of Afghanistan, its well-grounded suspicions of British intentions and the antipathy generated by the invasion and occupation of 1838–42, culminating in the disastrous withdrawal from Kabul. On many occasions during the century in which British armies held the north-west frontier, military emergencies resulted from the fomenting by the Afghan mullahs of enthusiasm for a jihad or holy war against their traditional Hindu enemies and their infidel protectors.

An even larger though more shadowy concern for British statesmen in London and Calcutta was the inexorable movement of Russian power to the south-west until the tsars had a border with Afghanistan. In each of the three Afghan Wars, of 1839–42, 1878–80, and 1919–22, there was an element of concern at the extension of Russian influence, mixed up, especially in 1919, with the work of caliphate agitators. Whatever the reality of the danger of a Russian invasion of India, the fear of it was a potent factor in British–Indian diplomacy, the disposition of Indian armies and, by extension, the provision of remount services.

Shadowy though the Russian menace may have been, the men of the Punjab Irregular Force (known after 1866 as the Punjab Frontier Force) had real and urgent military tasks to occupy them, which made the frontier a proving ground for generations of British and Indian soldiers. At the source of all its administrative and military problems was the complex character of its inhabitants, the Pathan tribes who lived astride the border between India and Afghanistan. Charles Trench describes them vividly in his recent book, *The Frontier Scouts*: 'By tradition and inclination, in some cases through economic necessity, they were predators; as

Moslem fanatics they fiercely resisted rule by Sikh or Christian; and as the ultimate democrats, with no man acknowledging another as master, they were difficult to hold to any agreement' (pp. 1–2).

Trench goes on to explain that no one, whether Afghan, Sikh or British, wished to govern these people of the frontier region. He describes the policy that was followed by Calcutta throughout the nineteenth century as one of the 'Close Border', which aimed 'to govern the plains and leave the hills as a sort of human "nature reserve"'.

> When the denizens of it became too troublesome—killing and kidnapping the dwellers in the plains, driving off their cattle and raping their women—they were subjected to punitive expeditions into a hostile tribe's country which killed a few of the men, blew up the fortified towers, pulled down the terraces of the fields, extracted a fine in cash and firearms, and then withdrew. This procedure was irreverently known as 'Butcher and Bolt.'[2]

One of the great figures of the north-west frontier during the formative years that followed the conquest of the Sikhs was a Scot who came from a distinguished military family, Lieutenant-General Sir Harry Lumsden. Appointed by Henry Lawrence to raise the Corps of Guides for frontier service in 1846 when he was still a lieutenant, Lumsden combined political and military duties and by force of personality and leadership, welded his combined force of infantry and cavalry, drawn largely from the Pathan tribes themselves, into a famous fighting unit. An idea of the character of the mounted operations that closed the campaign against the Sikhs is given by Lumsden's letter home from Camp Peshawur, dated 15 April 1849:

> On the 21st we took part in the general battle of Goojerat, which was an artillery action throughout, and much more like a grand review than a day which was to settle the destiny of the Punjab. A more beautiful sight could not have been on earth than the steady advance of upwards of one hundred guns—horse artillery going to the front at a gallop, and then 'Left about!' 'Action front!' supported by our cavalry, the heavy guns all the while smashing away at the Seikh artillery, and breaking up their masses of infantry and cavalry. Three times did the Seikh infantry form line to advance and charge at our horse artillery, who coolly watched for them until they came within the range of grape, and gave them a shower of such rain as had never come within the range of their conception. Their lines at first halted, shook backwards and forwards like a field of wheat in a heavy wind, and at last broke and bolted like a flock of wild sheep, the horse artillery following at a gallop, and keeping up a murderous fire on them for miles. Our cavalry took up the pursuit when the horse artillery left off, and finished as pretty a day's work as any army in India ever got through.[3]

By 1849 the Corps of Guides consisted of 400 irregular cavalry and 600 infantry, with headquarters in a rude fort at Mardan in the midst of Yusufzai tribal territory, well placed to watch the exits from the Yusufzai hills twenty-five miles to the north. Lumsden is described by his biographer as a 'daring sportsman, full of endurance, hardy and strong of frame, with an instinctive knowledge of men which gave him a power which none under him ever questioned'. It was said of the Guides, whose informal style of warfare was evoked nicely by their then unique use of khaki as a serviceable colour well suited to their sphere of operations,

Men from every wild and warlike tribe were represented in its ranks—men habituated to war and sport, the dangers and vicissitudes of border life: Afridis and Goorkhas, Sihks and Huzaras, Wuziris, Pathans of every class, and even Kafirs, speaking all the tongues of the border . . . Lumsden sought out the men notorious for desperate deeds, leaders in forays, who kept the passes into the hills, and lived amid inaccessible rocks. He made Guides of them.[4]

When the Corps of Guides was brought to full strength in 1849 it was merged in the Punjab Irregular Force, whose five cavalry regiments were trained and equipped for prompt action against marauders, and mounted on tough, agile horses, with sure, hard feet able to negotiate the hill country. General Elliott gives two examples of the Corps's effectiveness in this terrain. At the relief of Chitral in 1895, two troops of Guides came up to the 1st Brigade just as it was being threatened by 2000 tribesmen. Taking advantage of the opportunity of catching the enemy in the open plain, they charged with great determination and cut down thirty men, then drove the rest in headlong flight back to their hills. Again, when the garrison at Malakand was attacked in 1897, a message was sent to the Guides' post at Mardan and the cavalry left at midnight, covering the thirty-two miles in eight hours. Then the Guides charged across ground 'cut up with deep nalas [small valleys] and strewn with large boulders', inflicting heavy losses with little damage to themselves. As General Elliott comments, the performance was 'typical of the standards of fitness and readiness for action expected of troops serving on the frontier'.[5]

Lumsden's biographer describes an early incident in the career of the Guides when their khaki uniform became a matter of significance. In December 1849 they took part in a punitive raid on the Yusufzai town of Sango, which had positively refused to make revenue payments to the new government. The Guides were ordered to move along a spur to cut off the possible retreat of the Yusufzais, but so quickly did they carry out their task

> that an artillery officer deliberately laid a gun on them, and was on the point of ordering it to be fired when a keen-eyed gunner called out, 'Lord! sir, them is our mudlarks!' referring to their mud-coloured uniform, then for the first time seen in action by British troops, though now so generally adopted by the whole army in the field.[6]

Harry Lumsden unfortunately makes no comment on the quality of the Walers which we may assume to have gone into service with the Guides before he left the corps in 1862. Yet his detailed notes on the use of cavalry on the frontier assist our understanding of the circumstances in which Australian horses were used in India. His belief was that the effectiveness of cavalry had been greatly reduced by the huge weights that horses were expected to carry into the field, in spite of testimony— including that of Napoleon and Frederick the Great—to the superiority of light cavalry. As Lumsden expressed the point,

> Of all errors none is more fatal than that of imagining that by raising the weight on a horse's back you increase his momentum in a charge. Any weight beyond that of a light man and light equipment fatigues, and finally overpowers the horse, while in a charge it is rendered worse than nugatory by diminished velocity.[7]

It was this thinking that determined Lumsden's approach to the clothing, equipment and weapons of the Guides, which he cut down to the barest minimum, to their great advantage.

Anglesey shows that, throughout the nineteenth century, despite expert opinion that a cavalry horse should not carry more than fifteen stone (or 95 kilograms) all up, the actual norm was between eighteen and twenty stone. This was made up, according to Valentine Baker's calculations in 1858, of the following elements,

	stone	lbs
Average weight of men	11	0
Men's accoutrements	3	9
Horse equipment	3	11
Total	18	6

Not infrequently a supply of corn for four days weighing forty pounds was added, making a total burden for the horse of 21 stone 4 lbs.

The continuance of such practices reflects the conservatism of the cavalry and its reluctance to abandon the old belief that 'what really mattered' was the charge, carried out by heavy men on heavy horses, shattering and overwhelming the opposition, and that the light cavalry was contemptible by comparison. The same archaic thinking had kept the cavalryman, with such rare exceptions as the Guides, in uniforms as ill-designed as could have been imagined, with everything sacrificed to good looks on parade. As Anglesey explains, they were so notoriously close fitting as to hinder freedom of movement, as some troopers of the 12th Lancers discovered when they fought the Basutos in southern Africa in 1852. Falling to the ground, they were unable to remount because their overalls were too tight, so that they were all killed by the enemy![8]

But to return to the principles of Harry Lumsden. In line with his concern to reduce weight, he advised against troopers carrying pistols, which he pronounced to be utterly unreliable weapons, and thought that ten carbines amongst a whole troop would be ample. 'A cavalryman', he wrote, 'should trust to his spurs and sword, and have no other weapon'.[9]

On the subject of cavalry in hill warfare, he wrote:

> Infantry is the sheet anchor in all hill work, and guns its support; but it must be borne in mind that all hillmen have an instinctive dread of cavalry, and give this arm a position in their calculations which would not always be borne out by the effect actually produced. This feeling may extensively be taken advantage of whenever an open space admits of the movement of even a small body of horsemen, and in practice it will be found that a few sowars sprinkled along the flanks of a column of baggage give it a security quite out of proportion to the actual value of cavalry in such a position.

Another of the great leaders of *silladari* or irregular horse was Lieutenant-General John Jacob, like Lumsden, a soldier-administrator, appointed in 1847 as a mere brevet captain to be superintendent and commandant of the Upper Sind frontier, added by the recent conquests of Sir Charles Napier. His campaigns against marauders brought an unusual degree of law and order to the western border tribes, while at the same time he encouraged a great increase in the area of cultivation, so that the poor village of fifty inhabitants which he used as a base became at his death a prosperous city of 30 000. In 1851 it was given the name of Jacobabad.

The key to Jacob's military style was his readiness to take an offensive role. His frontier detachments were often posted in open country and taught not to depend on defensive works but to be able in a moment to respond to an emergency, with a self-contained transport system based on pairs of *sowars* (or troopers) who carried their own tents and camping requirements. Independence and flexibility were the glories of the *silladari* system, marked as it was by responsiveness and comparative cheapness, for the *silladari sowar* cost the state a third less than the regular.[10]

Cavalry style was gradually changing at mid-century in the matter of the military seat, which, partly for reasons of smartness on parade, used the long stirrup and straight leg, sometimes described as 'tongs across a wall'. This was a survival also of the days of armour, when an upright seat enabled a rider to bear the weight with more ease. But the more natural seat favoured by Captain Louis Nolan, the leading cavalry writer of the day, using a short stirrup and bent leg, was gaining adherents at this time, not least as a consequence of lessons learned in fighting the Sikh horsemen, whose use of short stirrups had given them an advantage over British cavalry in a skirmish.[11]

I have been arguing, somewhat in opposition to the Marquess of Anglesey, that a decade before the Mutiny, British cavalry leaders in India had begun to make significant adjustments to their ways so as to meet the challenges arising from great accessions of territory and the inheritance of turbulent new frontiers. Indeed, the most substantial change, from regular to *silladar* cavalry, though not completed till after the Mutiny, was anticipated at the beginning of the century with the outstanding successes of the irregular regiments raised by James Skinner and William Gardner.

Vital as this organizational change was to the efficiency of the cavalry, it could hardly have been more important than the adoption of new policies on the remounting of the cavalry and the horse artillery. Australian horses, or Walers as they came generally to be called in India to indicate their origin in New South Wales, began arriving in large numbers in 1846 to meet the growing needs of the mid-1840s. Geldings as they all were because of colonial pastoral eccentricities, these horses by their presence in Indian regiments demanded an urgent reconsideration of the relative merits of geldings and entires. When that debate was won by the proponents of the gelding, the way was automatically opened for the admission of mares to army ranks, thus increasing the flexibility of the remount service and improving the profitability of remount breeding. With the entry of new light and new ideas to the consideration of the needs of expanding mounted services, it was inevitable that hard questions should again be asked about the efficiency of the Bengal Central Stud. Commissions of Inquiry were told that Walers could be landed in Calcutta for a fraction of the cost of stud-bred horses, and there was an increasing reliance on these importations, limited only by a strategic and conservative concern that horse breeding skills and equine genes should be kept alive in India.

In this view of Indian equine history the coming of the Waler occupies a decisive place, so it is well that we should begin by looking at the reception accorded to the remounts that had been sent to Calcutta by Captains Dallas and Apperley in 1845 and 1846.

More than a thousand Walers were despatched to India by the horse buying deputation before it was withdrawn in 1847, upon the discovery that the output of the studs had caught up to the demand. Private speculative cargoes sent to Calcutta and Madras may have added a hundred Walers to the total number serving in the armed forces of the company, though it is likely that most of them went to the race tracks or into private stables for use as hacks or carriage horses.

Assessments made by commanding officers and veterinary surgeons during the first few years of Waler importations varied enormously. We may assume that Dallas and Apperley bought a high and fairly uniform standard of horses, given the co-ordination of their buying system and the extreme eagerness of the colonial breeders to make sales. Yet on the horses' arrival at their regiments, opinions as to their quality ranged from warm acceptance to explosive rejection. No doubt much depended on the horse's experience on board ship, which left many Walers emaciated and low in spirits for upwards of a year. The fact that they were all geldings also prejudiced many troopers against them. And they were less beautiful than the popular Arabs, while even the stud-bred colts made a better showing on the parade ground—a point of no small importance in Indian cavalry circles.

Writing on 20 August 1846 to the government of India, Lieutenant-Colonel P. Grant, the Adjutant-General, quoted the commander-in-chief as having mentioned 'the widespread feeling that the Australian horses may be too deficient in blood for campaigning in Asia, and though having great power and strength, they may lack the activity required for horse artillery'. This view that they were underbred was repeated many times in the early years in relation to questions about stamina and courage, which were seen as being dependent on a good measure of Thoroughbred ancestry. In the same letter, Grant expressed the common assumption that, being geldings, the Walers would be more timid than the stud-bred stallions.[12]

A batch of comments passed on to the government by Colonel Grant on 29 July 1847 shows the extreme variation in expert opinion. On the one hand we find Lieutenant-Colonel J. Alexander, of the 2nd Brigade of Horse Artillery at Ambala reporting on a month's experience with Walers:

> The N.S.W. horses in draught take the collar very kindly and firmly, not drawing by jerks, but pulling straight to the front, taking no notice of each other. Taking the mere question of a steady moving force without reference to speed or bottom, they draw better than the stud horses and having greater weight and substance, with more ease to themselves. With regard to pace, at a walk the Australians are faster than stud horses, and also at a trot, but in a gallop at full speed, the stud horses leave the Australians behind, having unquestionably the speed of them.

Colonel Alexander explained that neither set of horses was yet fit enough for severe trials and that the Walers had the disadvantage of arriving in hot weather with long Australian winter coats. He was most impressed by their ability to stand fire 'with very great steadiness with little or no teaching' and by the fact that in spite of being

Walers

Potential artillery horses: the chestnut (second from left) was rejected as too big and heavy

Good quality cavalry horses

worked regularly since arriving the previous October, they had steadily improved in condition.[13]

By contrast, Brigadier A. Campbell commanding the 3rd Cawnpore Division wrote in heavy disapproval of the eleven New South Wales horses that had joined the 9th Light Cavalry. They were, he exploded, 'of the very worst possible description and are not and never can be fit for any branch of the service. I consider the purchase of such horses a waste of public money'. Worse was to come a month later when he explained that on first seeing the Australian remounts he had assumed from their terrible appearance that they were set aside for casting, in which opinion he was joined, he said, by the veterinary surgeon.[14]

As the Walers settled down to life in India they tended to be praised for tractability and docility, qualities that were specifically linked by cavalry officers to their being geldings, and there was a widespread view that they spent less time than other horses in regimental hospitals. An illustration is given by the report of Lieutenant-Colonel Geddes, commanding a detachment of horse artillery at Meerut, who wrote of the miserable condition of the fifty-two Walers on arrival and of their slow recovery. But later, he said, they had much improved and after breaking in to saddle and draught they proved to be of gentle temperament. They had good bone and substance, good actions, and sound constitutions, with a commendable freedom from disease. He thought their rapid improvement was not unrelated to their being given an extra seer of gram (about one kilogram of grain) each day.[15]

Much depended on the care with which the Walers were treated in their first months in India. Initially few commanding officers made sufficient allowance for the strains the horses had undergone while standing in confined stalls on voyages of nearly three months, twice the duration of voyages taken by horses from the Cape, with which they were often compared. Captain Wheatley of the 5th Light Cavalry had charge of 450 Walers on the journey from Calcutta to the depot at Kurnool. Though in poor condition at first they improved visibly by the time they reached Benares but then encountered heavy rain, which pulled them down quickly in condition. Just before Aligarh fresh easterly winds set in and soon had the Australians in trouble with colds and catarrh, from which they recovered with great difficulty. Wheatley concluded, 'From the great sensibility of the colonial horses to the vicissitudes of weather and the difficulty with which they recover after every attack of illness, I am of opinion that they will prove almost useless in the service'.[16]

One of the most impressive testimonies in favour of the Walers comes from Veterinary Surgeon R. Hurford, who wrote cautiously about them in May 1847, that 'from their general appearance they seemed admirably fitted to dragoon purposes, since they were strong, sound, docile and free in action', though some had not yet recovered 'from their ships' sufferings'. He saw the best of the Arabs as the 'beau ideal of the troop horse', though the underbred Arab was 'a brute in every sense of the term, vicious and unthrifty, with no action and less stamina'. As to the stud-breds, they looked well on parade but on service any hardship told on them severely and they could not sustain effort under any privation.[17]

By 1851 Hurford was completely won over to the Waler and he told the Stud Commission under General Sir Walter Gilbert that he was

> now without a shadow of doubt that for artillery purposes the New South Wales horse is so superior to the stud bred as to render any attempt at comparison ridiculous: the

colonial is tractable, enduring, patient of privation, and of a courage no difficulty can damp. The most inveterate partiality can scarcely pronounce that these are qualities that characterize the stud horse.[18]

While the Indian army was making up its mind about the merits of Australian horses, a warm debate was taking place on the related question of whether geldings were as valuable as entires in the mounted services. The issue was an old one, though the last serious discussion had taken place thirty years earlier when a half-hearted experiment had been conducted in the Bengal army. Importations of colonial horses, whether Cape or Australian, were bound to revive the question, since in both countries the usual practice was to geld colts before they were two years old, in view of the expense involved in providing secure paddocks for stallions. From the time of the New South Wales impounding act of 1830, providing for heavy penalties on the owners of straying entire horses and bulls, only the best colts were left entire. It was a decision that augured well for Australian equine quality.[19] From January 1847 the military department of the government of India was collecting information about the relative merits of Arab, stud-bred, and New South Wales horses, and at the same time, of geldings and entires. The latter question was considered by Sir Walter Gilbert in a letter of 25 July 1846. He had frequently remarked, he wrote, on the 'extreme unsteadiness of the horses belonging to the mounted branches of our army', and during the recent campaign on the Sutlej had noticed the superior condition and behaviour of Major Grant's troop of horse artillery, in which a large number of geldings were used. On asking Grant for his views on the general question of the introduction of geldings to the mounted services, he had received the following reply, which is worth summarizing in detail.

Major Grant's long-matured thoughts on the matter had been confirmed by his own observations during the campaign and by conversations with wounded men, which suggested that losses were 'largely due to the fiery spirit of our entire horses, especially when opposed to the enemy's cavalry, many of whom were mounted on mares'. Virtually the only valid objection to geldings was that they did not carry as good a coat as entires but even this could be obviated by having the castration performed at the right season and by care and grooming. While the objections were slight, the advantages would be great, including economy of operation, the increased size of military horses and their improved steadiness in camp and action.

Under the existing system in the stud one syce looked after every three colts, so that they could only be exercised one day in three. With high feeding and little exercise, they grew heavy above and failed to develop adequate muscles or limbs. Geldings, by contrast, were much simpler to exercise, cheaper to house and manage and less liable to blemishes and injuries from kicking.

On service, the geldings' advantages were immense. The heavy head and heel ropes might be largely done away with. One man could take two or three to water, instead of one to one. In single combat, geldings were more easily managed; they were much superior to stallions on picquet duty—reconnaissance and guard duty—or in ambuscades and much less likely to be excited or put off their feed, whereas when a strange horse went past a troop of entires, it would set them all neighing and tossing their heads, and spilling half their fodder.

Grant's final point was that the adoption of gelding regiments would clear the way for the introduction of 'the fine mares of the country', once they had completed their time as dams.[20]

Another officer who wrote to General Gilbert advocating geldings was Lieutenant-Colonel J. B. Gough, who described the dangers he had encountered in the Sutlej campaign from vicious entires becoming loose in a hotly contested action:

> This I experienced especially at Moodkie [Mudki], where, after passing through the first body of the enemy, we came in contact with and were in the midst of the Sikh army, where our safety and success so much depended upon our compactness. We were much impeded in reforming for further action by the number of fighting, loose horses from our own and other brigades we could not get rid of.[21]

Gilbert himself told the Stud Commission of 1851, over which he presided, of a sergeant under his command. Because of the ferocity of the stallion he was riding, he was entirely occupied by the task of controlling his own mount instead of engaging the enemy and, though a powerful swordsman, had both his arms cut off in action.

Gough's second point had to do with the noisy disposition of the entire horse, which

> renders him almost useless upon outpost duty at night, and serves more to point out your own position than be a lookout upon the enemy. This I found everywhere, but more particularly at Ferozeshah, on the night of the 21 December, where, after taking up my position in the rear of our own division, the horses of my brigade became so noisy and troublesome that they plainly pointed out our position to the enemy, who immediately opened upon us, and I was obliged, with the Commander-in-Chief's permission, to change my ground during the night.

On the same occasion his men had been obliged to stand to their horses' heads throughout the night, which meant that neither they nor their mounts got any rest before going into battle. At the same time, because of the difficulty of unbitting stallions in these circumstances, the horses had been obliged to do without food for forty-eight hours before action.

Powerful testimony in favour of geldings was given by a famous cavalry commander, Colonel Cureton, whose own charger throughout the Afghan campaign had been a gelding that was never found deficient in courage. He reported that the same was true of his friend Major Havelock of the 16th Lancers; both of their horses had worked tirelessly and maintained good condition.

It may seem strange, in the light of these disadvantages, that entires were persevered with for so long. Part of the answer is given by Malcolm Kennedy, in commenting on the prejudices encountered by the first Australian remounts sent to India. He explains that Australian horsemen, unlike their Asian and Middle Eastern counterparts, were unconcerned to ride horses that were sexually intact. The point is developed in a fascinating footnote:

> The flying horse symbol used by an international oil company in Asia and the Middle East always exhibits a stallion with a large sheath and scrotum. When the Vacuum Oil Company used this sign in the Middle East during the 1930s without the sexual appendages their sales of petrol almost ceased as the Arabs stated that such a symbol represented a product that was of no real value or power. Many members of the Indian

army refused to ride geldings since such animals cast a reflection on their courage and manhood.[22]

Prejudice and sentiment were not the only factors in the retention by army stallions of their appeal, or of their testicles. An experiment of sorts had been conducted long before, as Lieutenant-Colonel John Angelo of the 3rd Light Cavalry informed the military secretary. He had seen the gelding experiment conducted from 1816 to 1820, including the whole of the Pindari campaign, one of the severest trials of the Indian cavalry. The gelding troop was commanded by Lieutenant (later Major-General) Sam Smith, one of the leading proponents of the change, and Angelo himself had been an advocate because of the dangers to the lives of riders from the violence of the locally bred stallions. But the results had been unsatisfactory, as the geldings did not bear up so well on the long marches or under exposure to rains, nor did they survive so kindly the passing of the years. As a consequence, the idea was abandoned and the gelding troop was broken up, though some doubts were expressed at the time as to the fairness of the test, for it was pointed out that the horses had been castrated at an age beyond that considered ideal.[23]

Angelo referred also to the trial conducted in 1809 by Major-General St Leger, into the suitability of mares for cavalry. One squadron of the 8th Cavalry at Kanpur was mounted on mares, and with some success until a squadron of stallions was drawn up behind them, when 'the uproar may easily be imagined'. As a result, many cavalry officers became rootedly and unreasonably opposed to the use of mares, much to the disappointment of St Leger, who believed that the result would have been very different if a whole regiment had been given mares.

From April 1847 Lord Gough, the Commander-in-Chief, directed that a separate gelding corps, the 11th Light Cavalry, should be created, made up of Australian imports and of horses bred by the Bengal Stud. It was decided, with the concurrence of the Secretary of State, that 20 per cent of the stud colts should be gelded before reaching two years of age, though the proportion was lifted in 1849 to 50 per cent.[24]

As may have been anticipated from the strength of Gilbert's views on the gelding question, one of the main recommendations of the Stud Commission of 1851, which he headed, was for the general castration of stud colts, though one of his colleagues, Lieutenant-Colonel I. S. Bradford, wanted more information from the gelding corps. Yet significant experimental evidence had already been obtained, notably in a recent march by geldings and stallions of Her Majesty's 15th Hussars from Bangalore to Hyderabad and back, a distance of 439 miles. The squadron, on escort duty with the new Commander-in-Chief, Sir Charles Napier, took the journey out in easy stages. On arrival at Hyderabad, Sir Charles could detect no deterioration in the condition of either class of horse; indeed, they were all in better marching order than at the start. In returning, they pressed on at forced marches and were examined on arrival by a board of officers, which concluded that 'the powers of endurance during the march of the entire horses and geldings appear to be equal'. This despite the fact that the geldings were older than the entires.

This experiment, reinforcing as it did the results of a similar test conducted with the Native Light Cavalry Regiment in 1849, was deemed by the commander-in-chief to be conclusive as to the equal merit of geldings and entires. So, taking account of the numerous advantages of the former, set out much as Major Grant had argued in

1845, Sir Charles urged upon the government the view that geldings were the better animal for mounting the Indian cavalry. Some reservations remained on the subject of horse artillery but here too there was an expectation of change. Again the army of the Madras Presidency took the lead and, as a result of an experimental march by F Troop of Horse Artillery which showed to the geldings' advantage, it was decided in January 1852 to mount the whole of the horse artillery on geldings, somewhat to the consternation of the Secretary of State.[25]

Armies, of course, are conservative bodies and slow to change, especially in such delicate matters as castration. The final shot in the great gelding debate was fired by the Secretary of State for India in a despatch of 27 January 1858, approving the decision taken by Commander-in-Chief General Anson to have all of the stud-bred colts castrated, except for those needed for stud duty.[26]

One of the landmarks in the history of stud and remount services in India was the Stud Commission presided over by Sir Walter Gilbert, which reported to the Council of India in August 1851. As this was the first major investigation of the Stud's work since the time of William Moorcroft, and one moreover made at a time of massive change within the mounted services of the army, it was bound to have significance for those services and for the countries and organizations involved in meeting their needs. Australia, as a newcomer to the fold of remount supply, could hardly expect to achieve more than a passing reference. In fact, the horses from New South Wales had a massive impact on the report, both directly in being singled out as the best available remedy for particular remount problems and indirectly as the factor that precipitated the change from entires to geldings.

Sir Walter Gilbert's feelings about the work of the government studs were made clear in a strong letter he wrote to the commander-in-chief prior to the appointment of the Stud Commission (published in the *Calcutta Sporting Review* and later in the *Sydney Morning Herald*—13 September 1851). Very possibly, it was a prime cause in the setting up of the Commission: the wonder is that after writing the letter, he could have acquiesced in the retention of the studs. But as the leader writer of the *Herald* realized, one of his two fellow Commissioners was Major Dickey, himself a stud superintendent, and no doubt committed to reform rather than abolition.

The letter offers a rare and lucid explanation of the working of the stud and remounting system in the Bengal army. About 1200 horses were allocated each year to the mounted services.[27] Most of those 1200 horses came from the government studs, some from the colonies and a small number from countries to the north and north-west of India. Stud horses had cost an average of Rs 758 in the previous five years, which with costs of transit and keep until five years of age gave a total of Rs 1000. By contrast, New South Wales horses were landed for £43 (Rs 516) and Cape horses for £47 (Rs 564).

There was almost universal agreement that the stud horses had deteriorated in the previous twenty years. In Gilbert's words:

> Even the best of stud horses, those the first selected for the Horse Artillery, are too often bad tempered and of insufficient substance for Artillery draught, and when they meet with any obstacle, which they cannot immediately surmount, they become sulky and will not renew the effort, and manual labour must be had recourse to, not merely to aid, but often in substitution of the horses.

It was for this reason, he said, that a gun was left on the banks of the Chenab by Colonel Lane's troop; if they'd had horses from the Cape, New South Wales, or Arabs, the result would have been otherwise.

Gilbert had special praise for the Cape horses bought by Colonel Havelock which had served on the march to Kabul, many having been chosen as officers' chargers. Walers had been under trial in the Bengal army for three of four years, and were 'much approved of, especially as draught cattle for the Artillery'.

A further weakness of the stud horses was their susceptibility to disease, notably the skin eruption peculiar to India known as *bursati*, which was spread quickly by flies, and most marked in the army preparing for the Sutlej campaign.

In summary, Gilbert saw Arabs and colonial horses as 'not only superior, as regards temper, docility, constitutional freedom from disease, power of enduring privations, and muscular power for draught' but they could also be bought at half the cost of the stud horses, saving the army perhaps £60 000 a year—or enough to buy another 1200 horses. He rejected the strategic argument, on the ground that in time of war the navy would be careful to keep the supply routes open from Persia, or the Cape or Australia. He anticipated the efficient working of a tender system by which the government would publish its annual requirements and call for supplies to be sent, subject to approval by remount committees. Poor as the stud horses were, Gilbert agreed with the view expressed in 1849 by Veterinary Surgeon Hurford, that their quality was bound to deteriorate further, so the time had come for urgent action.

Perhaps the most important recommendation of the committee was that, in spite of huge defects in the existing system, the government studs should be retained, largely for strategic and conservationist reasons. As to the former, it was considered inadvisable for 'the Bengal Army to depend entirely upon distant colonies and foreign countries for its horses'. They believed that the present system in the studs was capable of great improvement, sufficient to supply horses to the dragoons and light cavalry, while the special needs of the artillery were to be met by imports, especially from Australia.

> It is to be feared that if the studs be abandoned, the breed of horses in our provinces would still further deteriorate, as the original breeds which once existed are in a great measure extinct. It would be difficult to revive, for it appears always to have been necessary for the rulers of this country to furnish stallions to their subjects, and under the native governments we believe horse breeding was much fostered. For example the Kathiawar, so much prized, and now nearly extinct, is said to have been raised at immense expense by importing the parent stock from the shores of the Red Sea and the Persian Gulf. The abandonment of the studs would also doubtless tend to enhance the value of colonial and Arab horses, by creating greater demand for them.

The Commission surveyed the decline of the Bengal Stud since the high point attained by William Moorcroft, and attributed the principal fault to Lord William Bentinck's decision of 1831, on the grounds of economy, to successively cut down the numbers of brood-mares with a view to eliminating the Stud. When soon after an attempt was made to restore the stud, mares were hurriedly sent out, deficient in bone and substance and 'wanting that breadth which is requisite in brood mares'. They in turn were put to stud-bred stallions of inferior stamp, so that nothing but disappointment ensued.

Gravest of the faults remarked by the Commission in all the studs was that after being purchased from the *zamindars* as yearlings, the colts were treated as mature horses and stabled for the bulk of the day, receiving only two hours of exercise. This contrasted with the universal practice elsewhere of giving freedom to young horses in order to develop wind, muscle and agility, nowhere more so than in the open pastures of Australia. The result was to render the stud-bred horse the 'delicate animal he is found to be when put to hard work and exposed to the inclemency of the weather'.

To rectify the faults, the Commission advised the appointment of additional stud officers so as to supervise more closely the work of the *zamindars*. The deficient mares were to be ruthlessly weeded out and replaced by 'roomy Australian mares', which were to be brought in, fifty in the first year, and put to good Arab stallions. Major-General Gilbert had been particularly concerned at the widespread existence of diseased hocks, found to occur in one-third of the army's horses, and also ring-bone, spavins and other malformations. This again was a reason for his seeking to import Australian mares, which were 'remarkable for possessing fine clean hocks and freedom from ringbone'.

Not a single officer had a good word to say of stud-bred horses as draught animals. Only three of the thirty interviewed opposed the introduction of Australian horses, which showed a marked advance since the hostility encountered by the arrivals of 1846 and 1847. There was a general approval for Walers as the best available solution for the special problem of mounting the artillery, because they were seen as 'possessing greater strength, docility, and aptitude for draught than stud bred horses'. One of the most positive views was expressed by Brigadier Wheeler in writing to Gilbert on 2 January 1851. The troop of artillery under his command was horsed mainly by Walers and, as he put it, 'from their style of working I am satisfied that with such cattle our Horse Artillery might be given nine pounders instead of the comparatively useless six pounders now in use'.

The Commissioners advised the government to advertise in the Australian press that specified numbers of certain classes of horses would be bought at Rs 550, subject to their approval by remount committees in Calcutta. An arrival in July or August, they suggested, would give the horses time to recover from the sea voyage before marching to their regiments in the ensuing cold weather.

Just as remarkable as the improved standing of the Waler was the continuing regard felt by Indian officers for remounts from the Cape of Good Hope, which had been coming in numbers, especially to Madras and Bombay, for over thirty years. Their 'hardy constitutions rendered them capable of enduring great fatigue and privations' and therefore most suitable for the horse artillery, but the Commission regretfully concluded that 'in the unsettled state of the colony, the Cape was not a present source of supply'.[28]

Ironically, at the very time when the Australian breeders were about to receive the nod from the government of India, their ability to supply that need, of which Gilbert had felt so confident in 1850, was put in doubt. The gold discoveries in New South Wales and Victoria which began to be published to an excited world in mid-1851 had the effect of trebling the Australian population in a decade and, in the short run at least, of stretching to the limit the country's equine resources.

6

The Waler's Fortunes 1851–1900

T HE HOPES GENERATED by the Report of the Stud Commission under Sir Walter Gilbert, that India's remount needs would be substantially met by a steady flow of Walers from Australia, were quickly put in doubt by developments at both ends of the projected trade. Even before the ink had dried on the Gilbert report of August 1851, which condemned the failure of the Indian government studs and proposed reliance on Walers especially for the horse artillery, the ability of Australian breeders to meet the projected export demand was wiped out by the effects of the gold discoveries. Within a year of the brilliantly stage-managed rush to the Ophir field near Bathurst, much richer alluvial deposits had been found within striking distance of Melbourne, so that a flow of gold seekers soon began to arrive at the ports of New South Wales and Victoria. In those circumstances horse breeders had difficulty in keeping up with local demand, notably for the semi-draught types that had been earmarked by the Gilbert Commission for the horse artillery, and the rise in prices of quality stock put it out of the reach of the Indian shippers. With a prime cost ranging from £25 to £35 the landed price in Calcutta would have been far in excess of the Rs 550 (or £46) allowed by the Indian government. So it was that an official of the East India Company was able to write a pencilled note on a despatch of 17 January 1855, dealing with the remount needs of the Madras Presidency, 'Aust has not sent a horse to India for two years & will send no more'.[1]

Coinciding with the diminution of the Australian supply was a remarkable resurgence in the official approval of the stud-bred horse which had been so condemned by the Gilbert Commission. The high point in this brief rehabilitation came in an exchange between the newly created India Office and the government of India. In reply to the Governor-General's surprisingly warm praise of the stud-bred horse the Secretary of State averred in a despatch of 18 October 1860:

The Honourable East India Company's Depot at Bungarribee, New South Wales, *watercolour by T. Rider of Sydney, c. 1847*

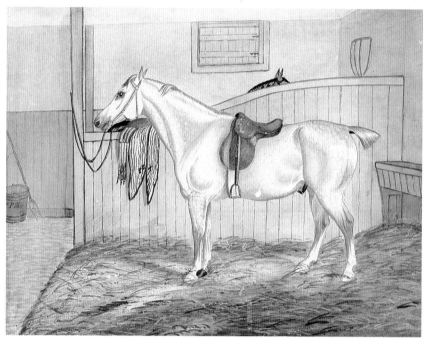

Beagle, an Australian bred horse, by Skeleton, the property of Captain P. P. King, R.N., *watercolour probably by J. Lethbridge Templar, 1839*

Landing Horses from Australia [at Madras], *watercolour possibly by J. B. East, 1835–45*

Shipping horses then and now: (above) Shipping Horses for the Government of India, Miller's Point Wharf, Darling Harbour New South Wales, *watercolour probably by Frederick Garling, c. 1846, and* (left) *loading horses on the* MV Centaur, *1977*

Walers for private use then and now: (above) *the Sultan of Pahang's polo team in 1965, and* (below) Pigsticking in India: The Picnic, *photolithograph after E. Hobday, 1907*

it appears . . . to be conclusively established that the first cost of stud-bred horses is less than the cost of horses imported from the colonies, and that, by the balance of testimony, their quality is superior and their powers of endurance greater. It is also to be borne in mind, that by the maintenance of the studs the breed of horses in the country is improved and the Irregular Cavalry well mounted, that the revenue is benefited, and India rendered comparatively independent of the foreign supply of horses for military purposes.[2]

In the light of the mass of contrary opinion, presented to both the Gilbert and the Troup Stud Commissions, this statement must be judged one of the most splendid examples of the human capacity for self-deception. It was the *desire* of India's governors to achieve certain results, not least an independence from distant horse imports, that formed the basis for those conclusions, not the evidence itself. The whole question of horse breeding and remount supply in India had a vast potential for confusion, distortion and special pleading, which is to be the subject of this review of the debate during the second half of the nineteenth century.

The view taken by this chapter is unequivocally Indian and military, tracing the Waler's fortunes as a war horse from the low point of 1860, when a biased and ill-informed inquiry prepared to dispense with Australian imports, to the resurgence ushered in by the Report of the Stud Committee of 1869, chaired by Sir Colin Troup. The story will be taken to the end of the century when the Waler had not only won a secure place in Indian military planning but also had its special needs accommodated by the erection of a new system of landing places, purchasing and holding depots, and reserves. It was this system that survived, virtually unchanged, till the end of the remount trade. The government of India indicated early in each year what its purchases would be at the three presidency ports during the following cold season and the Australian shippers, having sometimes battled for weeks to dispose privately of the horses rejected by the remount buyers, would return to their home ports and prepare for the next consignment.

Early in our period, the government of India settled comfortably into the practice of buying horses only in India, after minute inspections by veterinarians and remount officers. As we have seen, they had been prepared during the emergency of the mid-1840s to despatch a buying mission to Australia, and did so again during the greater crisis of the Indian Mutiny of 1857–58. Thereafter the government left all the costs and risks of purchase and transit to a small group of professional shippers, whose operations and adventures will be the subject of the following chapter. Many efforts were made by Australian breeders and even by Australian governments to bring about a change in the system, notably by having the Indian government set up a permanent buying agency in Australia, but they were steadily, and very astutely, resisted. What the government was prepared to do was to send out senior remount officials to go around the main breeding areas to acquaint pastoralists with changing Indian needs and to assess their capacity to satisfy them, as in the decisive visit by veterinarian W. Thacker in 1874.

Following the Mutiny in 1857–58, there was an urgent need to discover what shape the northern studs were in and whether they were still capable of performing their traditional function as the principal suppliers of cavalry and artillery mounts. A despatch of 1 September 1858 from the India Office reveals the deep initial pessimism with which the authorities approached the question. Stories had gone back to England of wholesale theft and destruction by the mutineers of the breeding stock, so that, particularly in the light of the criticisms of stud horse quality by the Gilbert Commission of 1851, the question of finally abandoning the studs needed to be seriously considered. As the Secretary of State put it, 'the question of continuing existing establishments is one thing; that of restoring establishments which have ceased to exist, is another'. The Indian government was therefore asked to consider the remount question with reference to the quality of the stud horses, their average costs in the previous ten years and the results of 'the late arrangements' (i.e. during the Mutiny) for procuring horses from the colonies and other sources.[3]

The results of this inquiry were summed up in a letter of 20 December 1859, conveying the surprising news that the losses of stud horses as a consequence of the rebellion were 'by no means as heavy as might have been anticipated'. From the Central Stud in the Buxar and Koruntadhee districts, the losses were only trifling, amounting to 12 stallions and 76 brood-mares, though the North-Western Division was harder hit, because of the carrying off of 341 colts from the Haupper Stud stables. Against this, there remained in the Central Division a total stock of 4993 horses, and in the North-Western, 3015, not including over 7000 brood mares in the hands of Zilladars.[4]

The crucial question, as it soon appeared, was the cost of the stud horse in comparison with remounts imported from the Cape, Australia and, to a much less extent, Argentina. Major Atkinson, though prefacing his estimates by remarking on the variations caused by different accounting techniques, claimed that the average cost of the stud-bred horse in the previous ten years was Rs 703. The unit cost, measured by dividing the total outlay by the numbers passed into the service, had fallen from an average in 1850–51 of Rs 1294 to one of Rs 674 in the years from 1856 to 1858, when much larger numbers had been provided.

According to the accounting method used by Major Atkinson, the cost of stud horses was substantially less than that of the two main imports, from Australia and the Cape. The former, for which alone full accounts had been presented, cost Rs 905, and the latter, Rs 631, before a number of heavy expenses were counted. He therefore concluded that, whereas an increasing importation of colonial horses would raise their unit cost, 'an increase to the out-turn of the stud may sensibly reduce the average'.

The advantages to be looked for in relying on the studs included the promotion of Indian horse breeding, the stimulation of the economy and, most desirably, the achievement of self-reliance in a vital area of military power. It seemed as well that these benefits could be won without sacrifice of equine quality, for Atkinson quoted the opinion of the commander-in-chief himself that 'Stud-bred Horses are exceedingly well-suited for Military purposes, both on account of their size, power, and capability to stand hard work and exposure to the climate'.

Responding to this unexpectedly good news in a despatch of 18 October 1860 the Secretary of State agreed to the Indian government's proposal that the Bengal studs should be maintained on a scale that would permit them to meet the ordinary demands of the service, 'leaving extraordinary demands to be met from the local markets or by importations of private dealers'. Not a word here of the horses from Australia and the Cape, of which more than 6000 had been imported to cope with the losses incurred during the Mutiny and to mount the regiments of cavalry and brigades of artillery that had been sent to India from the United Kingdom, as usual, without their horses.

Part of the reason for this extraordinary return to favour of the stud horse is to be found in the views of the Governor-General, who had taken the opportunity during a march from Kanpur to Peshawar of asking officers for their opinions on the relative merits of stud-bred and imported horses. 'I have found them all,' he said, 'without exception, in favour of the stud horse'.[5] One can only surmise that the noble questioner had indicated to his respondents the sorts of answers that would be preferred.

But why were the claims of the colonial horses so discounted? On the outbreak of the Mutiny remount officers had been sent overseas, Colonel Apperley to the Cape and Colonel Robbins to Australia. Apperley had despatched 3635 horses to India for which he had paid an average of £35, and of which 3465 or 95.3 per cent survived the journey. In Australia, Robbins had bought 3128, paying at first £32 a head but soon finding it necessary to pay £43 in a seller's market. The overwhelming bulk of shipments sailed from Melbourne, so initiating a predominance over Sydney that was to continue for eighty years. Of the horses embarked in twenty-three sailing ships, carrying an average load of 136, only 2535 made it safely to Calcutta, giving a survival rate of only 81 per cent, markedly less than for the Cape horses.[6]

Unfortunately I was unable to find in the India Office Library any detailed files relating to the Robbins mission or to the impressions formed in India as to the quality of these Australian remounts. One file that dealt with the allocation of 803 remounts from the Cape, Sydney and Melbourne recorded the committee's satisfaction with their soundness. Only four were found unfit for service,[7] and the contemporary *Reminiscences* of Sir Roger Therry quoted the encomiums of Colonel Robbins on the quality of the Waler. A letter of 1 March 1859 reported the loss in Torres Strait of all ninety horses carried in the *Chesterholme*. This was perhaps the last horse ship to leave Tasmania for India. The loss of this uninsured cargo reminded the Indian government of the expediency of not importing horses at its own risk. Far better, it was generally thought, to leave these worries to private enterprise.[8]

The critical factor in the disapproval of Australian horses was assuredly their greatly increased cost. At £43 a head the prime cost had more than doubled since 1850, giving a peak that would never again be reached. When the trade settled into a routine in the 1870s it was rare for Indian shippers to pay more than £20, even for the better class of remount.

It is perhaps chastening to reflect on the gap between the tone of Australian responses to news of the Indian Mutiny, which generated promises of noble and disinterested assistance to beleaguered fellow subjects, and the reality of the hard bargains struck by those who had horses to sell to Colonel Robbins. Though I cannot document a specific reaction to this experience of colonial commercial toughness there are many instances of the Indian government's determination to ensure that Australian horse breeders and shippers should never again secure the upper hand. Any approach to a monopoly was to be resisted at all costs and the oft repeated urgings for the government to set up permanent agencies in Australia, though offering such rewards as continuity and stability, suffered from the critical flaw of making an effective long-term commitment to Australian sellers that would give them an undesirable advantage.

Not that the protestations of loyalty and sympathy, such as those expressed by Gideon Scott Lang, M.L.A., in a letter published in the *Sydney Morning Herald* on 16 September 1857 and at a public meeting held the following week in Mort's Rooms, were entirely shallow. India meant a great deal to the citizens of the Australian colonies throughout the nineteenth century, not only by its appeal to the imagination and the hint of romantic adventures and great deeds, but also through a network of personal associations created in part by the arrival of ex-India hands for terms of leave or final retirement. So we should not be surprised at the collection by the New South Wales Indian Relief Fund of £5466, or at the allocation of Government House at Parramatta as a base for the accommodation of the remount buyers and the stabling of the horses while they were being broken and trained by a platoon of Indian syces, or Bengali Goorah wallahs, as the Sydney *Empire* described them.[9]

The true watershed of the remount trade was the Stud Commission appointed in October 1868 under the presidency of Major-General Sir Colin Troup. It was set up by the Governor-General, Lord Lawrence, as an official memorandum put it, in consequence of 'the almost unanimous reports of cavalry and artillery officers as to the badness of the remounts' sent to them from the government studs. Only one consideration prevented the committee from recommending the abolition of the whole Stud Department, the principle expressed by Sir Charles Wood in 1860, that government should assist in the process of making India self-reliant for the supply of horses. However, it recommended that the studs should be gradually wound down and breeding left to private enterprise with some encouragement from government. Imports of remounts from the colonies, notably Australia, were seen as a fact of Indian military life and it was urged that depots be created in which Walers could be acclimatized before they were drafted to their regiments.[10]

Sir William Mansfield, the Commander-in-Chief, commented on the Troup Report in a strong minute of 31 August 1869 that augured well for the future of Australian horse breeders and shippers. The only regiment he knew of as being wholly mounted on colonial horses was the Inniskilling Dragoons, which were horsed 'in a most admirable manner' when he commanded them in Bombay in 1860. The illustration was worth noticing, he said, because of the tendency 'to undervalue the resource we have in the colonies', a tendency especially strong in Bombay and Madras and also in Upper India, where horsemen were accustomed to the points of beauty of the pure Arab breed.[11]

It was impossible, he said, to rise from a perusal of the Troup Report on the Government Studs without recognizing that 'as a means of furnishing a sufficient number of remounts to the army, of causing such remounts as are furnished to be really good, or of economy in the art of production, the government studs are a gigantic failure'. Mansfield went on to make blistering comments on the extravagance evident in every department of the stud, but most particularly in retaining a quantity of useless mares and stallions that were either congenitally unfit or too old for stud purposes. The stud system supported a mass of young stock that could never be made suitable for the ranks and faced an eventual prospect of being sold at a dead loss.

Mansfield, even more than the members of the Troup Committee, put his faith in the efforts of private breeders but he saw India as depending indefinitely on imported remounts. Addressing himself to the strategic arguments against distant imports, he compared the supply of horses to the supply of troops. 'We import the British soldier,' he wrote, 'because he has special qualities which are not producible in this country; we do not attempt to have breeding establishments of Englishmen in India in order to lessen the primary expense of the British soldier. Well, there is no greater danger in relying on foreign parts for the supply of military horses than it is to rely on Great Britain for the troopers and gunners who have to ride and drive them'.

Because the armies of the Bombay and Madras presidencies, and native troops in general, relied on the open market for their horse supplies, the inquiry by the Troup Commission was limited to the question of replenishing the British troops of the Bengal army. As they numbered 6380 and the annual replacement figure was calculated at 12 per cent, a supply of 750 to 800 horses was thought to be needed.[12]

Such a number, the Troup Commission concluded, was far beyond the capacity of the Bengal Studs. A deficiency of 563 was expected in 1869, and of 510 in 1870, so the immediate task was to procure about a thousand horses from abroad in the two following years. Both the Troup Commission and the Special Stud Commission set up under Major-General C. T. Chamberlain to implement the report agreed that it was to Australia that the Indian government must turn. Even then, the prejudices to which Sir William Mansfield had referred were evident in the opinions expressed by commanding officers in letters sent to the Commission, several of which considered the Walers underbred and therefore unable to stand the stress of campaigning in India. Perhaps the best summary of the comparison of the stud horse and the Waler was made by Major-General Alfred Huyshe of the Royal Artillery:

> Whatever the cause, the Stud horse as a class, though tall, is wanting in breadth of chest and quarter, and in weight generally. He is tied below the knee, and is so weedy that he can draw only by the exercise of excessive muscular exertion and pluck . . . From their greater weight, the Waler draws much easier and more efficiently than the Stud-bred. Indeed, I believe this is not disputed; the unwillingness to employ the Waler in India lying in the supposed uncertainty of the supply, and in a doubt as to their working efficiently when exposed to extreme heat.[13]

The essential reason for the stud horse's deficiencies was the continuation of the same poor management of mares and young stock that had been condemned by William Moorcroft during his early years and by the Gilbert Commission in 1851. Brood-mares were rarely ridden by the *assamees*, and their legs became swollen for lack of exercise, with fetlocks almost touching the ground. Young stock were kept tied up for twenty-two out of twenty-four hours, making it impossible for them to develop tendons and muscles and inducing weak pasterns, narrow chests, twisted forelegs and cow hocks.[14] Those members of the Troup Commission who knew something of the life styles of young Waler stock saw their open range experiences as a good reason for preferring them.

Inevitably, the final decision turned on the question of comparative costs. Whereas the warm approval for the stud horse in 1860 had been a factor of its apparent cheapness, the Troup Commission was using a budget system that only came into force in 1861, requiring all relevant expenses, including those of the Civil, Public Works and Commissariat departments, to be charged to the stud account. As a consequence, the full and fearsome picture of the stud horse's cost was glimpsed for the first time by an Indian committee. Using the new and more complete system, General Troup and his three colleagues concluded that the cost of a stud remount had risen to the staggering average, for the three years from 1865 to 1868, of Rs 2194 or more than £180. This compared with the Waler's landed cost of about £55.[15]

The committee recommended the closing of two stud depots at Pusa and Korantadhee in the Central Division, the abolition of the *assamee* system, the creation of a new breeding stud in the Punjab on the Home System developed by Moorcroft, and the setting up of a new remount depot at which a reserve of 1000 horses could be accumulated. It was the latter point that bore especially on the prospects of the Waler.

Much of the argument in parts VI and VII of the Troup Report assumed that Waler imports would take an immediate and continuing place in the Bengal remount system. Colonial imports, it was pointed out, were now 'almost entirely confined to Walers', which had been bought by committees for some years past in adequate numbers and serviceable quality at Rs 600. Suitable Cape horses, it was believed, could not be imported at that figure. This was much regretted, since all members of the committee saw the Caper as the ideal remount. Its disappearance from the Indian scene was attributed to the decline of the Cape route following the opening of the Suez Canal in 1867, which caused immediate losses and the termination of the specialized breeding for the Indian market. What was not mentioned was the awful shadow of African Horse Sickness which imposed a cruel constraint on the main breeding areas of southern Africa.

At last there was an awareness of the need for Walers to be rested, well fed and acclimatized from the time of their unloading till the end of their first year in India. The report recommended that they should be bought in Calcutta only during the colder months from October to March inclusive and sent by rail to the remount depot, which it was proposed to establish at Saharanpur, north of Delhi. Urging this, the committee admitted that this old stud depot was climatically unsuitable for young stock:

> But . . . it has a very fine farm attached to it, and the best lucerne and carrot garden in the Stud with excellent stables for remount horses, abundance of forage of the very best description for fresh Walers as well as for any other horses likely to be sent there, and moreover has the great advantage of being on the line of rail . . .

All this may sound like an advertisement for a tourist resort; it is a measure of the distance travelled by the Waler in the estimation of the Indian authorities.

How was the report received in London? Oddly enough, it was not transmitted till 1873, when it evoked a somewhat uncomplimentary reply from Secretary of State, the Duke of Argyll. His despatch of 20 March 1873 referred to the 'startling conclusions' of the Troup Committee and declined to accept proposals for yet another breeding stud or even the eminently sensible remount depot. The Perry memorandum, on which the despatch was based, had made the nice point that the commander-in-chief had drawn sounder conclusions than the committee, in urging the abandonment by government of ground best occupied by private enterprise, and this would soon be the direction taken by Indian remount planning.

Another insight afforded by Perry's able memorandum takes us, perhaps, to the heart of the army remount question. His point deserves a lengthy quotation:

> It remains to be added, that the horse problem in India is a much simpler one than it is in European countries where Governments have occupied themselves with its solution. It has been seen that the Indian Government only seeks to supply about 750 remounts to its army per annum, but France, with a peace establishment of 50,000 horses has to supply over 7,000. And, although France contains over three millions of horses, and England nearly the same number, the demand for civil and industrial purposes in wealthy and advancing communities makes the supply to the armies of those countries every year more costly. India, on the other hand, is not a horse-using country. From time immemorial the animal has been employed for parade [*sowari*] and for war, and for those purposes only. His use is unknown in agriculture; he is rarely seen even in harness except in the Presidency towns. I marched all the way from Madras to Bombay and from Bombay to Umbala, over 1,900 miles, and did not meet a single horseman or a horse in a cart. For the supply, therefore, of the Indian Army, comprising in the whole about 24,000 horses, the Government, in looking to the Native breeder, need fear no competitors in the market.

In the meantime, Perry concluded, India had to continue to depend on a foreign supply, as it had for centuries. I would add one qualification to Perry's conclusions. The absence of local competition may have had the desirable effect of keeping the price to modest limits but it equally reduced the stimulus to produce locally a high quality product, which made all the more profound the consequences of the destruction of the Sikh state and the elimination of the last of the great native horsed armies in 1849.

While the Troup Committee was deliberating on the future of the studs in the bracing air of Simla, they were visited by R. D. Ross, an official of the South Australian government, who had been deputed to speak to the Indian authorities about a plan that would recur several times during the life of the remount trade. Very simply, it was proposed that the Indian government establish a depot at Port Darwin to which young horses might be overlanded from South Australia and Queensland, and acclimatized there to tropical conditions before being shipped to Indian destinations. Beyond the matter of acclimatization, the great advantage of the scheme was that it avoided the perils of the south-about route via Cape Leeuwin, with its fierce contrary winds, and of the still hazardous journey through Torres Strait. More than that, by cutting the journey from ten to three or four weeks (for sailing ships were still exclusively used in the horse trade), the organizers could deliver animals in far better condition, much sooner able to be used by Indian regiments and batteries. Ross urged the desirability of having the remount needs of all three presidencies supplied from this new source, so eliminating the need for the studs, and for recourse to other countries.

Though Ross made a good impression at Madras, Calcutta and Simla, and found his hosts quite charming (he was an Englishman, not an Australian), his proposal was quickly rejected. There were the utter imponderables involved in overlanding through some of the most inhospitable country in Australia and the uncertainties about how the young stock would thrive in the Northern Territory, which have been shown to be well justified by later experience even to modern times. The idea was submitted by the committee to Major-General Sir H. M. Durand, who had been made aware of the blowing out of the costs of breeding operations in India, and therefore expressed concern at the inflationary pressures that might be generated in remote Darwin. But the decisive obstacle perceived in his minute of 16 September 1869 was the danger of the government's relying on a single source outside India. He therefore recommended that Australia be seen as an ancillary source of supply and not as one to be absolutely depended on. These principles were held to for the next seventy years.[16]

Rather than embark on an untried scheme, the ongoing Stud Commission set up under General Chamberlain deputed a trusted staff veterinary surgeon, Mr W. Thacker, the remount agent at Calcutta, to visit the Australian colonies in the winter of 1874 and assess their capacity to supply remounts to the Bengal army. He visited Tasmania, Victoria and New South Wales and collected information that gave much comfort to his employers when he reported back to the Special Stud Commission on 10 September 1874.[17]

Looking first at the strength and quality of the equine population of the three colonies, Thacker noted an effective decline in Tasmanian horse breeding, which had been reflected in static numbers (the returns for 1873 showed 22 000 in the colony) and an inability to satisfy the local market, let alone continue exports. Victoria and New South Wales had steadily increasing numbers of horses with, respectively, 180 000 and 328 000 recorded in 1873, though in the latter colony perhaps as many as 30 000 wild horses, named brumbies possibly after the man who was reputed to have been responsible for their existence, escaped the musters.

Thacker attributed much of the stamina and quality of the Australian-bred horse to the 'fact that the grasses are much less succulent and far more nutritive than the grasses produced in England', though he denied that they had unique staying powers beyond those of England or the Cape. He went on:

> The Colonies I have visited present features in every way adapted for the rearing of horses; such as large enclosures, undulating ground, equable climates, and abundance of nutritive grasses and saline herbage. No protection is required for the young stock during the winter months, and the prevalence of bush affords shade in the hot weather. Entire horses can be depastured with the necessary number of mares, and therefore little expense is incurred . . . mares are kept in a state approaching nature, thus rendering them unusually prolific.

In the many stations he visited, where remount horses were bred as a sideline to sheep and cattle grazing, he found excellent stallions, descended from the 'best blood from England', though the quality of the mares had been brought down during the gold rushes, he thought, in an attempt to produce a more draught type of horse.

It was from Melbourne that the majority of Indian remounts were exported, most of them being purchased by shippers at the sale yards in that city. Though very satisfied with the strength of the supply, well evidenced, as he put it, by the fact that eight hundred horses had already been despatched to India by 14 August, Thacker felt sure that an improvement in quality would be effected by shippers becoming more mobile and going out to the stations themselves and to country sales, since many breeders were disinclined to assume the expenses and risks of sending their horses to distant selling points. As demonstrated by the operations of Henry Vanrenen, who shipped from Melbourne horses that were bought by him as far afield as the Darling Downs and the Hunter Valley, this was exactly what soon came to be done.

Looking towards the future, Thacker saw an ever increasing capacity of Australian breeders and shippers to satisfy Indian demands. Much greater attention was being given to the selection of mares and there was a widespread awareness of the market prospects in India, which had improved breeding practices, affording an interesting sidelight on the effect of the Indian remount trade on the development of the Australian horse. Adequate numbers of four-year-old horses, fitted for any branch of the India service, could be bought for £15 a head, direct from the breeders, and collected at the ports of embarkation. He made the recommendation, which the government immediately adopted, that the use of three classes of horses should be abandoned. He argued

> that a horse well adapted for Horse Artillery serving in India should possess as much breeding as one fitted for cavalry; that a Cavalry horse to carry a Dragoon in marching order satisfactorily, should possess strength as well as breeding; and that a Field Artillery horse should not be confined to one suitable only for draught. In short, horses of medium height, with breeding, well formed chest and legs, and proper development of muscle, equally fitted for riding, or the light draught of Horse or Field Artillery, would suffer less from climate, privation, or forced marches, and perform the work of each branch of the service most perfectly.

The government's decision was to pay a maximum of Rs 550 for all remounts instead of giving a Rs 100 advantage to the horse artillery, in effect adding an average of Rs 25 to the cost of remounts.

While Thacker was in Australia he was able to observe at first hand the working of horse breeding and selling schemes that had given the lead to Victoria and more specifically to Melbourne from the 1860s. He thought the decline of horse exports from New South Wales had resulted from a concentration on coal exports to China and Singapore, while at the same time, Melbourne maintained a pre-eminence that derived from the stimulus of its unrivalled gold fields.

Appendix 2 offers a statistical picture, adapted from Malcolm Kennedy's immensely useful Ph.D thesis, showing how the various Australian colonies shared in the horse trade to India from 1861 to 1900. Victoria's lead was clear by the 1860s, when 7292 horses were sent from that colony to India, more than half the Australian total. The advantage was even more pronounced in the 1890s, when Victoria's share was 30 336 in a total of 50 714. It was in Melbourne that deep water docks and sophisticated loading facilities were first developed, attracting visits from steamships when they began making runs to India with horses in 1881.

Kennedy's figures, it should be realized, show where the horses were shipped from, not where they were bred. A great proportion of Victorian horse exports originated in the Riverina and Upper Murray regions of New South Wales, whence they were driven, and later railed, to Melbourne. Wodonga, the Victorian sister town to Albury, just south of the Murray River, was a major centre for the sale of these animals, much resorted to by the Melbourne shippers.

Only about a third of the Walers were destined for military service. The Indian Army Remount Department's Annual Report for 1896–97 gives figures for importations at the Garden Reach Depot in Calcutta from 1891 to 1897, showing a total of 17 852, or an average of 2550 each year. During that seven year period, there was an annual purchase at Calcutta of 854 Waler remounts, intended chiefly for British cavalry and artillery.

That is, the bulk of the Waler importations in the 1890s must have gone to the buyers from the Native States and to private buyers, seeking hacks, carriage horses, polo ponies and racehorses. So we must see the increased flow of Walers into India as largely non-military in origin, reflecting an improvement in general prosperity that accompanied the extension of the railway system and the greater popularity of equine sports. One further feature of Appendix 2 requires comment: the total value of Waler imports in the 1890s fell by over £50 000, in spite of an increase of 12 055 in horse numbers. Critical to this was the impact on the trade of steamships, with their economies of scale and speed, and the growing expertise of the horse shippers and breeders.[18]

One of the questions addressed to Thacker in a supplementary letter concerned the likelihood of steamships being used in the horse trade. He pointed out that they rarely deviated from established routes, and were inhibited from seeking cargoes for India in Australian ports because of the difficulty of finding return freights. The

The luxury end of the Waler trade: the state coach, Dhar, 1913

Horse breaking at the remount depot

sailing ships, on the other hand, found Indian cargoes that were carried on to England.

Thacker also looked at the matter of 'buckjumping', and refuted the generally held opinion that Walers as a class had this vice:

> All domesticated horses, including stallions, I have observed to be very docile, and I have not the least doubt that 'buck jumping' is entirely the result of the hurried and imperfect mode of breaking so generally practised with young horses intended for the Indian market. Sufficient time is not allowed for instruction, submission being enforced, and not taught, and when opportunity arises, opposition or resentment is shown.

This view coincides with literary evidence that builds up a picture of Australian horse breakers in this period almost perversely encouraging young horses to put on a performance and then taking pride in riding them to a standstill. Nothing could have been more offensive to the principles that had been developed by the great American horse trainer, Rarey, in the mid-nineteenth century and disseminated in many countries, including Australia.[19]

Thacker's visit seems to have borne early fruit in the shape of greater expectations and improvements in the standards of Australian remounts. The second President of the Special Stud Commission, General Sam Browne, V.C., wrote a minute on 2 August 1875 which concluded, 'I think I may safely predict an unfailing supply of excellent animals. Hitherto a too coarse and underbred description have been purchased, causing much dissatisfaction, but the last year's purchases have been a great improvement and with the measures now [proposed] by Mr Thacker, the class of horse will improve'.[20]

The working of the system by which Waler remounts were bought for the Indian army during the final quarter of the nineteenth century may be conveniently followed in a history of the subject written on 7 November 1899 by Sir E. H. Collen, a senior member of the government of India.[21] He explained that the Special Stud Commission had completed its work in 1876, recommending the abolition of the Stud Department and the formation of two successors, the Army Remount Department and the Horse-Breeding Department.

Inspecting Veterinary Surgeon J. H. Hallen first exercised military control over horse breeding, with an attempt being made to improve local breeds in suitable districts throughout India by offering attractive prices, giving instruction in breeding techniques and importing stallions from England and Australia to mate with country-bred mares. The new breeding department's progress was very slow: though producing stock that was thought most satisfactory for the lightly weighted *sowars* of the native cavalry, it made only a marginal contribution to the needs of British dragoons and horse artillery, supplying a total of only 425 horses in the five years to 1888. Control of horse breeding was transferred in 1889 to a new Civil Veterinary Department under Revenue and Agriculture, though Hallen was still in charge. Soon after his death in 1901, his horse breeding scheme was declared a failure, and the reliance on Waler remounts became more absolute.[22]

The ever increasing importance to the Indian army of imported remounts was expressed after September 1881 by bringing all remount operations under the control of one director. Three purchasing depots were formed, the major and permanent one at Garden Reach, Calcutta and a temporary one at Madras being for the reception of Australian horses and a small number of New Zealanders, while at Bombay, Persians and Arabs were bought as well as Walers. Even the depot at Garden Reach was kept open for the purchase of remounts only during the cold weather, defined by 1880 as lasting from 1 November to 1 March.[23]

Another important innovation, recommended by the Special Stud Commission and adopted by the Indian government in spite of India Office protests on the score of expense, was the formation of remount depots in different parts of the country to which imported horses were sent for acclimatization and training before being drafted into regiments and batteries. Saharanpur and Kurnool were the depots used by the Bengal command, Hosur by Madras and Ahmadnagar by Bombay, while Hapur was the depot for country-bred stock.[24]

Associated with the depot system from the beginning was the practice of maintaining at the depots a reserve of up to 1000 horses. As Colonel J. D. Cooper, Director of Army Remount Operations put it to a commission held at Simla in 1880, 'As long as India is dependent on foreign sources for remounts, it will be . . . necessary to maintain a reserve of Government horses'. The need was exacerbated by the fact that Australian horses, and Persians and Arabs likewise, arrived only in the cold season. Major A. Capel, Superintendent at Saharanpur, pointed to the minuscule result from the breeding operations in the north-west for the previous four years as implying that no reliance could be placed on the local supply, most of all for the artillery. Another contingency to be provided against was the outbreak of devastating disease; in 1879 at Rawalpindi a battery had virtually been unhorsed by the Loodeanah Disease. The demands of the Afghan campaign of 1879–81 had quite exhausted the reserve, for it had employed three regiments of British cavalry, and three batteries each of horse and field artillery. The experience ensured the subsequent acceptance of the depot and reserve system, which had been so consolidated, if not quite initiated by the needs of the Waler.[25]

Not only was the depot system essential to the recovery of the Waler from its shipboard sufferings but in the view of Major Capel its use had an 'extraordinary good effect' on their tempers.

> I remember well, when this class of horse was first imported into this country, how constant were the complaints of their buck jumping, vice, timidity, intractability, &c.
>
> 'The brutes! I would rather not have them,' you used to hear officers say: 'they are such a nuisance to break in. I would rather have stud-breds; they are less trouble.' You scarcely ever hear these complaints about walers now.[26]

When the first major attack was made in 1887 on Hallen's horse breeding operations, he defended himself warmly by citing the marked success of the remounting of the army in Afghanistan, which had been effected smoothly without raising prices. In that campaign, he wrote, the bulk of the outpost and escort duty had fallen to the Native cavalry, comprising *silladar* units horsed with country-breds. He pressed the point that from the outset of the breeding operations it had been expected that reliance must indefinitely be placed on Australian and Persian imports. In military terms, it was an ideal plan, vindicated by the fact that:

> Among all the officers of the mounted branches whom I have consulted, I have found the unanimous opinion to be that batteries and British cavalry regiments in India were never better mounted than they are at present. Some even go further than this in declaring that they are now better mounted than similar corps in Great Britain and Ireland.[27]

This was praise indeed for the Waler, not least because the officer awarding it was a distinguished veterinarian who was attempting to breed local horses in competition with the Waler.

Eight years later Colonel T. Deane, Director of the Army Remount Department in India, gave similar praise, close to the end of this period. Deane was responding to remarks made by General Sir John Watson, V.C., who had been used in retirement in England as the Indian government's agent, charged with the task of buying English stallions for export to India. He had gone out to India in November 1895 to bring himself up to date with the army remount scene.

Watson, after advising a return to the pure Indian breeds, remarked on 'the much improved quality of the Australians, as compared with what they were thirty years ago; and the manner in which they were conditioned and issued to the Service left nothing to be desired'.[28]

Colonel Deane's response to the general's remarks on the improved quality of Australian remounts gives some explanation for this change. The quotation that follows is an early indication of the importance to the shippers of the currency in which they were paid; an earlier file had remarked on the losses they had experienced as a result of being paid in rupees at a time when the exchange rate was unfavourable. Deane noted that Watson's opinion coincided with the reports from commanding officers over a number of years, which showed a steady improvement in the Waler's quality. He went on:

> These results are mainly due to the Government of India having fixed the prices for Australians at a sterling rate, which was necessary as the shippers have to deal in gold. Improvement has also followed a much more careful system of purchase than formerly, with very strict veterinary examination, an open market, with free trade encouraged, and an enforcement of the rule that the entire shipments must be submitted to the Remount Agent, or else no purchases will be made from them. The supply is generally ample and good, and is made without any risk to the State whatever.

Finally, as to the comparison of the Waler with the country-bred, Deane noted that in the four regiments of the British service that were mounted on country-breds, there was much complaint because of their inability to carry the heavy weights involved. Yet they had good tempers and seemed better able than the Waler to work on short or inferior rations. More than compensating for this defect was the Waler's much greater life span when working under heavy weights in the British service, giving it the credit for significant economies.

The Waler was very soundly established at the end of the nineteenth century as the principal mount for the most demanding services in the Indian army—the British cavalry and the horse artillery. From the viewpoint of the Australian shippers and breeders, this was a most promising position to be in at the opening of a period of warfare in southern Africa and the Middle East that would create a tremendous demand for the Waler's services.

7

Ships, Shippers and Shipping

'IT IS A WELL-KNOWN SAYING in the American horse-trade', so ran a paragraph quoted by the *Sydney Morning Herald* from the Calcutta *Englishman*, 'that the Captain's horse never dies'. The writer had gone on to say, regretfully, that similar impositions were beginning to appear in the trade with India and gave the example of a valuable horse being reported to have died on the voyage, yet turning up in a Calcutta stable with the brand marks razed from his hoofs and wearing the captain's halter.[1]

Although in an earlier chapter we cited the example of a rascally skipper who had starved a consignment of A.A. Company horses in order to feed his own animals, the overwhelming impression given by the first hand accounts of the Indian horse trade is of a contrary nature. To be sure, there is plenty of evidence of horses suffering unspeakable privations, especially in the fifty years when they were carried by sailing ships and subject to being becalmed in tropical waters or battered by cyclones in the Bay of Bengal. But examples of blatant dishonesty were extremely rare, a fact that seems attributable to the way in which the trade was managed.

From the 1870s, Walers intended for the Indian markets were looked after by Australian grooms and Indian syces under the superintendence of shippers, or their trusted managers, who had bought horses in Australia largely in order to satisfy the published requirements of the remount authorities in Calcutta, Madras and Bombay. Presumably because of the impossibly high premiums that would have been involved in insuring individual horses against damage in transit, the shippers were covered only against the awful exigency of total loss. It behoved them, therefore, to watch over their large and powerful, but nonetheless delicate, charges with un-remitting care. Until sold after stringent tests by remount committees, or in private negotiation, the horses in a typical consignment of 200 animals owned by

Shippers having fun, c. 1930

an individual shipper, which may have cost him £3000 to get to the ship's side in Melbourne, were entirely at the shipper's risk.

This chapter tells the stories of some of the men who made a risky but often profitable living from the trade. Without them, the trade could not have survived, for it was their skills that overcame the dreadful hazards imposed by perhaps the longest haul on which livestock were regularly carried in the hundred years after 1834. The typical shipper spent from twenty to forty years of his life in taking horses to India, and accumulated an expertise that made him a formidable figure on both sides of the Indian Ocean. His knowledge of the Indian army's requirements, his judgement of the young horses that he inspected in gruelling journeys around the breeding areas of Australia, his attention to every detail in the management of his charges on board ship and finally his perseverance in selling the horses on arrival in India, all contributed to his financial survival and to the stability of the Waler trade.

I have chosen to reveal the workings of the horse trade with India by telling the stories of a number of outstanding shippers whose careers spanned seventy of its hundred years. Henry Vanrenen was a natural candidate for inclusion because he experienced the vital change from sail to steam and became the premier Victorian shipper at the end of the century. His forty years in the trade are the subject of one of the most important documentary collections in the La Trobe Library, thanks to the sense of history displayed by Henry himself and by his descendants. Steve Margrett had the rare distinction of taking Christmas dinner in Calcutta every year from 1894 to 1934, and of being the middle member of a family that had three generations in the trade. It was his grandson, Stephen Murray-Smith, who gave me an early impetus to study its history. Three shippers reflect the character and texture of the final decades of the trade: Charlie Pascoe of Eidsvold, Cosmo Gordon of Grosvenor Downs, who was a breeder rather than a shipper, and Bob Skene of Santa Barbara. Aptly, two of these men are from Queensland, the state which dominated the trade in its last decades and the third was a celebrated exponent of polo, the game that still attracts Walers from Australia to Asian and Southeast Asian destinations. Finally I draw on a unique document, the unpublished autobiography of William Hegarty, who with his brothers Henry and James came over from New Zealand at the end of last century and established one of the major firms shipping to India out of Queensland ports.

Henry Polman Vanrenen was descended from a Prussian aristocrat, Graf Jacobus von Rhenen, whom family tradition credited with having emigrated to the Cape of Good Hope in 1722 after killing his opponent in a duel. By the end of the eighteenth century the family had been largely anglicized and its members were prominent as landowners and as breeders of fine horses during the administration of Lord Charles Somerset. Henry's grandfather, Jacob, left for India, served in the Bengal army for fifty years and died at Kanpur as a brigadier-general in 1828. His father, John, served briefly in India but returned to the Cape and sired eight boys and one girl, many of whom had interesting careers in India or in other parts of the British empire.[2]

Our story concerns two of those sons, Adrian, the eldest, who attained the rank of lieutenant-colonel in the Indian Survey, and Henry, the third in line, who tried for a fortune on the Victorian diggings, had some experience as a mounted trooper and failed in the hotel business before trying his hand at the horse trade, as had his father before him. Henry Vanrenen's first effort was with a small consignment in 1864 to Mauritius, a market served chiefly by the Western Australian breeders, but he soon responded to the opportunity offered by the presence in India of his popular and generous elder brother. Adrian had told him of a cousin's success in bringing Walers to Calcutta and agreed to stake Henry in seven horses of a cargo that arrived in Calcutta at the end of 1866 in the French barque *Thetis*, chartered by William Cavanagh. Henry had to pay £12 a head freight, and received a free passage. The horses sold at Rs 600, and encouraged the brothers to try a bigger investment, with Adrian providing the capital, essentially interest free, so as to give Henry a start. So began a career that closed only with Henry's death.

The Vanrenen Collection makes possible a minute and intimate study of the classic days of the Waler trade. It documents the mechanics of horse shipping, much of it pioneered by Henry Vanrenen, because he and his correspondents—many within the family—kept letters that covered both business and personal matters and also insurance documents, charter parties, bills of lading, receipts for grooms' wages and reports of horse buying missions in which Henry Vanrenen and his stepson Edward Parsons put together their cargoes. The greatest illumination comes from the exchange of letters between Adrian and Henry. They show, typically, how the idea of participating in the 'Indian business', as Stephen Murray-Smith described it, originated in a direct personal connection, such as so many Australians had with India in the palmy days of the Raj. More importantly, they reveal the crucial contribution made by Adrian, not only to the initial financing of Henry's operation, but to his contacts with the remount people in Calcutta, including the two generals who successively presided over the dismemberment of the Bengal Stud, Sir Colin Troup and C. T. Chamberlain. Adrian Vanrenen also acted as a go-between for Henry with his fellow officers, bringing him special orders for chargers and sporting horses and arranging for the disposal of the remnants of cargoes after the remount officers had completed their purchases. More than that, the collection is a uniquely comprehensive documentary record of relationships within one great imperial family that sent its members into so many corners of the Victorian empire.

Henry Vanrenen's first major contract in the Indian trade was made on 28 September 1867 with the Melbourne firm of Boyd and Currie, which agreed to ship sixty horses for him to Calcutta, at a freight of £17 per head for each horse landed alive, on the barque *Albert Victor*. The vessel was to be fitted with stalls by the owners, providing water for seventy days at the rate of six gallons per horse per day, giving each horse a space of 2 feet 6 inches in width (or 762 mm) and one spare stall for every ten horses to facilitate cleaning. From the language of the document, 'The horses to be sent alongside on any day to be named by Boyd & Currie and to be taken from alongside in Calcutta' it seems that lighters were to be used at both ports, a sore inconvenience that was soon to be dispensed with in Melbourne. Vanrenen was to provide the fodder, as had been standard practice since the early abuses by scrimping masters, and he was to sail as a cabin passenger, while his six grooms were carried at the ship's expense.

It was apt that Vanrenen's 1867 contract was with Boyd and Currie. By 1872 Archibald Currie, a master mariner, was trading on his own, carrying horses to India and returning with cargoes of rice, oil, jute and tea. A sturdy, bearded and fair man, he was described as a 'dour Scotch sea captain . . . who looked as though he had never laughed in his life'. It was he who first applied a number of steamships to the Waler trade, craft of 2500 tons and more, capable of average speeds of twelve knots, which he ordered in the United Kingdom in 1882 and had specially fitted out for carrying horses. Though not the very first steamers in the trade, for Vanrenen himself had shipped a cargo of 325 horses to Calcutta in the steamship *Huntingdon* in 1881, the Currie Line gave to the Waler trade the qualities of speed, efficiency, size and regularity, which encouraged the Indian government to rely on Australian remounts.[3]

Sharing soon in this development was the big firm that was to dominate the horse trade in its final decades, buying out the Currie Line in 1913 on the eve of its greatest harvest. The British India Steam Navigation Company, or B.I., was attracted to form a regular Australian service via Torres Strait by the offer of a mail subsidy from the Queensland government, which was concerned to improve its share of British emigrants by giving Brisbane, or rather Moreton Bay, primacy over the southern ports. First of the B.I. ships on the Australian run was the SS *Mekara* of 2971 tons, which took emigrants and cargo through the Suez Canal and Torres Strait in 1881 and anchored in Moreton Bay on 13 April to an enthusiastic welcome. Neither Brisbane nor the other Queensland ports had the depth of access water or the loading facilities to compete at this stage with Melbourne as the base for the Waler trade. But by bringing the B.I. back into Australian commerce after a long absence, Queensland contributed to the growth by the 1890s of a period of keen competition from which the horse shippers benefited in the shape of low freight rates and highly specialized services. After about 1892, the B.I. ships came south-about to Australia, touching at Fremantle, Adelaide, Melbourne and Sydney and returning via Brisbane and the Torres Strait.[4]

Henry Vanrenen's venture in the *Albert Victor* proved to be disappointing—we learn from letters Adrian wrote to him in February and May 1868—because of a delay in Melbourne that added to the stress of the voyage and caused numerous rejections by the remount committee in Calcutta. Adrian gave vital assistance in disposing of the surplus horses by taking two for himself and his wife, and selling several to fellow officers, including a carriage pair of bays for £ 100. With the healing hand of time, they turned out remarkably well and gained for the brothers a useful reputation. Advice was passed on from their father at the Cape, warning against an attempt to ship two cargoes in one year because of the damage caused by contrary winds in winter via Cape Leeuwin and, in October, by cyclones in the Bay of Bengal.

On 1 August 1869 Adrian Vanrenen was able to pass on to his brother a private letter from General Troup, revealing the Stud Committee's intention of drawing on Australia for a regular supply of remounts and describing the stamp of horse desired. Henry took his next shipment, however, to Bombay and found a good market, though water had run low at the end of a long voyage. A charter-party signed by Henry in June 1871 provided for the payment of a lump sum of Rs 10 250 for the carriage of 120 horses to Bombay in the *Star of India*, specifying that the ship was not responsible for mortality, or for fodder. The cargo was to be loaded at Sandridge town pier, indicating that the system of winching the horses aboard by crane was now in use, as would continue to be the case until it became possible for horses to be walked on board directly from the railway trucks that brought them to the wharf. Ten Australian grooms were to be carried with this cargo, each paid a basic rate of Rs 87 for the voyage, with an extra Rs 10 for those that earned it by good service. By the time Henry Vanrenen arrived in Bengal, he had to comply, as Adrian informed him, with a new Vagrancy Act that protected the grooms from being left stranded at the port of disembarkation.

A letter from Adrian Vanrenen of 10 January 1873 draws our attention to one of the more bizarre dangers associated with the horse trade. He had noticed a newspaper report of a stampede by Henry's horses after being landed in Bombay, when two men were killed and many injured. Adrian assumed that the livery stable people belonging to Ali Abdoolah had been careless and sent a cheque to cover gratuities to the injured fellows in hospital. Of course, such incidents were predictable in handling large numbers of young horses that were brought to the ship in a wild state. That was to be even more the case in the twentieth century, when most horses came from huge stations in Queensland. The solution would then lie in the provision of ever more sophisticated landing facilities. By the 1920s, the vessels berthed within sight of the remount depot at Garden Reach, Calcutta, and walls of hessian stretching for perhaps half a kilometre from the ship's side were used to direct the horses to the remount yards.

Such labour-saving innovations lay well into the future when Henry Vanrenen loaded a cargo of 229 horses on the ship *Hereford* of 1439 tons, bound for Calcutta via Cape Leeuwin in late June 1873. As he informed the remount agent by letter before

Hoisting on board at Sandridge (Port Melbourne), 1875

departure, he had switched from Bombay because of losing £400 in his last venture and he trusted that the Calcutta buyers would liberally interpret the new guide-lines, because his own costs had risen sharply. Horse prices had been elevated by rural prosperity, and fodder for the same reason, while freights had also gone up because of the demand for shipping to California, a claim that is verified by comparing the Rs 85 per head charged on the *Star of India* with the £10 5s on the *Hereford* two years later.

But his hopes were not realized and he took up his disappointment with General Chamberlain in correspondence which reveals much of the working of the Waler trade. Chamberlain's letter to Adrian Vanrenen of 31 August 1873 conveyed the viceroy's rejection of Vanrenen's plea for the government to provide stabling in Calcutta for remounts brought by accredited shippers. 'Govt. has clearly set its face against it', he wrote, though expressing the hope that Henry would nevertheless 'do a good stroke of business' and dispose of two-thirds of his shipment to the remount buyer. The new rules, which set *maximum* prices of £50 and £60 for cavalry and artillery horses respectively, had been a response to the decline over the previous two years in the quality of Walers landed in Calcutta, with shippers expecting top prices for horses that they had bought in the bush for no more than £5 or £6.

Chamberlain suggested with the viceroy's approval that Henry might be induced to bring horses from the Cape, by the offer of premium prices, for he considered them

The modern way: Walers in their stalls on the deck of MV Centaur, *1977*

Improved landing facilities, Calcutta, c. 1927

'infinitely superior to Australians for work in India'. As the brothers well appreciated from their mother's letters, the rush from the Cape to mine diamonds in the Kimberleys had so elevated the cost of horses as to exclude them from the Indian market. Shipping space was almost unprocurable as a consequence of the opening of the Suez Canal and the captain of the *Hereford* had told Henry that he would need to charge more than twice as much to go to the Cape for a cargo than to Melbourne.[5]

Vanrenen's complaint was that, whereas in past years he had received the advertised price for all horses accepted by the remount buyer, this year Mr Thacker had paid an average of Rs 472 for the ninety-one taken so far. Chamberlain was immovable and pointed out that the alternative would have been to refuse all horses not worth Rs 500.

Some consolation was offered to Henry Vanrenen in the shape of eager requests for horses from Adrian's friends. Colonel Anderson wrote on 11 September to say that the grey sent from Bombay two years before, 'although a handsome nag, is not up to my weight. What I want is *Blood* and a weight carrier . . . I won't limit you as to price'.

Another friend who was prepared to pay a large sum for a *'swell horse'* was J. F. Harkness, an under-secretary who wrote to Adrian Vanrenen in mid-September,

> As I only ride twelve stone I don't of course require a massive animal. What I want is an extremely handsome horse to swell about on at Durbars etc., and of course he must have an angelic temper. I think I'd rather not have a mare for I haven't much faith in the sex.

By the early 1870s Vanrenen had a partner, Andrew Martin, who was chiefly responsible for the home front of the operation, not only buying four-year-olds for early despatch but also yearlings that were brought to maturity on holding properties in Gippsland. In mid-1875 when the partnership was about to be dissolved they had 1500 horses and 100 cattle on a station called Fulham, which Mr Thacker had so highly approved during his visit to Australia in 1874. Another long-term member of the team was Henry's stepson, Edward Parsons, later to be used as a buyer, who was sent off in the *Antiope* in December 1873 with 102 horses. Martin apologized for the sloppiness of the documentation for the cargo, but he had been nearly distracted by the trip to Gippsland, compelled at the last moment to buy horses that were supposed to be quiet to handle but turned out 'perfect devils'. They needed two or three men to load each horse and took two days to ship. One can imagine their behaviour on being unloaded into lighters at Calcutta![6]

On 23 August 1874 Vanrenen passed through the Port Phillip heads in the *Udston* with a cargo of 276 horses bound for Calcutta. It was an iron ship of 1695 tons built that year at Glasgow, which probably accounts for its surviving a cyclone that blew up in the Bay of Bengal when it was in sight of the lightship at the entrance to the Hooghly, sinking a score of vessels. Since Henry Vanrenen kept a journal of this fateful voyage, and it is the only such record which is known to have survived, we shall follow the story in detail.

It was a stormy passage of nearly three weeks to round Cape Leeuwin and Vanrenen was recording the loss of fine horses within three days of starting out, many from inflammation of the lungs, and all taken by his partner from the grass at their leased property at Lucknow without adequate experience of dry feed before embarkation. Twenty-four died in this way, including eight Thoroughbreds, seven three-quarter-breds, and nine half-breds, of a quality from which high prices would have been expected, and the language of Vanrenen's journal became increasingly despondent. On Monday 13 September, having already winched twelve horses overboard, he felt unwell himself and wrote, 'In all my voyages I have never felt so worried . . . it is quite distressing to see the shameful state in which the horses were shipped'. A little later he was consumed by homesickness and thought of his wife Kate and the prospect in her mind of the many lonely months still to be passed before his return.

In the final stages the wind was favourable and the ship made 240 miles on 14 October, bringing them within reach of the pilot ship. Vanrenen's journal entry— faithfully quoted here—for 15 October 1874 reads:

> This has been a sad and memorable day. We sighted the Lightship as expected at 2.30 A.M. and lay too until daylight expecting to get a Pilot on board, but ther was no Pilot brig there at about 6 A.M. it commenced blowing furiously, increasing in violence, and the horses being knocked about a good deal at about 11 A.M. the hatches and ventilators were covered up, I knew it was all over then, as the Horses would be suffocated. at 1 P.M. we carried away the fore and main topsail, and the Main Trysail was then set the water breaking over the Ship all the time I suppose if the Hatches had not been closed perhaps none of us would have survived to tell the tale, it was a melancholly sight to see the horses dying and dead.

After fourteen hours the gale moderated and next day all hands were busy getting the surviving horses back on their feet and clearing away the corpses, which were lowered with the steam winch. The smell, as Vanrenen put it, was 'something frightful', and on the seventeenth the crew refused to do any more, leaving him to clean out the hold with the help of his grooms, a group of Persians contracted to his service by Edward Parsons on an earlier voyage.

Only 138 horses were alive at the start of the journey up the Hooghly, towed by the tug *Challenge*, and 130 were landed at Calcutta. Slowly they were patched up and prepared for sale, some being taken by remounts and most by Cook & Company at Dhurrumtollah. Seven still remained unsold when the latter firm sent its statement on 3 February 1875. Writing to his brother Jacob on 14 May Henry Vanrenen estimated that the cyclone had already cost him £2500 though he faced a further cost of £500 for legal expenses incurred in a claim against the insurers. In January 1876 he learned that the High Court in Calcutta had found against him, on the ground that the policy had effect only when a total loss was suffered. As Basil Lubbock points out in his book, *The Colonial Clippers*, much depended on the luck of the draw. The *Thessalus*, like the *Udston* an iron clipper, had made a fast journey from Melbourne to Calcutta a week or so earlier and had landed the entire complement in prime condition.[7]

Far from being overwhelmed by this disaster, Vanrenen continued to take large shipments to Calcutta, as did Edward Parsons, and in March 1876 bought out Andrew Martin's interest in the partnership. They seem have thrived for the most part and in August 1881 we find Henry Vanrenen taking out insurance for a cargo of 325 horses that were to sail via Torres Straits in the *Huntingdon*, the first steamer known to have taken Walers to India.

The end of a Waler's journey: the ship was turned to ensure that the dead horse did not foul the propellers

Well-conditioned remounts in the depot at Calcutta, c. 1930

By the time of this arrival, the Indian government had responded to the shippers' requests for the establishment of permanent facilities in Calcutta by building a landing depot and stables at Garden Reach and a remount depot at Ballygunge. Stabling and veterinary help were to be provided free to approved shippers, together with the services of syces, food and medicines at cost. The institution of this reform, so vital to the stability of the horse trade in the coming era of steamships, coincided with the beginning of the Afghan War of 1878–80 and the sudden inflation of the army's remount needs.

With the advent of wartime prices, Vanrenen was able to make what he hoped would be a final effort to achieve wealth and the settled life of a grazier. Of particular interest is a collection of reports from Edward Parsons back to Melbourne as he was traversing the Riverina and the Upper Hunter regions, while Henry Vanrenen was simultaneously buying in Gippsland. In the first region, Parsons was introduced by his stock and station agents in Sydney to a number of famous breeders, including Geo. Main of Groongal, J. H. Spiller of Tubbo, J. H. Douglas of North Yanko, and Devlin & Co. of Ganmain, in the Wagga district. In fact, after seeing hundreds of horses, Parsons bought a total of twenty-seven on the Murrumbidgee including eleven from J. Dallas of Wagga at £15 a head and a superlative batch of seven from Donnelly's at an average of £25 14s, for which seeming extravagance he apologized profusely. Swearing to reduce the average to an acceptable £16 a head, he went on to look at William and Henry Bowmans' horses at Muswellbrook and then bought forty-seven head from H. C. White at Woodlands, near Denman on the Upper

Hunter, for which he paid £20 when White showed himself immovable. He reported on 11 May 1880:

> I am afraid I shall not see many more such as White's horses this year at any rate, as for a large number they are undoubtedly the grandest I ever saw in my life, not one amongst them but would carry 15 stone, and with such amount of substance, style, and breeding, while their action is faultless. They are all got by 'Meteor' by 'Lord of the Hills' out of large well bred roomy mares, are all broken in quiet to the saddle but three and those I have had handled.

One hopes that Parsons followed his boss's advice, to take delivery of the horses as far as possible from their home paddocks. His plan, in a time of plentiful grass, was to have the northern horses driven to Wodonga in stages of seventeen to eighteen miles a day, and then railed to Melbourne. On other occasions they were collected by coastal steamers, which were also used to carry the huge amounts of fodder that were needed in Melbourne by embarkation time.

Profiting by the *Huntingdon* venture to the extent of perhaps £2000, Henry Vanrenen felt able at last to bid for domestic felicity and a settled life. He bought two properties, the leasehold of Tiltagoona in the Western Division of New South Wales and the freehold of Avoca Forest of 2465 acres, north-west of Ballarat. Within ten years he had been brought to his knees by a combination of drought, rabbits and depressed overseas markets. Tiltagoona had to be sold and Avoca Forest was only retained by the family because Vanrenen was prepared and able, old and sad as he was, to go back into the 'Indian business'. This is now the home of Donald and Rae Vanrenen, who have gradually got Henry Vanrenen's huge collection of papers into order, typed copies and deposited originals and copies in the La Trobe Library, Melbourne.

Vanrenen's final ten or twelve years in the horse trade were made easier by the universal use of steamers, supplied mostly by Archibald Currie and British India, so that the time at sea was reduced from eight weeks to three. The documents relating to his 1895 voyage in the *Clitus* show that he paid freight of only £8 per head for each horse landed alive in Calcutta. They collected their cargo at Newcastle, equipped with walk-on facilities, and after sailing through Torres Straits arrived punctually on 1 November, the first day for admission to the remount depot, losing only three horses. A letter to his wife Kate from Calcutta on 4 February 1899 laments the slowness with which his last horses were being disposed of, while he was being tortured by attacks of lumbago (for which he was taking liquorice). The good news was that the government had adopted the system of giving specific orders to trusted shippers, so that the press of competition would be less fierce. A 1900 charter for the 3451 ton B.I. ship *Unita* shows Vanrenen sharing with the redoubtable Steve Margrett and other shippers who made up a total of 550 head, to be taken on board at Melbourne, Newcastle and Gladstone. This combination of men, ports and big steamships is nicely suggestive of the final era of the trade.

A twenty-four page publication entitled, *Army Remount Department, India. Instructions for the selection of remounts*, belonging to the 1880s and found amongst Henry Vanrenen's papers, offers a contrast with the narrative material so far presented. The booklet begins by referring to the notification given in March by the Indian government, for publication in India, Australia and the Cape, of the remount needs of the three presidencies in the ensuing year. At Calcutta there was a government depot at Garden Reach 'where horses can be taken *direct off the ship on to a pier* leading into the Remount Depot enclosure' (my emphasis). Articles of Agreement were to be signed by shippers, and remount agents were empowered to advance the sums required to clear their obligations to ships' captains.

On the question of breeding, the main distinction is between cavalry and horse artillery, which required a good deal of breeding, and field artillery, for which size and weight were more important.

[Para] 22. There is no difficulty in distinguishing the well from the under-bred horse. Young horses fresh from grass, even when well-bred, are often long in the coat, and look coarse and under-bred in consequence; but the shape of the head never changes. The signs of under-breeding are large coarse head, thick throat, short and thick neck, large body and joints, and thick legs, short pasterns, curly hair in the mane and tail. Such horses are more adapted for draught, for in the saddle they are unwieldy, difficult to bend and turn, rough to ride; and they cannot gallop. On the other hand, a well-bred colt has a small lean head, flat and broad forehead, ample and fine nostrils, throat fine, neck thin, legs fine, pasterns long: and the hair of the mane and tail is straight and fine.

Paragraph 26 tabulates the heights preferred for horses in the different branches of the service. British Cavalry horses were to be bought at four years in a range from 15 hands to 15 hands 2 inches, attaining a maximum of 15 hands 3 inches at full age. Native Light Cavalry remounts were bought at 14 hands 2 inches to 15 hands, attaining a maximum of 15 hands 1 inch, while Field Artillery and Horse Artillery requirements ranged from a minimum of 15 hands at purchase to a maximum of 16 hands 1 inch at full age, with wheelers averaging an inch less than leaders.

[Para] 28. *Colour.*—As a rule remounts should be selected that are what is called *whole* coloured, that is, those which have no or very little white about them. Well-bred chestnuts, however, generally possess more white than horses of other colours . . . Light 'mealy' bays, with bay legs, and very light, washy, irritable chestnuts should be rejected, and other horses, except chestnuts, which show much white. The various kinds of roans are good colours, also bays and browns. Blacks must be taken, but it is not such a good colour as the preceding. Greys now are seldom purchased for Artillery purposes.

[Para] 29. . . . The two greatest essentials in horses intended for all military purposes, are:—1. A short and broad back and loin.

2. A broad and deep chest.

Horses which possess these two essentials are invariably robust, of sound constitutions, hard, and enduring. If either of these two conditions are wanting, many other bad points are sure to be found in the same animal, such as the following:—

Narrow chest	Fore legs close together, toes generally turned out, 'Brushes', 'Speedy cut', unsafe to ride. Elbows 'tied in', girth galls, often flat-sided, weak constitution, predisposed to lung diseases.
Long back and narrow loin	Badly ribbed up, scraggy hips, never carries flesh, hind legs long and far behind. Hocks often 'curby', can not carry weight, no endurance.

The paragraphs that followed looked in detail at the good and bad features of military horses, and set out the procedures that would be followed at the Garden Reach remount depot at Calcutta and also at Madras and Bombay. It may be well to conclude by quoting advice given to remount buyers on the subject of the initial examination.

> [Para] 52. Much of the success in obtaining good remounts depends upon the method of examination at the time of selection. If a horse stands in a constrained attitude habitually there is generally something wrong. It is well to examine a horse when he is tranquil and not after having been 'warmed up'. The eyes, nostrils and mouth should be first examined, and the horse should be placed on level ground with his head held up. The purchaser should then walk round him and carefully note whether he stands well; whether his legs are properly shaped; that his feet are neither odd, nor too small; that his coat gives indications of good health, and that his movements are perfectly natural, and that there is no deformity.

A second document, taken from a book so far unidentified, is addressed to horse masters in India at the end of the nineteenth century and provides similarly valuable insights into the trade. The appendices were written by a veterinary surgeon who had toured the breeding districts of Australia and returned to Madras in the B.I. steamship *Bancoora* of 2880 tons.

> *Veterinary Notes.*—Horses certainly thrive most wonderfully in Australia; and whilst there seems to be absolute immunity from the most fatal diseases, as Anthrax, Glanders and Farcy, the ordinary ills to which horses are liable, affect them less in Australia than in England or India. In the winter I am told that cases of Chest Affections occur, and in the hot season cases of Disordered Liver and Fever. Abdominal diseases are rare; this fact is doubtless due to the simple, clean, and good feeding the horses get. Roaring is said to be rare amongst Australian horses ... Diseases of the Skin are exceptional. As far as I could learn, the Eczematous disease so common and troublesome in India, is practically unknown.[8]

A second appendix is entitled, *Notes on a voyage in a horse-ship from Melbourne to Madras via the Torres Straits*. The writer believed he was the first Indian army veterinarian to travel on such a voyage and certainly the rarity of the account gives it great interest for our purposes. The *Bancoora* had been chartered by the Melbourne shippers, Krcrouse and Madden, who in addition to sharing in the general remount trade to Madras made a specialty of supplying Australian Thoroughbred stallions for use by Indian military breeders. Reasons for turning to Australia for this purpose were explained by Lieutenant-Colonel A. E. Queripel of the Civil Veterinary Department in a letter of 12 February 1895. He was finding it ever more difficult to import suitable Thoroughbreds from England and proposed to buy at least six Australians every year, since, as he put it, 'There can be no doubt that these are, as a rule, better limbed than English ones'. While in Madras he had been struck by the 'quality, power, action and bone' of Walers imported by Mr H. Madden, who offered to land six stallions in Calcutta or Bombay later that year at £350 each. Queripel's advice, which was readily accepted, was to effect this by making a similar reduction in the numbers of Hackney stallions which had been imported from England under the regime of Colonel Hallen.[9]

Before proceeding with the veterinarian's account of his voyage, we should notice a technological development that confirmed Melbourne's primacy as a horse ship-ping port. The *Illustrated Australian News* of 4 October 1882 drew attention to the adoption of the practice of walking horses aboard by means of staging, so obviating the need for slings. A *Sydney Morning Herald* report of 31 July 1886 described a scheme just introduced at the Port Melbourne town pier by Mr Warren, who refined his earlier system by an arrangement with the railway authorities that enabled each horse to be walked by a stage directly from the railway truck to the ship's upper deck and down to its stall 'as regularly and quietly as if it had received a circus training'. A hundred horses had been loaded and stalled in an hour, effecting a saving of time and labour that prompted Mr Warren's fellow shippers to make a valuable presentation to him.

The stalls on the *Bancoora* were made of jarrah, those on deck being 2 feet 6 inches broad and roofed with deal, while those below were 2 feet 8 inches broad and 9 feet deep. Stout battens were placed in the stalls to give the horses a foothold and the stalls were separated by two round movable bars. Each horse had a hempen head-stall and a leading rope, and to the headstall were fastened pillar chains, the T-shaped ends of which were passed through staples in the stall posts, making it an easy matter to set a horse loose, though with his head rope still on.

Ventilation on the ship was complex and thorough. In addition to large hatchways fore and aft, wind-sails were used to convey air to the more distant parts of the ship. The lower portholes were also opened when possible and air-scoops were fitted to the scuttles 'tween decks. Even so, the horses with their long winter coats felt the heat in the Straits of Malacca, when the temperature remained at 86°F night and day, and one died suddenly from 'Heat Apoplexy' in the aft part of the ship.

Daily cleaning the stalls All the stalls were thoroughly cleansed every morning and the floors sprinkled with slaked lime . . . Two or three horses were taken from the stalls at one end; these stalls were cleansed, then the bars having been removed from the adjacent stalls, the horses were moved up as the stalls were cleansed, and the dirt thrown overboard. When the line was finished, the horses from the end at which the work commenced were put into the stalls at the other end . . . There was no system of flushing the stalls, the urine is almost entirely absorbed by the dung, and the subsequent sprinkling of lime assists in drying and purifying the stalls . . . when there was any breeze, there was but little smell in any part of the ship; whereas . . . after flushing, it is impossible to dry the decks, and there is in consequence a constant humid, oppressive atmosphere all day; moreover the continued moisture is very in-jurious to the feet of the horses.[10]

The horses were watered twice daily, at 4 a.m. and 3 p.m., and fed four times with a mixed feed of oaten hay, chaff and bran at 5 a.m., noon, 4 p.m. and 8 p.m. A more detailed diet given in an Australian Archives file at the time of the Boer War lists the daily food for each horse as 5 pounds of oats, 5 of bran and 10 of hay, with about a pound of carrots per day for sick horses.[11]

On the subject of feeding, the veterinarian told of a Thoroughbred entire horse, usually a docile animal, which had a curious attack of 'phrenzy' or 'mad staggers' on the twenty-second day out, partly from the heat but chiefly, he thought, from im-patience at feed-time at being so far from the point where feeding began.

A piece of good advice for ships encountering heavy seas with a live cargo was to

Shippers going out for supper, c. 1930

avoid the temptation to force the vessel through the waves, which would necessitate the closing of hatches and the shipping of waves that might knock animals down. A day or two longer at sea would do less harm than the shipping of one big sea.

The *Bancoora* lost only four horses from 391 during the thirty-day voyage to Madras. Even in 1894 the *masullah* boats were still used for taking the horses through the surf and it is interesting to compare the fourteen hours taken by that operation with the four hours required in 1886 to embark the same number using Mr Warren's technique.[12]

To balance the dour professionalism of the last two sources, I shall now refer to the more lively and impressionistic writings of Captain Horace M. Hayes, for decades one of the most respected judges of matters equestrian in India and other parts of the British Empire. In his *Among Men and Horses*, published in 1894, he recounts the stories of such men as Teddy Weekes, the greatest 'character' of the horse trade, a man whose language was 'loud, copious and foul', but with the redeeming point of being a thorough sportsman. About five years before Weekes had plunged heavily while in his cups and lost £1200 on a horse but, instead of being cast down, he returned to Australia, worked like a slave and sold a shipload of horses to pay his debts, returning to the betting ring 'beaming with delight to find himself again in his old paradise'.

A fine horseman before he became fat, Teddy Weekes

> liked, during a sale of his horses, to get the leaping bar put up to a respectable height, and having mounted one of the animals with more assumed than real difficulty, would take the obstacle in good style, to show the people, as he would explain, how clever his horses must be to jump with a fat old man like himself. And then he would describe in a manner few could resist, how marvellously the animal would perform over a country with any of the on-looking *jeunesse dorée* on its back.

I mentioned the notable firm of Krcrouse and Madden in connection with the importation of Australian Thoroughbreds to India. The name of the former's father appears in a beautiful story told by Horace Hayes:

The only regular London dealer in the whole lot was Kerouse [sic], whose people kept a livery and commission stable in Edgeware Road. He used to bring out cart horses from England to New Zealand and Australia, and then used to work back via Calcutta or Madras, with a shipment of Colonial horses. He was certainly the cleverest man in the trade at inducing a shy man to part with his money; but then we must recollect that he had a London training. He had not a thought in the world except for horses, pure and simple. 'It was as good as a play' listening to him when he was explaining to would-be purchasers how his 'five-year-olds' had lost all the 'marks' in their teeth by grazing on pasturage the sand of which used to grind down the teeth, so he said, in less than no time; and how the absence of hair on the knees of some of his animals was merely the temporary result of their sleeping in stalls which had not a sufficiency of straw bedding. The poor fellow died miserably from cancer in the throat; yet so strong was his ruling passion even in the presence of death, that when the friend who was tending him wanted to send, on the day before he died, a servant to stop the noise of some horsebreaking that was going on in the yard below the sick man's room, poor Kerouse, overhearing what was said, feebly whispered: 'Let them be. I love to hear the sound of the horses.'[13]

Hayes also introduces us to the shipper, Steve Margrett, a man who was born and bred in Gloucestershire but spent most of his life in the Indian horse trade.

Although an ordinary lad, he said, could readily learn to sit a buckjumper in a colonial saddle, Margrett was the only man able to do so in an English hunting saddle. In one buckjumping contest in Australia,

when Steve was mounting a terribly vicious brute, he pulled off the bridle, the throatlash of which he had purposely left unbuckled; so that the animal, while he was on its back, was free to do everything it possibly could to unseat him. As Steve stuck to the horse, without having any reins to steady himself during the desperate plunges made by his mount, he won the prize amid the frenzied plaudits of the delighted spectators.

Margrett, commonly known as 'the colonel' because of his military bearing and dapper appearance, was another of the characters of the horse trade, who lasted in it longer perhaps than any other man. His first cargo was taken for James Cavanagh in the *Nighthawk* from Dunedin to Calcutta in 1884, and the last in 1936. There was a break for several years when he was a police horse breaker in Melbourne, but from 1891 he claimed to have missed not a single Christmas dinner in Calcutta, or a Viceroy's Cup, in forty-five years.

According to biographical notes prepared by his daughter, Alice Murray-Smith, Margrett was born on 13 October 1859 at Cheltenham in England, the thirty-first child of his father Henry, and the fifteenth child of his second wife Elizabeth. Arriving in Melbourne in 1879, he went on to New Zealand and there had his first experience of the Indian trade. In Calcutta on that occasion he met Thomas Derham, an experienced shipper, whose daughter Maud he married in September 1892. They honeymooned at the Windsor Hotel and left in a horse ship for Calcutta two days later. Alice was born in December 1894 and she too was early accustomed to travelling on the big B.I. horse ships. In about 1921 she married W. D. Murray-Smith, who joined his father-in-law in the trade in 1926 and eventually operated in his own right, finishing only when the mechanization of the Indian Army brought it effectively to an end. His son Stephen, one of the outstanding editors and literary personages of our time, was born in 1922, and recalled vividly the day when his father received the telegram from the Indian remount authorities in 1938, saying that no further shipments would be required. The impending loss of income by the father was not allowed, however, to interfere with Stephen's education at Geelong Grammar School, for James Darling, the headmaster, insisted on the continuation of his attendance. And to good purpose, we might all agree.

Although, sadly, the Derham–Margrett–Murray-Smith dynasty did not collect and preserve its horse documents, we have in tapes made by Alice Murray-Smith in 1959 and 1979 some fascinating perceptions of the trade by a woman who had visited Calcutta twice before she was three. Alice, who was rarely allowed to penetrate the rough world of men and horses on board ship, thought the hygiene was so well managed that one could have taken morning tea on the 'tween deck without risk to the appetite. Even the sounds seldom disturbed passengers in their comfortable, first-class cabins, though on laying her head on the pillow at night she would be occasionally aware of vibrations from the stamping of heavy feet and her father was liable to be called to deal with such emergencies as sickness, or falls in heavy seas.

Life for the Margretts on arrival in Calcutta was, at least for Steve, a busy routine that began at sunrise with the exercising and breaking of horses, and the selection and preparation of those most deserving to be shown first to the remount buyers. By the time Alice came on the scene the depot had moved to a big open ground at Alipore, though disembarkations still took place at Garden Reach. Contemporary photographs show horses being swum in the long pool at the Alipore depot to test their wind, then to be closely examined by a veterinarian when they emerged dripping from the water.

In Calcutta, the Margretts stayed at the Hotel de Paris, the Continental, or the Grand, and enjoyed, Alice recalled, an 'absolutely marvellous' social life. In the cool season the city attracted army people, officials and planters from all over Bengal and Assam to attend the great race meetings and polo carnivals, of which the Viceroy's Cup and the Governor's Cup were the most important. Some of the atmosphere of this carefree period after the First World War is caught by a picture showing Mrs Steve Margrett presiding over a tea party held at the Calcutta races in about 1925, with the ladies, including her daughter Cleeve, dressed in the height of fashion.

They could, of course, afford to do so. Steve Margrett had made £1000 in his first solo venture in 1891 and thenceforth never looked back. During the First World War he was making a profit of between three and five thousand pounds on each shipment, with the opportunity of adding 25 per cent to this from currency deals. Back in Melbourne the family was able to move steadily up market, going from Flemington to Ascot Vale and finally building 'Cotswold' in Macquarie Street, Toorak. Steve Margrett's son-in-law, W. D. Murray-Smith, felt more keenly the chill wind that came with the decline in remount buying in the mid-1930s, but he economized by living in quarters supplied at the remount depot instead of an hotel. In the last year or so before the beginning of the Pacific War he took as many as seventy racehorses to

The swimming test

Calcutta in the one ship, which paid almost as well, he said, as a full load of remounts.

Charlie Pascoe was another of the truly lovable and popular figures of the trade from the late 1920s. He had left school at ten and worked in western Queensland until the chance came in 1928 to sail to Calcutta on the B.I. ship *Janus*, employed by Jim Hegarty as a groom for £2 10s a week. Always skilled with horses, he stayed on to ride and show horses and when Hegarty's manager, Tom Shortis, died suddenly in 1929, Charlie was offered the job at £10 a week, amongst men much senior to him. So it was that the photograph published in the Queenslander of 7 April 1932, entitled 'Prominent Purchasers of Horses for Indian requirements assembled in Calcutta' shows Charlie Pascoe amongst an impressive company. Aptly, Steve Margrett had a place of honour next to Brigadier-General Scott, Director of the Remount Department, and looked utterly at his ease.

In spite of his youth, Pascoe was often the first of the shippers to complete his private sales and take ship back to Australia, usually disembarking at Fremantle and taking the overland train. On meeting a prospective customer he would immediately match him mentally with a particular horse and then go on to ask solicitously exactly what his wants might be and how much he wished to spend. The reply made no difference at all to to what then followed. Pascoe reappeared with three horses including the chosen animal and two very inferior ones, and the purchaser delightedly embraced his destiny and paid a top price.

Five years with Jim Hegarty, which included a private arrangement to take 128 horses to Afghanistan at a handsome profit, and Charlie Pascoe was able to return to Eidsvold, marry his lovely wife Irene and buy a small grazing property for £900. Expressing a nice sense of having arrived, he gave the name of 'Belvedere' to the handsome home that he built at the crown of a hill near Ceratodus, recalling the

Calcutta races, c. 1925: from left, Mrs Stephen Margrett, Miss Cleeve Margrett, Mrs Willy Robinson (the wife of the leading jockey), others unknown

Prominent purchasers of horses for Indian requirements assembled in Calcutta, 1932: back row, J. Robb (second from left), R. Elliott (third from left), C. Pascoe (fourth from left), A. Robb (fifth from left), W. Robb (sixth from left), W. Murray-Smith (second from right); front row, S. Margrett (third from left), Brigadier-General Scott (fourth from left)

Jim Robb and Charlie Pascoe with syces

name of the governor's mansion in Calcutta, which he had passed every day on the way to the race track.

The epilogue to Charlie Pascoe's story finds him at the start of the Pacific War sharing with Bill Woods of Toowoomba in a commission from the United States Army to supply 1000 horses for service in New Guinea, half for riding and half as pack-horses. His first batch of twenty or thirty he bought in at £10 and they were inspected in the yards at Belvedere by Colonel Dawnblazer, found satisfactory and a cheque for £15 a head paid on the spot. Eventually they were brought together and loaded at Pinkenba, the deep water anchorage in Port Brisbane, and sent north. We might see this commission as the end of the Waler trade in its classic military form but I am glad to say that Charlie Pascoe and his wife are still thriving and working seven days a week 'because that's all there are'.

The unpublished autobiography of William Hegarty, dealing with his experiences in the horse trade along with his elder brothers, Henry and Jim, balances the nineteenth-century material of Henry Vanrenen with the narrative of a twentieth-century operator, offering detail and colour on every aspect of the trade from the purchase and droving of the horses in Queensland to the brilliant pageantry of formal occasions in Calcutta. The boys' parents were Patrick and Mary Hegarty who had emigrated from County Derry to Melbourne in 1857 and then on to Dunedin. Patrick Hegarty was a carrier to the South Island goldfields and his boys all became involved in stock, dealing with anything from dogs to sheep, cattle and horses. Henry Hegarty's first venture to India with a Dunedin syndicate in 1889 fell foul of the maritime strike and lost £1950 because the horses arrived in Calcutta when the season was over. It was an expensive but potent lesson. After some years trading between Dunedin and Australia the brothers moved their base to Sydney and resumed their interest in the Calcutta market. By the end of the Boer War they were supplying 700 a year, most of which went to the Princely States such as Bikanir, Boroda, Hyderabad and Jaipur and to private buyers.

Henry and William Hegarty took half each of Queensland for their buying, moving mobs of hundreds of horses in great droving journeys from the Gulf to Townsville and from Bowen to Dalby and Toowoomba. Like the formidable Sidney Kidman, they were teetotal and non-gamblers, at least so far as horse racing was concerned, though land and stock were different matters altogether. It is no surprise to find that they both bought fine homes at Pymble on Sydney's North Shore and took pride in being regarded throughout the bush as men of honour, if they were seen as a little eccentric in their preference for water over strong liquor. Jim Hegarty was chiefly involved in the Indian side of the operation, though in 1910, when both he and William were married, they took their brides to stay in an old palace they had leased five miles from Calcutta, close to the docks and the government remount depot.

One of the best places in which to show off a promising horse in the then Indian capital was at the Eden Gardens. At 6 p.m. the viceroy's band played popular airs and the quality paraded in their finery on the Red Road, some eighty-eight yards wide, and carrying always a variety of impressive carriages and hacks.

William Hegarty tells of his brother Jim selling twenty-three horses to a particularly smart troop that used only black horses, with saddle-cloths of tiger skins. It was, he recalled, the Imperial Service Corps. His greatest thrill came when he watched a show put on by a mounted band of twenty-one performers at a special occasion in Calcutta:

> A drum major rode in front twirling his pole, about six paces behind him came the drummer mounted on a most beautiful black and white horse. As the drummer and all the other bandsmen had their hands fully occupied, the horses' reins were attached to the riders' feet. However, the horses needed no guiding. The Drum Major made the pace, and each horse kept his exact position in the troop. I really believe the drummer's horse was the proudest thing in India, as he kept his step with the music, and the whole show was really a wonderful sight. I was just as proud of the horse when I had a good look at him and found that he was one of the black and white horses I had sent from Floraville the first year I was there. There was our brand on him so there was no mistake, but he had grown and improved so much that without the brand, I would never have recognised him.[14]

The Hegartys and their wives were much impressed by the pageantry of the Viceroy's Cup. There might be 100 000 brightly dressed people in the centre of the course when the viceroy and his party arrived:

> Perhaps three carriages with six horses in each and ridden by postillions and with his wonderful troop of Bodyguard, 300 beautiful well trained horses before the carriages

and 300 behind. These were all big bay horses, over 16 hands high, and beautifully turned out, each horse was ridden by a native over six feet who was dressed in blue uniform with a red and blue turban and red and blue sash, and each man carrying a red and blue pennant. When the whole troop came up the straight between thousands of cheering and brightly dressed natives, it was truly a wonderful sight.[15]

But to return to the Queensland side of the Hegarty operation. The drum major's black and white horse mentioned in William's story had been bred on a station named Floraville in the far north of the Gulf Country, with seventy miles of land on either side of the Leichhardt River. The property had been established by a man called Barry in 1889 with a mob of largely draught horses intended as the nucleus of a breeding station. Henry Hegarty had bought eighty horses there in 1902, the year Barry was killed in a fall, and soon after William Hegarty had the idea of buying the station and mustering the wild horses that had bred like a plague on this and adjoining properties. He paid £1550 for the run and all its assets, which comprised not much more than 'one gun, 4 billycans, a galvanised iron hut and about 25 broken-in saddle horses, and an unknown number of horses running wild'.

Much to the relief of the owners of other properties who suffered from the incursions of the brumbies in this unfenced country, William Hegarty brought in a brumby runner named Davidson, a tall old man from Mudgee, to muster the brumbies. He was to be paid two shillings a head for the first hundred, and an extra shilling for each further hundred. The horses were then held in a rented paddock ten miles long and five miles wide and when they were drafted out, 160 really high-class gun horses were selected for sale in India, which Henry Hegarty took south for shipment with a party of drovers. Other drafts were regularly taken to Charleville, for this was a period when semi-draught horses were in strong demand for delivery purposes and they could be supplied for less than £8 and yet return a good profit.

It was a lonely and rough life for a young chap from Dunedin and William Hegarty sorely missed the comforts of a proper home and the skill of his mother's cooking. Not infrequently he succumbed to Barcoo rot, a skin disease that responded well to an adequate supply of fresh fruit and vegetables. In the wet season of 1904 he left a man in charge, rode north to Burketown and took ship to Brisbane, where he loaded 250 Hegarty horses for sale in India. Though there was always plenty of work to do around the horses, he was relieved in India of the chores of bush life and enjoyed the Indian curries after a monotonous diet of salt beef and damper.[16]

Let me conclude this chapter by recounting William Hegarty's story of a Floraville horse which he recognized from its brand at the gate of the Calcutta remount depot. A nice-looking brown, it was being ridden by one of the Melbourne shippers, who told William that his groom, a north Queensland drover, could give an account of the horse's history prior to its sale at Kirk's Bazaar in Melbourne. His boss had seen the horse at a waterhole at Floraville and, being short of broken-in horses and knowing that Barry was dead, he simply helped himself. They drove a mob of cattle to Charleville, where the horse was sold to a dealer who sent it to Bourke. There it was sold at auction and taken to Wodonga and eventually offered for sale at Kirk's Bazaar in Melbourne. As the crow flies, the journey taken by the horse was about 1370 miles, or 2285 kilometres, with only the final stage from Wodonga affording the dubious luxury of a railway truck. It was the sort of journey to which Sidney Kidman's drovers were well accustomed.[17]

8

Walers in India at Work and Play

THE EMPHASIS OF THIS chapter will be on the role of Australian horses in the sporting life of India. Most of the evidence, which covers a period of almost a century after stories of their performances began to be published in the early 1840s, concerns the part played by Walers in the equine sports to which the British rulers of the subcontinent were so thoroughly addicted. Chief amongst them were horse racing, an activity that was soon dominated by the Waler, and increasingly such team and field sports as polo, pigsticking, tent-pegging and paper-chasing.

The military function of the Waler also belongs here, since the military and sporting uses of the horse in India were so intimately connected. This flowed naturally from the fact that many owners of quality horses in India were British military officers, not only such obvious candidates as cavalrymen but also those from artillery and infantry units. More significantly, we must notice the stress that was placed by commanding officers on the value of equine sports in the total education of their subalterns, both in the formation of character and the development of specific skills.

No less an authority than Lieutenant-General Sir Robert Baden-Powell, twice a semi-finallist and once a victor in the Kadir Cup, famous later as the founder of the scouting movement, wrote on the eve of the First World War that the merits of his nation's cavalry officers had been shaped largely by their devotion to polo and pigsticking. By participating in those sports they taught themselves horsemanship and handiness with arms rather than by parade ground drill as was the case in the German cavalry. He went on, no doubt with the exaggeration common to all storytellers:

> In addition to the natural training involved they have completely driven out from the British subaltern the drinking and betting habits of the former generation, and have

'Yi-hai!'

Tent Pegging, *drawing by 'Snaffles'*

given him in place of these a healthy exercise which also has its moral attributes in playing the game unselfishly; and above all the practice of quiet, quick decision and dash that are essential to a successful leader of men.[1]

The New South Wales Sporting Magazine published in Sydney on 1 November 1848 is an important early source of information on the place of the Thoroughbred in Australia and the incipient horse trade with India. Its founding editor was David Scott, brother of Robert and Helenus Scott of Glendon, the pioneer stud masters and founders of the Indian trade. What is quite fascinating is that as early as this, the editor of an Australian magazine was writing nostalgically of the 'good old times, when the Sydney Hounds and the Cumberland Hunt flourished', while a contributor regretted his inability to replace 'an old favourite hack, one that has often carried me sixty miles a-day without making a mistake —finishing as fresh as when he started'. The supposed deterioration, which was thought to harm the prospects of the Indian trade, was attributed to two factors, the introduction during the late 1830s of 'wretchedly mis-shapen animals' from Valparaiso at a time when brood-mares were in desperately short supply and a frequent cross of the established colonial horse with 'heavy and hairy legged' Clydesdale and Lincolnshire cart horses, which had thrown the colony back for years beyond calculation in the search for perfection in horse breeding.[2]

An article in the first issue of the magazine made the point that the Australian horse had been shaped by 'numerous and select' importations of English and Arab blood, the progeny of which enjoyed the benefits of 'our dry rich soil, and arid climate, with the unlimited range permitted to the growing stock'. As a result, even the commonplace colonial horses achieved a high level of muscular development and constitutional vigour and a reputation for hardihood and endurance. This, thought David Scott, had been threatened by the importations and cross-breeding of the previous ten or fifteen years, though he thought the 'contamination has not yet reached the core', in that some studs kept their blood free from 'any spurious admixture'.[3]

It may seem surprising, given the popular image of South America as a great horse breeding region, to find the *Sporting Magazine* so thoroughly discrediting the Chilean imports of the 1830s. A correspondent in the second issue saw the decline of the original Andalusian breed as a consequence of 'centuries of mismanagement . . . in their breeding and rearing', and the effects of 'in and in breeding . . . amongst widely dispersed and neglected herds'. I have no means of judging the fairness of this criticism in relation to Chile, but it is relevant to notice that by the end of the nineteenth century, when an Indian mission was sent to Argentina to assess that country's ability to compete with Australia as a source of remounts, the decision was emphatically negative. Soon after, at the Boer War, Argentinian horses distinguished themselves by being judged consistently by remount authorities as the worst of all the breeds purchased for that unhappy and fearfully destructive conflict. Not that the Waler fared much better, for reasons we shall later examine, though the ones that were brought by Indian regiments to serve at the Cape maintained their high standing.

The notion that the golden age of equine quality in Australia had passed was also expressed by Edward Curr in his 1863 classic, *Pure Saddle-Horses*, and in another forty years, equine writers were wallowing in such sentiments, ascribing a supposed deterioration to the influence of the misguided preference in the racing industry for sprints over distance events. I am inclined to see this as a manifestation of the human tendency to idealize a past age rather than as an objective measure of declining standards for, while Australian equine experts were full of despair and predicting a collapse of the breed that might endanger its performance in imperial wars, the final reality was that Indian remount authorities and sportsmen acknowledged the Waler as their undisputed beau ideal. As to the horse's ability to campaign efficiently under sustained pressure, this was completely resolved by its performances in the Desert Campaign of the First World War.

One of the virtues of the short-lived *Sporting Magazine* is that it reveals the early contribution of the remount trade to the development of Australian equine excellence. This happened most obviously through the opportunities offered to breeders and shippers by the large and durable Indian market, and it is beautifully satisfying to find the magazine recording importations of high quality Arab stallions in the mid-1830s by Captain J. G. Collins, the founder of the remount trade. The animals were Phantom, a grey from the stud of General Macdowell, which stood at Petersham, and Saladin, a bay that was employed in the Cowpastures. The trade with India went both ways, for the shippers themselves used their return voyages to import well-bred stallions. In 1848 George Plaistowe brought back Crab, an Arab that had won a major distance race in Calcutta, and which was sold to George McLeay for £230, also Scheik, a silver-grey Arab of 14 hands 3 inches that was destined for the stud of J. B. Bettington, a noted breeder of Walers on the Upper Hunter.[4]

The flavour and detail of the sporting pursuits for which Walers were used in India —as well as the type of men who rode them—are well conveyed by the following story which, though not specifically concerned with Walers, is remarkable for being probably the first account published in Australia of Indian pigsticking.

> The usual way of journeying in India is by relays of horses or ponies every ten miles; so twenty or thirty miles are knocked off in no time. Then comes the breakfast; ours was all ready awaiting our arrival, and consisted of rice, eggs, kaboobs, salt and fresh fish, sardines, ham, and a few other trifles to tempt the appetite, but ours required no tempting, for we were as hungry as wolves, and did ample justice to each and every delicacy in its turn. Just as we had finished this satisfactory feed our head huntsman, rejoicing in the name of Ranoo, made his appearance, and gladdened our hearts by reporting that he had tracked a boar of immense size into a thick jungle of grass and thorny baubel trees . . . All jumped up in a moment; cigars were thrown away; boots, spurs, spears, lustily called for, and, mounting our nags, off we started without one moment's unnecessary delay.
>
> It was a glorious morning—a day worthy of a gallant deed; even our horses shared in our excitement, and pawed and fidgeted, with extended nostrils and eyes of fire, eager to engage in the noble sport; indeed I have known them to enjoy so thoroughly a hog hunt that, without any guidance, they have followed, and dodged, and bit with a zest equal to that of the rider's . . .
>
> On the right of us lay a dense forest of underwood, quite impenetrable to man and horse, which, if the hog once succeeded in reaching, we must bid adieu to all hopes of gaining his tusk; but to the left and straight a-head the country was capital; a corn field here and there, a ditch or two, some hedges of prickly pear, and a few dry wells. Ranoo

had collected out of the neighbouring villages two or three hundred men to beat the jungle, in order to frighten out any animals which might be lurking there; some of these had crackers, rattles, and small drums, called tom-toms, to heighten the noise, as if their own unearthly howlings were not sufficient to terrify the king of the beasts himself. A few sharp sighted fellows were stationed on the tallest trees to give information where any bursts took place . . .

By heavens there is no excitement like a real good boar hunt, it beats fox hunts out and out; the screams of the beaters, the noise of the tom-toms and crackers, the anxiety of your horse, the throbbing of your heart, the fear, the hope, the dread, that the monster might start out nearer your companions than yourself, and thus deprive you of the honour of the first spear, all conspire to render this sport the prince of sports; and thus it was for us, for suddenly a tremendous shout arose, and slowly, aye, at a walk, stepped forth the mighty patriach of the stye, as if he had just been aroused from his mid-day slumber and came out to see who had dared so to disturb his rest. He shook the dust from his grey hide, cast his small, fierce eye around, and seeing nothing, (for we dared not move till he left the cover), was about to return and finish his nap, when the near approach of the beaters aroused his attention, and then for the first time believing danger was nigh, forced himself to a half trot, in the direction of the right-hand scrub, but seeing us there, and hearing the beaters still advancing, he boldly took to the plain, and made towards the corn fields . . . When he had quite cleared the grass and jungle, we started off at racing speed, and at racing speed he led us for two miles, over ditches and creeks, through corn fields, tearing us to pieces amidst thorny baubel and prickly pear bushes, until his wind at last began to fail . . . he now cast his eye behind, and seemed undecided whether it was better to run on, or turn, and manfully fight. He chose the latter, and suddenly wheeled about and charged the staff officer before he was aware of it, ripped the horse, and brought both thundering to the ground; he then charged the old one, who cooly [sic] received him on his spear, and laid the heavy mass of bacon dead at his feet, but not until he had ground the spear to bits in impotent rage.[5]

At the time this story was published it is unlikely that Walers had experienced their first blooding as hog-hunters in India, though in later years they were to win fame in what many writers saw as the blue ribbon event of Asian sport, the Kadir Cup. As was noted in an earlier chapter, Walers made their first impression on Indian sport at the Calcutta meeting in the winter of 1844–45 with the victories of Lara and Young Muleyson, which resulted in Walers being put on the same weight handicap as the Caper. Young Muleyson had been bred by Henry Dangar at Neotsfield on the Upper Hunter and sold in Calcutta for Rs 1100, while another Dangar horse, Waverley, fetched Rs 1600, treble the price of the average remount.[6]

H. A. Wyndham's account 'The Cape Horse in India' suggests a link between successes on the race track and in the market-place. The Caper's impending decline in the private and remount markets of India coincided with the rising prestige of the Waler, which was shown vividly by the results of the Calcutta meeting of 1849–50. Walers won fourteen races, Arabs six, country-breds six, and English horses three. The only performance recorded by a Caper was that of Rat Tail, which ran last in the Colonial Stakes.

In spite of this, the Cape horse had one great final contribution to make to the remount trade, when Colonel Apperley was sent to southern Africa in 1857 to buy horses at the time of the Mutiny. Though the initial requisition was for a thousand, he remained till 1861 and shipped a total of 5482, as well as 104 mules, at a cost of £215 645.[7]

While Apperley was buying at the Cape, Lieutenant-Colonel W. P. Robbins was putting together cargoes in eastern Australia, which suffered far more heavily in losses at sea and cost more than the Capers. Both had their special moments of glory in the campaigns of 1857–58, for Sir Henry Havelock made his official entry into Lucknow riding his Cape horse, Blue Peter, and the great George Hodson of Hodson's Horse rode his 'magnificent, powerful and courageous bay Waler' at the relief of Delhi in 1858.[8]

Wyndham concludes by asking why Cape breeders failed to maintain their position in the lucrative Indian market. The first difficulty was that their methods failed to produce the size and substance required by buyers, whereas at this very time Australian stud masters 'electrified racing circles' by the importation of Thoroughbred stock of outstanding quality, buying Fisherman for 3000 guineas and three of Lord Londesborough's mares for £1200, £850 and £630. Secondly, the main horse breeding districts of George, Caledon, Riversdale and Uitenhage lost their capacity to produce surplus horses of quality because of the devastating effects of drought and the virulent epizootic disease of African Horse Sickness, so that at the Caledon Show of 1860 there was only one entry for Colonel Apperley's prize awarded to the best span of four horses suitable for Indian remounts. As Captain Horace Hayes, the equestrian writer, put the point in 1894 after his visit to southern Africa: when one considered that the disease killed 20 000 horses a year, it was hardly surprising that the fear of heavy mortality should make for the neglect of horse breeding. At the same time, many of the open ranges on which horses had been bred were turned over to the farming of merino sheep, as happened also in the pastures south of Perth in Western Australia in the final decade or so of the nineteenth century.[9]

Both Horace Hayes and his younger colleague, J. C. Galstaun, saw the time spent in India by Lord William Beresford as military secretary to the viceroy as crucial to the popularity and prestige of the sport of racing in India. He supplied more horses to the native rulers than all the other dealers put together and brought many princes into the sport, including the Aga Khan and the Maharajahs of Mysore, Patialia, Cooch-Behar, Gwalior and Kashmir.

One of Beresford's first horses was Myall King, bought for him by Teddy Weekes, the Australian shipper. It was, Galstaun writes,

> a mean looking, light-fleshed bay gelding, without any pretension to class. When Lord William saw the animal he was very annoyed with Weekes for buying him a 'damned Sydney Cab horse' as he called it.

But Weekes was a shrewd judge, and Myall King won the Viceroy's Cup three times, bringing his owner plate worth Rs 1000 and Rs 7000 in cash.[10]

The Calcutta season of 1892–93 brought to the fore the 'popular Maharajah of Cooch Behar', whose newly imported black Waler gelding Highborn 'swept all before him'. This was a time when Galstaun was not directly involved in racing and he persuaded his solicitor and friend, Gal Gregory, to buy a noted Australian racehorse named Courallie for Rs 16 000 at Cook's Auctions. During the 1896-97 season he won eight out of twelve starts in Lucknow, Calcutta and Bombay.

Another aristocrat who contributed mightily to the Indian turf was Lord Ulick Browne, a senior civil servant who was joint editor and proprietor of the *Oriental Sporting Magazine*. As early as 1852 he rode the Waler gelding Emperor in a match race against the English horse Bedford and beat it, then built up a stable based on the Walers Beeswing and Boomerang and had a successful season. One of his concerns was to do justice to the colonial horses, whose time of foaling—from August to November inclusive—meant that they suffered a disadvantage against English and other horses, which took their ages from 1 May. So Lord Ulick drew up on the English principle a table of weights for age and class that was soon adopted throughout India. The allowance for class, which stood for a long time, was that English horses gave Walers 7 pounds, Capers 21 pounds, country-breds 35 pounds, and Arabs 49 pounds. Eventually the concession given by the English horse to the Waler was abolished.[11]

By the time Captain Hayes published the first edition of his classic *A Guide to Training and Horse Management* in India in 1875, both Cape horses and country-breds received class allowances from Walers of 2 and 3 stone respectively and even then only two Capers, Echo and Merryman, could hold their own against the Australians. Hayes thought English horses suffered in India from the severity of the climate and the hardness of most of the race courses, which jarred the legs so continually as to make them shin-sore. The Waler derived an advantage from its native climate and terrain and, as Hayes reminds us, the high cost of English racehorses ensured that 'there has been hardly a single horse sent out here with even second class pretensions'. The latter style of English horse would have cost from £1200 to £1500, whereas the Waler colt Kingcraft, seen by Hayes as 'the very best horse ever imported into this country', had cost only £500, though he was estimated to have won Rs 30 000 (or about £2500) in his maiden year of 1873. With the famous Pathan-born jockey Jaffeer Khan in the saddle he carried off all the big events for Mr Kelly Maitland, including the Viceroy's Cup, the Colonials, and the Burdwan Cup. Taking account of the limited prize money and racing facilities available in India, owners were bound to see Walers as offering better value for money.[12]

Nearly twenty years later, in a new edition, Hayes made it clear that the Waler's supremacy on Indian tracks was even more absolute, chiefly because of the virtual disappearance of its English rivals. He then made a point that bears on a recurring contention of this book, that:

> racing stock of even the most moderate pretensions cannot be bred in India without the blood being constantly renewed by suitable importations, whether from Europe, the Colonies, or America. The effect of the climate, which is manifest in the indigenous equine type, will not allow, without constant foreign aid, the production of animals fit either for the turf or for heavy saddle work.[13]

In another book, *Among Men and Horses*, Hayes writes of the racing scene in Calcutta in 1894, when English bookmakers were accustomed to arrive for the winter meeting that ran from about 1 December to the end of February, after fielding in France and Italy. He refers also to an aspect of Calcutta life that was still being experienced by Australian shippers in the 1920s and 1930s, the early morning exercising of horses which began when the mist was still rising from the Hooghly.

Calcutta affords to its inhabitants unrivalled facilities for breaking horses either to saddle or harness; for it has, between the English part of the town and the river Hooghly, a level plain of about three square miles in area, over which everyone is free to ride; and there is ample space set off for the breaking of horses to harness. For making animals quiet to carriage work, some of my Colonial dealer friends used to employ an ingeniously-constructed trap, called a 'jingle', which had such long shafts that if the horse which was harnessed to it began to kick, he could not reach either the splinter bar or the body of it with his heels . . . few things make a horse stop kicking so soon and so effectively, as finding that he has nothing to kick against.[14]

Hayes describes another sport that was popular among the European population of Calcutta by the 1890s. Paper-chasing was conducted in the cold weather over a 'made' country that might range from three to four miles, with the course marked out by a paper trail and perhaps twenty hurdles made from stiff mud walls varying in height from 3 feet 6 inches to 4 feet 4 inches. The horses were almost all well-bred or Thoroughbred Walers and the pace was as fast as they could go. Hayes saw little of the sport, because it took place in the early mornings, when he was occupied as a trainer, but his wife was addicted to it, and on the morning of a meet would be up at five o'clock for a cup of tea and slice of toast, before driving to the course in a dog cart.[15]

Hayes had an explanation for the Waler's success in Indian sport:

These Australasian horses, even when only lately landed, are wonderful jumpers, principally, I think, from the lightness and obliquity of their shoulders . . . the fact of the large majority of them being allowed to wander over large tracts of country in a state of perfect liberty during their youth, say, up to four years of age, confers on them great freedom of shoulder as well as soundness of limb. I am also under the impression that horses brought up on hilly ground have better shoulders than those reared on level soil.[16]

Frank Maxwell, the cavalry officer who won the Victoria Cross on a Thoroughbred Waler gelding he called English Lord, recorded in unusual detail his career as a sportsman and trainer of horses from 1900 to 1915 and revealed the tenderness of his feelings for those that remained in his stable for many years. The height of Lord's sporting career came with his win in the Calcutta Cup for paper-chasing, as described in Maxwell's diary for 15 March 1904. It is apparent that Frank saw the horse as the true victor.

Paper chase cup at last. En. Lord won comfortably, his only serious rival—Deakin's Blue Bill falling ½ way. Long course of 4 miles with some dreadful sharp rinks . . . so 18 BL [Bengal Lancers] win Challenge cup, Paper Chase Cup and H.H. [Hoghunter's] Cup. K. [Kitchener] out there & very happy at us winning something at last.

Polo, even more than pigsticking and paper-chasing, was the sport with which Walers and British officers were closely involved in India from the 1860s. No better introduction could be given to the subject than to quote at length from Winston Churchill's *My Early Life*, which describes his arrival in Bombay as a subaltern in a

Dolly, a fine Waler polo mare

troop-ship at the end of the 1890s and his induction to the work and play of a cavalry station at Bangalore in the southern highlands. The first task was to establish proper domestic arrangements:

> Daylight brought suave, ceremonious, turbanned applicants for the offices of butler, dressing boy, and head groom, which in those days formed the foundation of a cavalry subaltern's household. All bore trustworthy testimonials with them from the home-going regiment; and after brief formalities and salaams laid hold of one's worldly possessions and assumed absolute responsibility for one's whole domestic life. If you liked to be waited on and relieved of home worries, India thirty years ago was per-fection. All you had to do was to hand over all your uniform and clothes to the dressing boy, your ponies to the syce, and your money to the butler, and you need never trouble any more. Your Cabinet was complete.

With two colleagues, Churchill took a palatial bungalow with a heavy tiled roof and deep verandas, the white columns of which were wreathed in purple bougain-villaea.

> We built a large tiled barn with mud walls, containing stabling for thirty horses and ponies. Our three butlers formed a triumvirate in which no internal dissensions ever appeared. We paid an equal contribution into the pot; and thus freed from mundane cares, devoted ourselves to the serious purpose of life. This was expressed in one word —Polo. It was upon this, apart from duty, that all our interest was concentrated.[17]

Churchill then describes how he and his friends arranged for the regimental polo club to buy the entire polo stud of the Poona Light Horse, and they then committed themselves to 'an audacious and colossal undertaking', the capture of the Inter-Regimental Cup. Duties occupied the mornings and every afternoon at five o'clock, after siesta, they played between eight and twelve chukkas before having a hot bath, and dining to the strains of the regimental band.

In the tournament at Hyderabad, Churchill's team, from the 4th Hussars, had been unlucky enough to draw the Golcondas, considered the best team in southern India.

The whole ground was packed with enormous masses of Indian spectators of all classes watching the game with keen and instructed attention. The tents and canopied stands were thronged with the British community and the Indian rank and fashion of the Deccan. We were expected to be an easy prey, and when our lithe, darting, straight-hitting opponents scored 3 goals to nothing in the first few minutes, we almost shared the general opinion. However, without going into details which, though important, are effaced by the march of time and greater events, amid roars of excitement from the assembled multitudes we defeated the Golcondas by 9 goals to 3. On succeeding days we made short work of all other opponents, and established the record, never since broken, of winning a first-class tournament within fifty days of landing in India.[18]

Frank Maxwell and English Lady (far left)

One of the most authoritative early histories of polo was contained in the recollections of Lord Curzon, former viceroy of India, published in 1926. He tells of the ancient origins of the game in Persia, centuries before the Christian era, whence it spread westward to Constantinople and east to China, commencing as the pastime of princes and nobles but 'developing whenever the ponies and the means were forthcoming, into the popular recreation of the people'. The Emperor Akbar was addicted to the game but somehow it vanished from the scene in India until in the mid-nineteenth century it was rediscovered in the tiny highland state of Manipur, having probably been introduced from China. European planters in Assam learned the game from the Manipuris, and Lieutenant Joe Shearer of the Indian Army founded the Silchar Polo Club, the first of its kind in the world, in 1859. From this point, the spread of the game throughout India, particularly amongst British and Indian officers, was mushroom-like and it was soon brought to Calcutta where the Polo Club was founded in 1863. During this process a panoply of rules was added and in the 1870s the game was taken to England and Australia by army officers who, like Churchill, made it almost a vocation.[19]

Devotion to polo is a theme common to that large body of literature written by former officers about their time in India. Sir Stanley Reed, sometime commanding officer of the 4th Bombay Light Horse, editor of the *Times of India* from 1907 to 1923, wrote that, for the Britisher, 'India was pre-eminently the land of the horse. If compensation was sought for exile . . . it was found in the cheapness of horseflesh'. The new chum, or 'griffin' in Indian terms, could sally forth to the Arab stables in Bombay and for thirty or forty pounds take his pick of the new arrivals. 'For those in search of bigger game there were the Australian Walers', which might be brumbies or descendants of the famous Carbine. He went on to say that if kept in 'cotton wool for a year after landing to be acclimatised, the Waler was good for ten or twelve years' service, standing up to the hard ground of India far better than the imported English horse'. This is a useful reminder, incidentally, of the disappearance in the last decade or so of the nineteenth century of the belief that Walers were too underbred to stand the severities of campaigning in the Indian climate: it was a matter of acclimatization and of recovery from the awful strains of the voyage, though from the mid-1880s this was cut down by steamships from ten weeks to three.[20]

General the Lord Ismay, who began his service career as a cavalry officer, confronts the popular misconceptions of the profession by his charmingly written *Memoirs*. He describes as a great piece of good fortune his failure in the scholarship examinations for Cambridge, which allowed him to pursue the career for which he had had a sneaking desire since the Boer War, in spite of the ideas of his father, who 'never tired of telling the story about the cavalry officer who was so stupid that even his brother officers noticed it'.[21]

Ismay took a simple delight in his profession:

Most of us played polo three days a week, and schooled ponies on the other afternoons. In addition there were occasional race meetings at neighbouring stations, and rough shooting for all who wanted it. I could not help thinking, as I drew my admittedly meagre salary at the end of each month, that it was very odd that I should be paid anything at all for doing what I loved doing above all else.[22]

Even more thrilling was 'the occasional excitement of hunting a gang of raiders'. He tells the story of one day at Risalpur Cantonment on the north-west frontier when two squadrons had to move quickly to intercept a raiding party from Mohmand country which had killed a policeman, looted and set fire to a village and carried off some Hindu women. The squadrons moved off by moonlight but saw no raiders and so drove on to Mardan, the home of the Corps of Guides, played polo and then attended a dance at Nowshera. 'The next day I was due to ride in two steeplechases. I was still under twenty-one years old. How I blessed my ineptitude at examinations.'

In his latter days as a shipper, Henry Vanrenen often took ponies to India as special orders for customers who desired Walers as polo ponies in the days when they were still very small, in the tradition of the pony-sized Manipuri horses. By the time of Steve Margrett the horse used for polo was much the same as an average remount, about fifteen hands, and many of those that went into the game from Calcutta were rejected remounts, though in Bombay the Arab was more commonly used.

It was Curtis Skene, himself a highly rated player on a handicap of eight goals, who injected an element of professional specialization into the supply of polo ponies to Calcutta. Born in 1880 in Hamilton, Victoria, he spent nearly thirty years as a tea-planter in Assam, where he married and had a son, Bob, who in 1940 became the first Australian to achieve the maximum ranking of ten goals. Curtis Skene retired from planting in the mid-1920s and bought a property near Wagga, but was almost ruined by the Great Depression. Moving to a small property at Campbelltown in 1930, he began responding to the frequent requests of his friends in India by purchasing horses suitable for polo and taking them to India. Bob was withdrawn from the cloisters of Geelong Grammar School and during the following eight years was engaged with his father in what proved an extremely profitable trade.[23]

The Skenes bought horses within an arc of New South Wales that ran from Maitland to Blayney and south to Jindabyne, paying in those tough early days not much more than £10 each for horses and then giving them basic polo training. Cargoes were usually loaded on the big fast British India ships at Newcastle, where their batch of seventy to eighty horses would be stalled in the very bowels of the ship, the 'coal hole', which offered significant advantages to its occupants. There was a minimum of rolling and an abundance of space, which permitted the Skenes to set aside loose boxes in which their animals could take turns for exercise and a good roll in the sand. It was hot down there but Bob Skene recalled losing only one horse and his charges were disembarked at Alipore in Calcutta in better condition than the remounts.

In Calcutta the Skene family stayed at the Ritz Hotel and both father and son played polo while they were disposing of their horses. In 1937 Bob Skene had his introduction to international polo when he played in England with the famous Ashton brothers, who had put Australia on the world polo map in 1930 during a successful tour of England and the United States. After war years spent largely in Changi prison camp, Bob played professionally in America and now lives in Santa Barbara though he is in demand still in Australia as a lecturer.

A recurring theme of the writings on Indian equine sport is that not only the riders but also the horses hugely enjoyed themselves. Consider Sir Robert Baden-Powell's account of the keenness shown by an opposing pony in a race for the ball:

As my pony was gradually inch by inch passing his, it suddenly turned its head and, gripping hold of my fore-arm, dragged me off my mount and held me firmly, refusing to let go in spite of the efforts of its rider, and only a smashing blow on the nose caused it to relax its grip and release me. My arm was black and blue for a week afterwards.[24]

Hog-hunting, or pigsticking as it came generally to be called, though not pursued as widely as polo, claimed the highest place in the pantheon of south Asian sport. It appealed certainly to the blood lust and love of a sense of danger that characterized many Britishers, gentle as they were in private life. For the cavalry officer, it offered the closest approximation to the desperate thrill of a charge, with danger coming not only from the hazards of the terrain but also from the weapon of the adversary, in this case the razor sharp tusks of a mature boar—an animal which stood more than three feet high and was capable of outrunning most horses in a sprint.

Colonel Walter Campbell wrote in 1864 comparing the difficulties of Indian terrain with those in England in words that suggest why the formative environment of the Waler prepared it so well for the sport:

True, the fences of Leicester, or Northhamptonshire, are not met with in India; but deep ravines, to which the Wissendene is a ditch; dried-up water-courses, with under-mined banks, which render falls inevitable; steep rocky descents, which in cold blood appear impracticable to any animal but a goat; holes and cracks wide enough and deep enough to receive a horse up to the girths; and last, not least, 'cockspur thorns'—three inches long—which absolutely nail a man's feet to his boots, and make his horse's chest and forelegs look like a pincushion, are difficulties, I think, sufficient to redeem hog-hunting . . . from the character of easy riding.[25]

Campbell looked also at the qualities demanded of horse and rider. For the latter courage and even recklessness were essential to success, and for the horse a combination of speed, staying power and anticipation.

Mere hard riding will not do. You must know how to handle your spear, as well as your horse; and mounted on a stiff-necked, hard-mouthed brute—be his speed what it may—you have not the ghost of a chance against the man who rides a well-trained hunter, even though he be a slower horse. A perfect hunter will twist himself about, by the pressure of the leg, or motion of the body, without assistance from the reins; and some horses become so fond of the sport, as to stick to a hog like a greyhound coursing a hare; keeping a bright look-out, at the same time, to wheel off and avoid a charge.[26]

The Kadir Cup, described by the 1901 winner as 'the blue ribbon of Indian sport', was a silver trophy valued at £120, presented first in 1874 by Major-General Hardinge and the Meerut Tent Club. Meerut had long been the Mecca of pigstickers because it brought together a concentration of cavalry and artillery officers in a city that lies near the Ganges plain. Annual inundations made the Kadir, or grassy bed of the river, a habitat for wild pigs, which had been the sporting target for horsemen since ancient times. Each contestant in the Kadir Cup might enter a number of horses. Contending spears were to be divided by lot into heats of not more than four and the takers of the first spear in each party would contest the final spear and the cup.

Lined Up for the Kadir Cup, *drawing by 'Snaffles'*

When Frank Cornish won in 1901, the contest was held in the Kadir thirty-two miles from Meerut in northern India, in a vast sea of high reeds and grass which abounded in pig, deer, leopards, hares and partridges. On either edge of the Kadir were ripening fields of corn in which the pigs revelled at night, only to be disturbed by the beaters who flushed them out towards the riders. Frank's Arab mare Hermia was the fastest in the field, so he was able to get in the first spear, 'the merest prick', and was soon being congratulated by a dozen sportsmen with Kodaks who insisted on photographing the victorious duo.

In his posthumously published *Letters and Sketches* Cornish explains that the cost of actually making the Kadir Cup was borne partly by his regiment, because the possession of this trophy by a regimental mess was highly prized. Within six months of this triumph, he took his own life with his service revolver, apparently in delirium caused by a fever that was his recurring companion in India. For the men who rode the Walers there, life was not all beer and skittles; the pressures of climate and fever, and medication with quinine and arsenic created some awfully dark patches of the mind, so powerfully evoked by Kipling in his 'City of Dreadful Night'.[27]

Coming closer to the present day the place of the Waler in polo and pigsticking can be documented. Brigadier Thurston Edward-Collins, who transferred to the Central

India Horse in 1935 and remained there for the remainder of his service, has put together information about two great horses that were associated with the regiment after it returned from service in Palestine, where their team had won the 1920 Inter-Regimental Polo Tournament at Cairo, mounted almost entirely on Walers:

> One of the most famous walers was a pony named Myra who stood only 14.3 hands. The little mare had been purchased by the First (38th) Regiment in the silladar days in 1914 and had accompanied the Regiment to France. She carried a Sikh dafadar during the first two and a half years of the Great War and was later allotted to Michael Cox as a charger. At the end of the war Michael bought her and put her to polo. She was played by Bill Williams in the Inter-Regimental in Cairo and thereafter she was played regularly by both Williams and Cox in all the tournaments for many years. Perfectly balanced, and with a wonderful front, she was as fast and staunch as anything on the polo ground and she could hold her own in any company.

Edward-Collins recalled many brilliant Waler polo ponies that established the fame of the Central India Horse in those days, amongst them Nikky (ridden by Richard George), Starlight (Bill Williams), Kitten (Michael Cox), Snapshot (Jeff Alexander), Bosun (Charles Harvey), and Golliwog (D. B. Edwards). Equal to any of the 'line' ponies was Corner Boy, a chestnut Waler that probably played in more tournaments than any other pony in the regiment. 'He had a heart of gold and a mouth of iron and he carried Jeff Alexander, never anything but a heavyweight, in a partnership that was highly successful.'[28]

Jeff Alexander also described his days in the Central India Horse, which began in 1918 when the regiment was in Palestine. At the depot in India there were five squadrons, four of Walers and one of country-breds. As Jeff put it, 'We much preferred Walers as troop horses and polo ponies because they stood up to the hard going much better than English or Country breds'. Most of the Central India Horse remounts were bought in Bombay from a shipper named Baldock who carried horses to that destination for decades. He was succeeded by Bob Gove, a South Australian shipper who probably bought extensively from the Kapunda sales held by Sidney Kidman from 1900.[29]

Much of the charm of Jeff Alexander's description comes from what he reveals of his relationship with his horses: it has a tenderness that occurs again and again in this material. He writes, 'the few of us at the Depot played polo on troop horses—to my great good fortune I got a chestnut called Corner Boy—he was a trained pony & taught me more than I ever taught him!'

On reaching retiring age Corner Boy was given by the colonel to Jeff Alexander, and after a time in his stables he went to a paddock kept by the viceroy's bodyguard, where he finally died. 'When he was in my stables [Alexander continues] my orderly used to bring him—running free—with my ponies to polo—and I have seen him lying by my sticks quietly watching the game! I have no doubt that he chatted to my young ponies'.

'Snaffles', the great equestrian artist, drew a sketch of Corner Boy in his retirement, and depicted him, as he put it, with an ethereal background below a line from Kipling's 'Mandalay', 'But that's all shove be'ind me—long ago an' fur away. . . .'. 'Snaffles' felt sure that the old horse dreamed about his gallops and jinks after the polo ball, and also that his two-legged friends shared 'his dreams and memories of those not so long ago days before we "abandoned ship" in India'.[30]

From Lieutenant-Colonel P. Massey of Hampshire comes an account of two Walers that were thought to have been racehorses in Australia, and perhaps sent to India after being warned off for life from Australian tracks. Regent was a big, bay, Waler Thoroughbred gelding 'with flop ears and a beautiful temperament'. After winning an open point-to-point with him by half a mile, Massey put him into training, but he was surreptitiously entered in a sprint, heavily backed and mercilessly flogged by the jockey. When next seen by Massey, Regent was 'sweating and obviously terrified of his surroundings'. At his next run on a course he 'simply bolted to the first fence with his eyes shut, took it by the roots and broke his back'. A similarly built Waler of Massey's that was never defeated as a steeplechaser was Dunsling, a 'fearless pig sticker' on which Massey also played good polo just before the Second World War.

Massey's closing remarks are of particular interest:

Most of my 'line' ponies were Walers, as for polo I weighed twelve stone and country breds were seldom up to weight. Of course Walers took a lot of training, having often been brutally treated on their way to India and all of them were fearful of men. When I was Adjutant, I used the Lichwark tackle on Walers with which one could handle, saddle and mount them in 20 hours. With it one could gain their confidence without getting killed in the process! After a month I used to put on a Remount Ride Display with the remounts in line and the men climbing along the saddles and then through the tunnel made by the horses' legs back to where they had started. Then they would vault on over the horse's tail and slide down its head, walk forward ten paces and call their horse to them. It was quite impressive and by then the Walers were just as amenable as the country breds. Indeed there are no bad horses; just ignorant riders![31]

Colonel Douglas Gray, former commanding officer of the famous *silladari* regiment, Skinner's Horse, drew on his unmatchable experience with Walers as a sportsman, cavalry officer and Director of Remounts in a letter referring to an impending visit to India and Skinner's Horse in 1986: 'They are still tremendously keen on maintaining all the old customs and traditions which they inherited from us and their mess is immaculately and nostalgically preserved. But they are armed with the latest mark of Russian T 72 tank!'[32] In the following passage he describes the Waler on which he won the Kadir Cup in 1934.

the best horse I ever owned was a Waler. He was a grey and, being that colour, became a Trumpeter's mount in my regiment, Skinner's Horse. The nature of that job meant that they were not worked as hard as the troop horses and, consequently, were not 'cast' at 14 years—the age limit—and could be bought out by Officers at a cheap price. This particular horse was 15 when I acquired him and he proved to be a fantastic cross-country performer. I rode him for three years as a Pigsticker and he never once gave me a fall because he seemed to have a spare leg when galloping flat out over rough ground—so I could trust him absolutely and scarcely needed to guide him at all. I called him 'Granite' and he won the Kadir Cup for me in 1934. He remained with me until the outbreak of War in 1939 when we Cavalry Officers had sterner things than Pigsticking to attend to. He was 23 when he had to be put down. Then the regimental syces dug his grave, lining it with flowers, and we were all in tears over the death of this great Australian horse. His tail, mounted as a fly whisk, now hangs beside my desk.

Lieutenant-Colonel Douglas Gray and Granite in pigsticking attire, winners of the 1934 Kadir Cup

Colonel Gray also wrote to me of the work of the Army Remount Department which, supported by the Veterinary Corps, continued to purchase remounts for the mounted services before mechanization. It administered a large breeding area in west Punjab in a scheme that aimed at enlisting the skills and energies of ex-servicemen. About a hundred stallions distributed over ten stables served some 4000 mares and the resultant crop was selected and purchased from the Indian breeders before being sent to depots at Sargodha and Mona (now in Pakistan) and to Sahar-anpur and Babugarh.

At the same time the Remount Department continued to buy thousands of Walers every year from official shippers who took the horses in B.I. ships from Melbourne and the eastern Australian ports to Calcutta, Bombay and Madras. Gray describes how on arrival the horses were herded from the dock side to the remount depot:

> This was cleverly done by a party of ARD Rough-riders who held up the walls of tents to form a space about the size of a tennis court inside which about a dozen horses at a time were slowly walked along in a sort of moving paddock. It was an effective way of dealing with many semi-wild horses and it became the standard reception procedure. At the Depot the Walers were introduced to head-collars and being led, before they were allocated to their intended Units, where their real training as troop horses or Gun teams was done under regimental arrangements.

He emphasizes the contrast between the training of Walers and country-breds. The former were mature horses and raised on the open range, and so needed extreme patience for they were clever at avoiding or resenting discipline, while the native horses were easily biddable, having been constantly handled since birth. Yet it was only the Walers that were found suitable for the heavy British troopers and the gun teams. Apart from their suitability for regimental duties,

> The bigger walers made superb Pigstickers because they stood the heat well, had legs of iron and were courageous in the face of a charging wild boar. They could not have the quality of thoroughbreds and few could be termed 'oil-paintings' but Walers were simply the best horses for the job thay had to do. In conclusion without the Australian Walers, the cavalry regiments in India could never have achieved their very high standards.[33]

It remains to convey something of the flavour of the punitive actions and military engagements in which Walers were involved during their final decade or so as the standard cavalry horse of the north-western frontier.

Two stories will have to suffice. The first is a summary of Charles Treharne's account in the *Cavalry Journal* of a small-scale action by his unit, the Emergency Squadron, against a gang of Mahsud tribesmen which had raided the village of Zakka Khel, some twelve miles away. Led by an outlaw named Badshah Gul, a dozen or more Mahsuds had crossed the border and attacked the village, burning two houses, killing several people, and had cantered off with two money lenders for whom a ransom would later be sought and booty loaded on donkeys.

Much of what followed was quite typical of the recurring experiences of *silladari* regiments stationed in small posts dotted along the north-west frontier from the time of the conquest of the Sikh kingdom in 1849. It was typical in all respects but one; the

Emergency Squadron succeeded in catching up with the Mahsuds and engaging them before they regained their native hills.

With several British officers and a hundred *sowars* or Indian troopers behind him, the squadron leader had reached the village by dawn and set off again at a cracking pace enabling the squadron to cut down the two-and-a-half-hour lead of the Mahsuds, who were slowed down by their booty and hostages. But the crucial advantage to the forces of law and order was that the Frontier Constabulary, which had received the breathless news of the raid at midnight and had passed the news on to brigade headquarters by telephone, had themselves engaged the raiders in a running fight, forcing them to disgorge their loot and captives and take shelter in a cave with a breastwork of stones below a cliff.

Massively outnumbered, the raiders were attacked by fire from rifles and Hotchkiss guns until only one man remained alive. It was Badshah Gul himself, who had been buried to his shoulders by a fall of sand and rock. He was taken to the nearest police post to be summarily dealt with by the Political Agent and hanged from a tree to pay for his many murders.[34]

So much for the Mahsuds and the small-scale punitive action of the frontier. Another writer in the *Cavalry Journal* of the inter-war period describes a much larger operation involving the use of horse artillery as well as cavalry against Mohmand forces in the vicinity of Risalpur Cantonment on the north-west frontier. This was a major reprisal, the political origins of which are not brought out by the writer, but it culminated in charges by squadrons of a magnitude that belonged rather to an earlier era.

Very simply, the charges were ordered to deal with a threat by Mohmand troops seeking to outflank a body of infantry and cavalry occupying some dunes overlooking a canal, beyond which lay tall crops of corn. Near mid-day,

> when the tribesmen were now streaming down from the spurs and over across the canal, we were thrilled to see a part of [the Risalpur Cavalry Brigade] . . . mounting for a charge. Out they galloped into long extended lines, two squadrons of British Lancers, one of Indian, and on they clattered, lances and swords flashing in the sun, officers on their blood horses far ahead, down the piece of bare plain between our end of the dunes and the canal. But, before they had covered half the distance, there was nothing on that flat open stretch of ground to charge; the tribesmen, seeing them coming, had vanished again under cover. They galloped on; a withering fire burst on them from the spurs in front, where the horses could not go; a yet more galling fire, at shorter range, from the crops bordering the far bank of the canal . . . In a moment, it seemed, the space between us and the canal was littered with fallen men and horses, lying still or struggling. We saw some, chiefly officers, jump it clear and vanish in among the crops. But the obstacle was too big for ordinary heavily-loaded troop horses. They blundered and fell; and as the men tried to scramble up the far bank, we saw tribesmen appear out of the high standing corn, and shoot them point-blank, the muzzles of their rifles held almost against the troopers' bodies.

To the onlookers who saw the wreckage of dead and wounded men and horses on the plain below there seemed little glory or victory in the first real cavalry charge they had witnessed. After a few moments, a swarm of tribesmen rushed out of the crops to take their spoil from the victims, and the writer 'knew that our moment had come'. In a cold, calm voice Colonel Holland-Pryor gave the order to mount.

There was great noise. The men yelled their piercing war-cry, 'Himat i'mardan, madad i' Khudda!' (The help of God and bravery of man!) From boyhood onward I had often pictured myself in a cavalry charge on this wild frontier, and now the reality had come. All was there: the dust and thunder of hoofs rattling over the stony plain, the shouting of the men for blood, the 'phit' 'phit' of bullets through the air, the crash and clatter as horses, hit by these bullets, pitched neck and crop among the stones. And in front, the plain swarmed with the grey figures of our enemy.

Our appearance had evidently taken them by surprise. They had seen the remnants of the previous charge melt away back on to the rest of the mounted column, in a position a mile or so behind. Our horses had been so snugly hidden in the fold at the end of the dunes that they probably had not realised that we, too, were cavalry. When they saw us coming, they began to run; in two directions, some towards the spurs, some towards the shelter of the crops across the canal.

Holland-Pryor rode in front; I, just behind him to the right. There came to me the sense of power and mastery which riding a well-trained, mettlesome horse will give. Ahead of me a group of slate-shirted figures crouching over the body of a British Lancer, rose up and started away in a running slouch. I quickly came up with the hindmost. Jabbing my revolver against his back, I pulled the trigger. I had the impression of knocking over a nine-pin with a light touch of the tip of the finger. He was, I think, an unarmed youth. Moving on at a canter, I had only a fleeting glimpse of a crumpled heap on the ground, and two lance points thudding into it with hoarse shouting. I rode on at a great bearded fellow, snarling back over his shoulder like a wolf as he ran. He whipped round and pointed his rifle at me. I touched my pony with the right heel; it passaged to the left as the rifle spurted. The bullet went up my sleeve and out at the elbow without touching the skin. The Mohmand reached for his knife, but before he could draw it, I thrust my revolver between his shoulders. He slid to the ground like a limp sack, unconscious, no doubt, of the lances behind me which instantly transfixed his body.[35]

After more desperate fighting, which included the loss of Colonel Scriven, the cavalry retired, having fully achieved its object. While doing so they were fired on from the neighbouring village of Bires Ghundhai, in which some of the Mohmands had taken shelter. Next morning they received orders to destroy the village and lay waste the crops as a reprisal for the part its people had played in aiding the Mohmands.

It was the sort of 'example' that is a common experience for an army of occupation, as the British in India were in the last resort. What made the destruction the more poignant to the writer were two considerations. The villagers had undoubtedly been forced into an aggressive role by the Mohmands, who were very hard men indeed. And when he rode forward with the colonel to arrange with the headman of the village for its evacuation before the artillery got to work, they met

a tall stately figure with one arm in a sling, striding towards us with long dignified steps, anger on his face.

'Sahib,' he said, 'less than three months ago I was in Buckingham Palace, before the King, who gave me this, for some work in France.'

He moved the shattered arm, displaying, pinned on his coat, the Indian Order of Merit—(corresponding at that time to the V.C., for which Indians had not yet become eligible).

'And now,' he went on, 'after being wounded across the sea in the King's service, I come home and find you, the King's servants, about to destroy my house and crops.'

Between Razmak and Bannu, Waziristan campaign, 1940–41

Holland-Pryor quickly took down his name, regiment, particulars, and sent an orderly flying back to Headquarters. But the answer came to proceed with the demolition according to plan.[36]

British officers continued to use Walers in India in the 1930s and in a limited way during the Second World War, even after the army was mechanized. Alex Walker was a subaltern in a mountain battery on the north-west frontier and therefore a member, as he put it, of one of the last units to succumb to the 'rot' of mechanization. He has written of these final military duties of the Waler:

I think it probable that the last time that Walers came under enemy fire, while part of an Imperial force, was during the Waziristan operations of Nov. '40–Jan. '41. Operations, within sight of the Afghan border, were conducted by a brigade group with artillery and air support—the latter lost a plane due to a hillside-sitting tribesman shooting the pilot while he and his observer were carrying out low-flying reconnaissance. Part of the artillery support was provided by the mountain regiment (Kipling's 'screw-guns')

A moment full of symbolism: letting the cavalry overtake on the pass to Razmak during the Walers' last campaign

of which I was then Orderly Officer, namely, assistant adjutant, survey officer and general 'Dogsbody.'

Walers were used as officers' chargers and for key personnel among the signallers and surveyors, the rest being mounted on Indian-bred horses. Guns and immediate-use ammunition were pack-carried on Argentine mules—necessary because of the weight of the loads and the need to be able to negotiate obstacles while carrying them. Both mules and walers were 'acclimatised' at the remount depot before arriving at the unit.[37]

A photograph from this period shows dismounted Walers and pack animals carrying survey equipment and parts of screw guns, waiting at the side of a road through a mountain pass on the Afghan border as a column of tanks overtook them. In fact, the horses themselves are not revealed by the lens of the camera, only their shadows on the road. No more potent image could be imagined to represent the passing of the horse, and more specifically the Waler, from the military life of India.

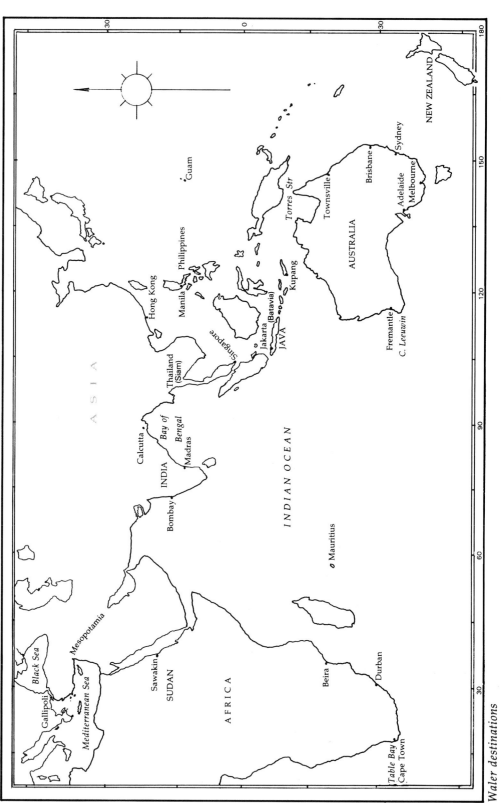

Waler destinations

9

Waler Exports

W ALERS WERE EXPORTED from every colony and state of Australia at one time or another. The trade lasted more than a hundred years in New South Wales, and only slightly less in Victoria and Queensland, while both Western Australia and Tasmania faded out rather more quickly. South Australia was a slow starter but became interested in the late nineteenth century in what proved to be abortive projects for Waler breeding in the Northern Territory. From 1900 onwards the huge sales conducted by Sidney Kidman at Kapunda contributed greatly to the trade by drawing horses from wide areas of central Australia and western Queensland and attracting the big Indian shippers.

In the chapters that follow, I aim to show how the trade varied from one colony (or state) to another, giving an idea of the characteristics of the major regions and of how they differed one from another. What is strikingly evident is the impression made on every aspect of the trade by forceful personalities, amongst them the astonishing Bishop Salvado of New Norcia in Western Australia. Another dominant character was J. S. Love, one of the hard men of Queensland, who superintended a pastoral empire in north and central Queensland from his suite in the Queens Hotel, Townsville, importing significant numbers of Thoroughbreds and exporting in the most lucrative years of the trade a large proportion of the Walers that left Queensland.

This regional study will begin with Western Australian horse exports. The attempt that was made between 1849 and 1852 to set up on the western pastures a horse breeding operation aimed at the Indian market has been mentioned earlier (see chapter 4). It will be remembered that even in the earliest days of the Swan River

Colony the colonists had looked hopefully at their proximity, albeit on the south-eastern extremity of the Indian Ocean, to the established horse markets of the three Indian presidencies. Plans had been laid in Madras for a horse breeding company based in Western Australia, financed with Indian capital and using imported Arab stallions and local mares to breed young stock that might supply the remount needs not only of Madras but also, in due course, Calcutta. Madras veterinary surgeon Thomas Hagger came to the colony in March 1851 and again in 1852 to select brood-mares, along the lines of the Bengal system, but found the stock too slight in bone and substance for the production of cavalry mounts. The extravagant hopes expressed by the Perth newspapers, of supplanting the breeders of the eastern colonies in the Indian market, were brought to a sudden and embarrassing end.[1]

One obvious factor in the failure of the Hagger plan was the inadequacy of the western colony's equine population, which stood in 1851 at only 2978 head, far too slight a base in numbers or quality to support a durable trade. With the stimulus given to the colony by its decision to accept British convicts in 1850, at the very time that Van Diemen's Land was preparing to dispense with them, the local need for horses made it the more difficult to procure some for export. Another problem was the emergence of a split between two rival colonial groups, both of them led by men who had strong Indian backgrounds and connections, W. L. Brockman and T. N. Yule. The former, a well-to-do pastoralist and horse breeder of Herne Hill and Gin-gin to the north of Perth, hoped to set up a breeding establishment on the Greenough River, 200 miles north of Fremantle, whereas Yule, himself a former Indian army officer, headed a group that wanted to locate south of Fremantle in the far more accessible Williams River district.[2]

Thomas Hagger was not completely disappointed—he sent off two cargoes to Madras in 1851 in the ships *Mermaid* and *Minden*, valued at nearly £2000. And the plan for a pastoral and horse breeding operation in the vicinity of Champion Bay in the north came to fruition in the leases taken up by S. P. Phillips and Edward Hamersley on the Irwin River in 1850, while Thomas Brown and his sons went to the Greenough River, where they set up a successful stud based on imported bloodstock, from which exports were drawn for thirty years.[3]

The flow of exports was slight until 1858, when the western breeders joined other Australian colonists in taking advantage of the opportunity created by the Indian Mutiny of 1857. Horse numbers in the west had increased by 1858 to 7214, at a rate faster than the Australian average, and two substantial cargoes were bought that year by missions acting for the presidencies of Madras and Bengal.[4]

Both of the 1858 cargoes were a result of purchases made in the west by remount officers. The Perth *Inquirer* of 10 March 1858 reported with some pride and perhaps, no small surprise, the successful completion by Mr Phillips of a contract with Lieutenant Oliver Probyn of the Bombay army to provide a minimum of 100 horses suitable for remount purposes within a space of three weeks. Only three districts required to be visited in order to secure 139 horses of fifteen hands and above, which were walked to Fremantle and slung into lighters that took them out to the *Caduceus*, a ship of 1106 tons lying in Gage's Roads. As was absolutely typical of the colony's approach to the trade, the transfer from beach to lighter was needlessly slowed up by the shortage of slings, and one fine animal was lost in the sea when the straps broke on his being hoisted on board. The second of these cargoes, of 132 horses, left on the

Albuera bound for Calcutta on 12 December, with an extraordinarily large complement of forty-one syces to look after them. On the way out the ship had brought a consignment of eleven Indian convicts to serve sentences of transportation in the west, following a tradition started in the mid-1840s of a voyage out to Van Diemen's Land with convicts and a return to Calcutta with a load of New South Wales horses.[5]

It seems that these cargoes must have been well received in India, because during the 1860s that country imported 2126 horses from Western Australia, making it the second largest supplier amongst the Australian colonies during that decade, following Victoria with 7292 but ahead of New South Wales with its 1081. One of the factors in this success was the eagerness of W. L. Brockman, who built on the connections with his brothers in the Indian army, and went to Madras in 1862 to negotiate an arrangement with the governor, Sir William Denison, to supply 200 to 300 horses a year to that presidency. Brockman's letter of 30 June 1862, published in the *Inquirer* after his return to Herne Hill expresses his disappointment at having netted only £20 a head from the sale of the horses, in spite of their being a 'very superior lot'.[6]

Brockman's result would have been welcomed by most Victorian shippers of the period, unless they were dealing in Thoroughbreds. Viewed in the light of a report in the *Perth Gazette* of 20 March 1863, it suggests that good money had been spent by the western breeders on foundation stock, for it describes the sale in Madras of ten horses from the stud of S. P. Phillips of the Williams River district at prices ranging from £50 to nearly £100. The report also makes the significant point that one of the Phillips horses taken to Madras by Brockman had already won seven races under the name of Van Diemen, contributing to the colony's equine reputation.

What is amazing about the success of the western breeders in the Indian horse trade of the 1860s is that it was won in the face of staggering disadvantages. Facilities for receiving ships and loading cargoes remained primitive, inefficient and quite dangerous at all the colony's 'ports' on the Indian Ocean until the artificial harbour was built at Fremantle at the end of the century. The bar at the entrance to the Swan River forced vessels to wait miles out to sea at Gage's Roads, discharging and receiving cargoes by lighter, often waiting for the swell to drop sufficiently to reduce the peril of a transfer to an acceptable level. This normal danger was greatly increased by the special risks of shipping young horses newly brought in wild from the bush.

An illustration of this is given by the Perth *Herald*'s account of the loading of the iron sailing ship *Astracan* of 1040 tons at Gage's Roads. It left for Calcutta on 24 October 1872 with a cargo of 147 horses from the studs of three breeders on the Victoria Plains, W. L. Brockman, Donald McPherson and James Clinch, horses described as 'without exception, handsome well bred animals' and 'as fine a shipment as has ever left this colony'. As was by now peculiar to the western horse trade, the breeders themselves acted as the shippers and young Aeneas McPherson sailed as supercargo, returning in March 1873 with a tale of 'highly satisfactory prices'. The report mentioned 'a few trifling accidents' in getting the horses down the jetty. 'One man was severely kicked, and Mr Harwood in leading a young and restive animal down the jetty had his finger badly crushed. It is wonderful that more casualties did not happen, as the present jetty is most inconvenient, not to say dangerous.'[7] No simple solution was evident to the *Inquirer* when it considered the problem on

19 March 1873. The proposal to build a jetty in Gage's Roads long enough to take large vessels alongside was simply impracticable, because of the risk of damage to hull and rigging caused by the ground swell in the Roads.

Further south at the minor port of Bunbury matters were in even worse case. The *Inquirer* of 23 January 1867 described the loading of the ship *Clutha* of 1060 tons with ninety-one horses, predictably 'as fine a shipment as ever left the colony'. The reporter hoped that the recent increase in the business of the port would cause the authorities to improve facilities, for as things then stood the only water for ships to use lay at a distance from the jetty, and the light was so dim it was not visible until the ship was within twelve miles of shore.

It was this unsatisfactory port of Bunbury that was resorted to by Henry Prinsep, the young scion of a distinguished Anglo-Indian family who had come to the colony in 1866 to manage the properties of Belvedere, Prinsep Park and Paradise for the East India Company. His diary for the years 1869 and 1870 conveys at almost every page a sense of the hazards to life and property experienced by horse breeders and shippers in the west. Consider the entry of 23 January 1869: 'We got to the shipyard about 1 o'clock & after haltering & lunging the horses, we led them down—after great plunging & scattering in fact every sort of struggle that horses can make they did make. Very tired & sleepy'. Again on 25 January: 'Luttah was nearly killed by a kick in the chest & a fall—by Brick colt 165—who also staked himself inside the near hind leg'.

Yet there were moments of exhilaration which helped to explain why men like Prinsep engaged in horse breeding at all, when more reliable returns were available from sheep and cattle. On 28 November in the midst of mustering the horses that ran wild in the bush at Prinsep Park he wrote, 'In all we had passed 165 of them & it was a grand sight to see the whole herd of them careering round the field—the start of the Derby was nothing to it'.

Prinsep was twenty-five years old on 5 September 1869, and his wife Josephine a week over twenty. On 17 March 1870 they embarked at Bunbury in the ship *Heimdahl* which Henry owned, bound for Calcutta with a cargo of his own produce, forty horses and a load of jarrah logs intended as sleepers for the Indian railways, a common combination for Western Australian exporters. His diary describes how they settled down in the captain's cabin with their new baby and saw the police come aboard to poke pitchforks into the hay to check that there were no escaped convicts. The voyage was slow and hot in the final stages in the Bay of Bengal and the pilot was taken aboard on 27 April. Prinsep declined the offer of a tow from a big steamer, thinking the fee of £80 severe and was unlucky enough on 30 April to see the pilot run the ship aground on the constantly shifting shoals of the Hooghly. After struggling ashore in the gig against a roaring ebb tide Prinsep and his little family were taken to Calcutta, a city where fortunately they had many friends, but the loss from the failure of the voyage effectively brought his career as a pastoralist to an end. Returning to the colony, Prinsep became a public servant and had the compensation of finding the leisure to contribute to its cultural and scientific life as an artist and a correspondent of the botanical collectors of Kew Gardens.[8]

Embarkation problems were the subject of a letter in the Perth *Herald* of 12 September 1874 by W. Padbury, who had sent eleven well-bred horses to Calcutta in the *Wimmera* on 6 November 1873. They had been taken by remount buyers at from £50 to £55, and had netted him £163 6s 10d, or less than £15 each. He could not fail to compare this result with the likely profit on a bullock of £10, for a much smaller risk. Few people seemed to realize that quite a tiny injury, especially to an eye, which would have been negligible in the case of a bullock or sheep, rendered a horse worthless.

Padbury went on to doubt the common western claim that the colony could ship horses more cheaply than Melbourne, which had become the principal exporter. In Melbourne the ship lay at the pier and was able, even before the adoption of the walk-on ramp system in the 1880s, to load horses by crane twice as fast as the lighters could operate in Fremantle. All too often the wind would get up just when the horses were ready to load, so that the boats could not lie alongside either jetty or ship. All hands might have to remain with the horses for a week waiting for the weather to improve. With the increasing use of steamers in the trade in the 1880s and the need for economies of scale to bring freight rates down to an acceptable level, the major shipping companies and exporters saw the uncertainties associated with the Western Australian 'ports' as intolerable.

Important as were the Brockmans, McPhersons, Clinches and Browns in establishing the trade which often occupied the second position to wool in the export statistics of Western Australia, none of them could compare with Rosendo Salvado, Bishop of Port Victoria. Dom William's article in the *Australian Dictionary of Biography* is of course a first step towards an acquaintance with this dedicated Benedictine missionary and horse trader.

Salvado was born into a wealthy Spanish family in 1814 and discovered a talent for music that would have won an international reputation had he not chosen the life of a Benedictine monk. Even after taking his vows in 1830 he distinguished himself as an organist, pianist and composer; these gifts came to his aid in 1846 when, soon after making a start on the Aboriginal mission at New Norcia on the Victoria Plains with his associate Serra, he walked into Perth to give a piano recital and so earn the money to provide for food.

Through the formative years of the mission, which took the gospel to the Murara-Murara people of Victoria Plains, Salvado lived 'by the sweat of his brow', dressed in dungarees, driving bullock carts, felling trees, ploughing, sowing and planting, as Dom William puts it, 'to turn the desert into a land rich in corn, wine and honey'. Salvado used the opportunities of agriculture and stock raising to win the tribes-people from their nomadic ways and in due course made use of their great natural skills as horse handlers.

I do not know when Salvado decided to embark on the remount trade but his horse stock was described by the Perth *Herald* on 17 June 1871 as perhaps the best in the colony. That comment was excited by the news of the arrival at the mission stud of a beautiful grey Arab stallion named York, of 14 hands 3½ inches, sent by steamer from Calcutta to Albany, and insured for Rs 2600, or about £216. By the following October, Salvado was participating in a small way in the export trade with his neighbour Donald McPherson, but the first substantial cargo he sent to India was a load of forty-six horses taken by the *Ellora* to Calcutta, leaving Fremantle on 7 January 1877, and arriving on about 21 February. This was so late in the season that Salvado was perhaps fortunate to escape from the venture without a loss; twenty-eight were taken by remounts at an average price of Rs 500, and the remaining fifteen survivors from the voyage sold at auction eventually at an average of Rs 193. Gillanders Arbuthnot, the Calcutta agents, paid the freight and other charges and remitted the balance of Rs 6556 to the bishop. This amounted to an average of just over Rs 142 on the forty-six horses embarked, a far from handsome return on the costs and labour involved.

Salvado's agents made the most earnest attempt to advise the bishop as to the best means of avoiding such disappointments in future. Their first report, of 28 February 1877, drew attention to a feature that seemed almost inseparable from the western horses, bred as they were on huge unfenced runs and rarely sighted, let alone handled, till they were mustered for sale. The animals were thought by the agent to be 'excessively wild and unmanageable', and two broke away soon after landing, one injuring itself so badly as to have to be destroyed. They had landed in miserably poor condition, having been shipped with less than half the food required for a voyage of forty-five days, and had been kept alive only by the generosity of Melbourne shippers travelling also on the *Ellora*.[9]

Captain W. A. Roberts, the remount agent, made a detailed report about the forty-three New Norcia horses which brings out the essential amateurism, or rather inexperience, of the Salvado operation. Many of the horses were too old either for the remount or private markets, for eight were absolutely rejected as being over six years, while fifteen were at a discount because fully six years old. Secondly, they were leggy, with the length in the wrong place, below the knee, and they had rather weak necks and short shoulders, though with the redeeming feature of wiriness and appeared well bred. Roberts described his ideal troop horse as being: 'from 14.2½ to 15.0½ hands high; on short, straight legs, with large joints and good bone; long sloping shoulders, strong neck, and, above all, with good action—a point in which the W. Australian horses are deficient'.

Roberts found it remarkable that the Melbourne horses, though suffering the worst passage—around Cape Leeuwin—had arrived in 'splendid condition', far healthier than the mission horses. This was chiefly due to the adequate provision of food, water and grooming, though it may have been contributed to by their having taken the best places in the ship. Far better in future to combine with other western breeders to make up a cargo of about 200 horses and charter a ship to start at Fremantle. He advised also the purchase of some new blood, especially mares, for the legginess of which he complained was taken as a sign that the mares were deteriorating. 'All the Western Australian horses', he added, 'present very much the same defects', which were especially evident in the McPherson and New Norcia Mission horses.

One further effort was made by Salvado to 'crack' the remount trade, with a consignment of thirty-five horses collected rapidly from the bush and sent down to Fremantle to make up a batch of Victoria Plains horses for consignment by the *Cingalese*, a ship of 689 tons which had brought a partial cargo of horses from Melbourne. Salvado attempted to ensure that his local agent, Habgood, Absolon & Co., loaded ample food and water but was disturbed to find that the provisioning assumed arrival at Calcutta in thirty-five days. In fact they nearly achieved this and Gillanders Arbuthnot wrote on 25 February 1879 to report that the mission horses had arrived in 'very fair condition'. In spite of the anticipated lift in the military demand for remounts on account of the projected invasion of Afghanistan, only

Aboriginal grooms with New Norcia horses

sixteen of Salvado's horses were taken by remount buyers, at an average of Rs 479, and the rejects sold at auction at an average of Rs 213.[10]

When he did his sums at New Norcia on receiving the accounts from Calcutta and Fremantle, Salvado found that the Indian profit of Rs 4141 converted to £333, from which had to be deducted the local costs, principally loading the horses and providing fodder, which came to £174. So there remained a profit of £159, which took no account of the costs involved in bringing thirty-five horses to the point of saleability. Spread over thirty-four horses (it should have been thirty-five) it came to £4 13s 6d per horse, on which he commented 'I consider this is a very poor business. I am coming to the conclusion that our horses are not fit for the . . .'. But he did not finish the sentence. It may have been a consolation to work out at the same time that James Clinch had made only £4 15s 6d from his twenty-five horses.

The report from Gillanders Arbuthnot of 25 February 1879 included a further and vastly enlightening comment from the remount officer, 'The horses I have take from Bishop Salvado are a fairly good lot, but the horses from Western Australia generally are very unsound—such a number of cases of side bones and ring bones'.

This comment may take us towards the heart of the failure of the western breeders to maintain, let alone develop, their share of the Indian remount market. Statistics adapted from Malcolm Kennedy's doctoral thesis which appear in Appendix 3 show the Western Australian share of the Indian horse trade falling away steeply after the 1860s until in the 1890s it had virtually disappeared. While that was happening the *direct* New South Wales share in the trade was steadily increasing (a great number of horses bred north of the Murray River had been exported from the closer and better organized Port Melbourne and so recorded in the Victorian statistics); at the same time the Victorian share remained dominant and the Queensland export, though starting modestly and experiencing massive reverses, became after 1901 and remained the major element in the trade (see Appendix 4).

The prospects of the western horse export trade with India were frustrated not only by deficiencies in port facilities and management skills, such as the absence of a body of professional shippers who could build up a corpus of knowledge and a team of grooms who could learn gradually how to convey spirited and sensitive animals across the ocean from pasture to remount yard. Less obviously, but even more decisively, their chances of success in the trade were undermined by the effects of trace element deficiencies that remained unsuspected until the use of soil analysis techniques in the late 1930s.

W. J. de Burgh writes in *The Old North Road* of the problems experienced in the scrub-covered plains of the north, including the country occupied by New Norcia and the McPhersons and Clinches, as a result of cobalt deficiency. This, however, was not so important with horses as with ruminant animals. Far more decisive was the copper deficiency of the coastal country to the south of Bunbury, where many of the horse studs, including that of Henry Prinsep, were situated. Little has been written about the importance of this deficiency in relation to horses, but Professor Marsh Edwards of the University of Sydney writes:

> Copper deficiency was not a common subject of research or extension papers on horses. However, when I was in Bunbury (between 1954 and 1962) I saw quite a number of young horses with what I believed was copper deficiency. I checked my suspicions with Dr. Bennetts and he agreed that I was probably correct. In young growing horses the deficiency mainly affected bones and general growth. Affected foals were growing poorly. They were usually owned by a person with one or two mares which were running on unimproved pasture which was, rarely, if ever top-dressed. The affected bones were usually the shins of the forelegs (cannon bones or metacarpals) which had quite obvious even, bony, painless enlargements near the joints and especially the fetlocks. In severe cases the hindlimbs were similarly involved.[11]

Professor Edwards added that farmers in the affected region 'on the Stirling' developed the habit of shifting their stock to 'sound' country in the hills to the eastward for part of the year to minimize the effect of the deficiencies, but later stud owners used copper supplements with complete success.

It seems very probable that this pasture deficiency may have had a lot to do with the degeneration noticed by the Calcutta remount people in the late 1870s. This health problem was decisive at the Indian end. At the same time inadequate loading facilities kept the experienced, professional shippers out of the western horse trade and excluded the steamers once they began to carry the bulk of the horses after 1882. The result was that the western breeders, if they wished to remain in the export business, resorted to the smaller scale and less discriminating markets of Mauritius and Southeast Asia, as illustrated by the table which is printed in Appendix 3.

Bishop Salvado's diaries show that after the disappointment with the *Cingalese* cargo to Calcutta in 1878, he exported chiefly to Mauritius and Singapore, as did his colleagues of the Victoria Plains and the Stirling, until at least the early 1890s. Many of the ships combined timber and horses in their cargoes, taking jarrah to India for railway construction and sandalwood to Southeast Asia and East Asia, where it was prized for its aromatic qualities.

Writing of *Old Toodyay and Newcastle* in 1974, Rica Erickson described the form taken by the annual muster of bush horses in the Bolgart Springs district, which like its counterparts in the colony was unblessed by fences. Twenty people had an interest in the mobs there and in preparing for the muster the stockyards around the springs were repaired and wings of brushwood fence built to catch the wary wild horses when they were rounded up by teams of horsemen. One of the techniques was to close the gates and keep the horses away from the only remaining spring of pure water, while kerosene was poured on the other pools so as to drive the thirsty horses eventually to the reopened gate of the stockyard. One can imagine how this procedure prepared the horses for the experiences of being loaded, shipped and sold; the comments of Indian regimental officers show that they well knew why the first six months or so of a Waler's life required so much gentle nurturing to remove the layers of accumulated terror.

One of the reasons for the Waler's timidity, it was suggested in a letter from the government of India, was what many commanding officers saw as the unnecessary size and depth of the brand mark used by the Australian colonies. Concerned not only with timidity but also with the unsightliness of the large brands on the back and the point of the shoulder, the Indian Adjutant-General suggested that preference might be given to horses with light brands, under the mane, for example. Malcolm Kennedy gives the example of the Queensland Brands Act which required a brand of two letters and one figure (to cope with the widespread problem of rustling) each of which was one and a half inches square.[12]

Even in the less discriminating Singapore market there was dissatisfaction with the presentation of the colony's horses. An article in the *Western Australian Times* of 14 March 1879, discussing the complaints about the unprofitability of the trade, quoted the criticisms published in a Singapore newspaper:

> The appearance of some of the animals when landed from the ship is wretched. Some are so badly cut and knocked about that it takes months of nursing to bring them into anything like working condition. Much of this is due to the ships used for carrying horses from Western Australia to the Straits, being badly provided. Horses are huddled together on deck, exposed night and day to the inclemencies of the weather.

Henry Taunton told the story of a speculative journey he took to Java in about 1886 with a cargo of eighty horses that had been brought in wild from the Victoria Plains. There was trouble from the start and the departure from Fremantle was delayed by a north-westerly gale, a common winter experience. Helping Taunton were only four grooms, all new to the game, and for thirteen days there were hopes for a quick and prosperous venture. He describes the curious spectacle the horses presented as he looked along the lower hold from one end,

> and as the vessel rolled to starboard some forty horses' heads appeared outside the stalls; and as she rolled back to port, all these would disappear and forty other heads would emerge on the opposite side . . . It was a strange sight, and reminded me of an

incessant 'knight's move', or of the old fashioned weather indicators where Jack comes out as Jill goes in.[13]

On the thirteenth day out of Fremantle, after an easy passage, they sighted the mountains of Java and there the breeze failed utterly, leaving the horses suffering in intense heat, with water running short, and, in the absence of ventilation, built-up ammonia fumes. For fourteen days the dead calm lasted and the ship drifted with the tide up and down Wynkoop's Bay, while twenty of the best horses died, to be hoisted overboard and fed to the sharks that circled the ship night and day. Thirty of the remaining horses were eventually landed and sold at Batavia, in a depressed market, and Taunton sailed on to Singapore, where the horses were landed in bad condition and sold in another overstocked market.

Taunton does not mention prices but a report in the *Inquirer* of 3 September 1879 gives an average of Singapore $90 (or about £24) as having been realized by two cargoes of Western Australian horses sold at the Singapore Horse Market. In those days, as the *Western Australian Times* leader writer had complained, the idea seemed to prevail in the colony that 'anything in the shape of horse flesh is good enough for Singapore'. Yet the trade to these Southeast Asian markets and to Mauritius, combined as it was with sandalwood exports, offered the colony an important source of foreign exchange, and sales of any kind, at a time when the domestic economy was so sluggish, were welcome. Records in 'Arrivals and Departures' show Mauritius, Batavia and Singapore as the main destinations, with Guam becoming important after 1885. From 1887, horse departures were rare, though sandalwood continued.

Horse exports from the colony declined rapidly in the 1890s, falling to a total of 916 for the decade. The change that occurred after 1887 was a consequence chiefly of an elevated domestic demand responding to the discovery of gold nuggets in the Kimberley region; by the end of 1886 an estimated 2000 diggers were on the fields and with the strike at Coolgardie in 1892 horses were virtually unavailable for export. This condition of affairs continued for more than a decade, during which time many of the pastures on which horses had been bred were fenced as the big estates were cut up for closer settlement. It is ironical that the establishment of the artificial harbour at Fremantle, which removed the main practical obstacle that had frustrated horse exports for fifty years, came too late to be of service in this trade. In 1902 the Prime Minister sent circulars to the state governments, asking about the capacity of their graziers to breed horses of remount quality. The Western Australian Stock Inspector's reply made it clear that the colony's resources had been exhausted by the demands of the southern African contingent, for, as he put it, 'all the principal breeding stations have been broken up'.[14]

Queensland became an independent colony when the Moreton Bay settlement was separated from New South Wales on 10 December 1859. Three days later the *Sydney Morning Herald* carried one of its first news items about the new colony by reporting the total loss of the ship *Sapphire* of 749 tons on a reef near Raine Island at one of the entrances to Torres Strait. It was bound for Madras with a cargo of horses, the property of Captain Maurice O'Connell, which had been loaded with much éclat and more difficulty at the primitive new harbour at Port Curtis, where O'Connell combined official duties with grazing. Though the horses had come aboard in early September and had been wrecked on the twenty-third, this can be seen as the first of the Queensland horse cargoes. Of course there had been a few other horse cargoes from Moreton Bay, going back to the days of George Leslie at Canning Downs in the late 1840s.

The *Sydney Morning Herald* report on the *Sapphire* wreck was one of the most poignant relating to the long history of the horse trade. News of the disaster was brought back to civilization by lifeboats belonging to another Liverpool-owned ship, the *Marina*, which had been wrecked a fortnight later within sight of the *Sapphire*. On Sir Charles Hardy Island the surviving crew of the Marina had found a bottle tied to a tree containing some letters; one from a young seaman dated 4 October 1859 makes a raw appeal to Victorian sentimentality:

Dear Mother,
I write these lines, perhaps the last I shall ever write. We are about leaving. We have been wrecked in Torres' Straits, and are now proceeding along the coast towards Port Curtis, in an open boat, with starvation staring us in the face. The poor Sapphire has gone to Davy Jones. If I never see you again, you can say your son died like a true Briton. Tell Mary Ann Ordish that I love her to the last. Love to all sisters and grandmother, aunt, and every one. Farewell. Dear Mother, pray for me.
Your loving son, Tom C. Clark

The venture had gone badly from the start; a correspondent of the *Moreton Bay Courier* of 26 October 1859 described how O'Connell had loaded his young horses on the *Sapphire* at what was euphemistically called Port Curtis. The mob of unbroken horses was brought to the waterside on a long rope, and one by one they were attached to a sling at the end of another rope that passed over a pulley on the ship and then back to the shore. A team of bullocks provided the motive power that dragged each horse through the mud, on into the water and then up to the hold of the ship. As the correspondent remarked, it was rude and primitive treatment for young horses; far better, he thought, to have driven them 100 miles north to be loaded at the superior port of Rockhampton.

It was an unpromising beginning to the new colony's trade. For the horses especially much worse was to follow. On 23 September when the ship was making for the Raine Island Passage through Torres Strait breakers were seen unexpectedly at 7.30 p.m. and it went broadside on to a reef with such violence that there was no chance of getting off. Leaving the ship and its live cargo to perish, the crew of twenty-nine made off in two boats. After some days at Sir Charles Hardy Island, where messages were left in the bottle, they tried to beat against the prevailing south-east trade winds to return to Port Curtis. Failing in this, they turned north and in the vicinity of Friday Island the lifeboat was attacked by Torres Strait Islanders who killed Captain Bowden and all but one of the men. The survivor was picked up by the pinnace, which had been attacked in a separate incident but escaped by the effective use of firearms.

Returning to the wreck to reprovision the pinnace, the crew of eleven found a goat still alive after eight thirsty weeks amongst the putrefying horses. Just as astonishing, on the same reef they found and boarded the wrecked *Marina*, with which they had lain at anchor in both Liverpool and Sydney. A brave but sensible decision was made to patch up this less wounded ship and try for Port Curtis, as the *Empire* newspaper put it, 'in a ship with her bottom out, water-logged, and so scantily provisioned that they finally had to put themselves on half a biscuit a day'.

On 19 February 1860 the *Marina* reached its destination and earned for Tom Clark and his lucky shipmates a share in salvage money of £600. Robert Towns bought the ship, had repairs done and despatched it for Sydney in company with an escorting schooner but its seams opened off Moreton Island and it sank.

One of the effects of the disaster was to lead Governor Sir George Bowen to press for the establishment of a station on Cape York or nearby to offer aid and protection to mariners who used the Straits. Another was to confirm insurance companies in the policy of charging additional premiums on vessels using that route and continuing to do so long after the statistical evidence showed it to be no more dangerous, with the adoption of a system of pilots and beacons, than the journey by Cape Leeuwin.[15]

The *Courier's* description of the primitiveness of the facilities for loading Captain O'Connell's horses on the *Sapphire* in 1859 makes a useful introduction to a discussion of horse exports from Queensland. A coastline of over a thousand miles from Moreton Bay to Cooktown offered a dozen inconvenient ports to serve the needs of what remained for decades a huge sheep and cattle run, with sugar plantations occupying the coastal fringe. Without exception those ports required large expenditure to make them adequate for the special demands of the horse trade, whether by the dredging of a river port like Brisbane to a sufficient depth or the construction of an artificial harbour as at Townsville. Until the end of the nineteenth century there simply had not been sufficient public money available to pay for such work and the competition amongst the contending ports ensured that no single harbour reached a satisfactory standard.[16]

Melbourne's pre-eminence in the horse trade from the 1880s had been made possible by the combination of an efficient railway system drawing custom to the capital and deep water wharves at which ships could receive horses direct from the railway trucks. Queensland, of course, was a complete contrast, and with the application to the trade from the mid-1880s of steamships of 1500 to 2500 tons, her ports were effectively excluded until after 1892, when the man-made harbour at Townsville was ready for big ships. At the end of the century the dredging of the Brisbane River to a depth of 20 feet (or 6.1 metres) enabled it also to contribute to Queensland's coming dominance of the remount trade. One effect of deficient local facilities had been that Indian shippers commonly bought horses at the great Darling Downs horse market of Toowoomba but exported them from Melbourne, as Henry Vanrenen did as late as 1904. By then, however, Pinkenba on the Brisbane River had become the chief southern outlet for Queensland horses.[17]

Queensland may have been effectively excluded from the mainstream of the remount trade during the first decade or so in which the big steamers were employed as carriers. But as her port facilities became more adequate, Queensland developed an ever increasing advantage over the other Australian states. From the 1890s the trade with India had been large and constant and there was a rapid enhancement in the military and civilian demand for horses in the countries of Asia, Southeast Asia and the Indian Ocean. War and the threat of war in China, Korea and southern Africa, together with military preparations by the Dutch in Indonesia and the United

States in the Philippines ensured that the supply of remounts became a large and profitable industry, with the prizes going to those suppliers who enjoyed the economies of scale.

Although the breeders of Victoria and New South Wales continued in the business, they were gradually disqualified by the trend to closer settlement and the appreciating values of their pastures. As war broke out in the Transvaal, in China and Korea, and at length in the Middle East, the military market for artillery, cavalry and mounted infantry horses became huge. The campaigns in southern Africa became notorious for the terrible wastage of horseflesh and contributed perhaps to a decline in the standards aimed at by remount buyers. Under these pressures the cheap and extensive pastures of Queensland became the principal suppliers to what had become a mass market and the typical unit of production was not the immaculate, freehold grazing property of the Hunter Valley or the Western District but the 550 square miles, say, of Grosvenor Downs near Mackay or the even larger leaseholds held in western Queensland by Sidney Kidman. So it was that Queensland, which had been ranked second last amongst the Australian colonies in horse exports during the decade from 1881–90, with a total export of 301, had become the clear market leader in the decade 1901–10, with a total of 59 187, compared to Victoria's 44 434.[18]

At the end of that decade the Chief Inspector of Stock in Queensland, P. R. Gordon, formerly a Victorian horse breeder, wrote an article for the *Queenslander* of 27 May 1911 that summed up the claims of the state as a supplier of military horses for the Imperial Army. One of the keys to economical horse raising in the state was that the climate permitted stock to remain in open pasture all the year round, dispensing with the need for cultivation and artificial feeding. He went on:

> The heavy seeding native grasses are also conducive to the development of bone and muscle. Horse diseases may be said to be unknown in Australia. Many grasses are peculiarly adapted for horse pasture. The extensive sub cretaceous formations, all artesian water bearing, which form such a large area of the Queensland pastures are impregnated with salt, lime, and other chemical constituents that go to form bone and muscle development in horse stock . . . The free, untrammelled life and the large areas over which they graze also tend to muscle development, hardiness, and endurance in Queensland horse stock.

But the special thrust of Gordon's article came from his appreciation of the Queensland breeder's advantage in economy of operation over competitors in other states. A grazing run of about 100 000 acres suitable for horse breeding, in a district free from the prospect of closer settlement, could be very cheaply secured. Freehold tenure would cost less than 10 shillings (near enough to a labourer's daily wage) per acre, or on an extended lease about £2 a square mile. The improvements needed would be the subdivision of the run into eight or ten paddocks, the sinking of a few wells, erection of a manager's cottage, huts for employees and yards for stock.

Gordon's article expressed nicely the shape of things in the Queensland horse trade. In Appendix 4 is a table that looks at the market leaders in the Indian horse trade from 1891 to 1930. It reveals two striking features of the state's performance, its numerical dominance of the Indian trade in the twentieth century and the comparative cheapness of the Queensland horse before shipment. The prices paid by the

Indian shippers at the great horse sales conducted at Toowoomba, Longreach and Bowen were for twenty years less than half those ruling in other states (that is, about £10 a head compared with £20 to £25), giving them a much higher profit margin when they came to sell in India, especially to the remount buyers, who operated on a fixed average maximum price, ranging from £45 to £55 during this period.

In Queensland, as in other parts of Australia, leadership in the production of horses for export came from a few outstanding men who gave to the breeding of horses skills, attitudes and sentiments developed over generations. That was true of Thomas Lodge Murray-Prior, who arrived in Moreton Bay with the explorer Leichhardt in 1843 and became a pioneer pastoralist in the Logan and Burnett districts, eventually settling at Maroon Station near Fassifern. His son, also Thomas, established a reputation as a breeder of Shorthorn cattle and Arab horses. After a tour of India in which he canvassed the prospects for Queensland horses in the remount trade, he brought together a number of breeders during the Brisbane Exhibition week of 1892, seeking to interest them in regular participation in the trade. His concern as a horse lover and public man was to improve the breed of colonial horses, which he considered to have deteriorated as a result of the growing dominance of sprint events at race meetings, designed to maximize the opportunities for gambling. Thoroughbreds were sought for speed rather than stamina, making for the production of fast, weedy horses in place of the stayer whose qualities had been bred into the Waler. Similar complaints had been made by Edward Curr as long ago as 1863 and Murray-Prior's warning in the *Pastoralists' Review* was echoed in New South Wales by Richard Rouse of Guntawang in a lecture to the United Service Institution in July 1895.[19]

Another leader in the colony's search for equine excellence was De Burgh Fitzpatrick Persse, born in 1840 to a Protestant landowning family in County Galway, steeped in literature and with abiding interests in hunting and farming. Tabragalba near Beaudesert became his home, where he bred cattle and horses that stocked his stations in the Burnett district, including Hawkwood. From here came the horses that he sent to India, forty-six of them in 1902 at a price of £15 15s apiece, and forty-five in 1903 at the same price. As he told the Select Committee on the Improvement of Horse Stock in August 1903, he put a Thoroughbred stallion to Norfolk Trotter mares. The foals were handled from the time they were taken from their mothers and each succeeding year until they were sold as four- or five-year-olds, so that they were much quieter than most of their compatriots, which were bought for not much more than half the price.[20]

At the same select committee, which was appointed largely because of the criticism of the Queensland horses sent as remounts to southern Africa, Patrick Gordon, on the basis of thirty-five years as chief inspector of stock, commented on opinions expressed on the suitability of Australasian horses for British army purposes. After extensive inquiries, Lord Downe had classed them in the following order, New Zealand horses first, Victorian second, South Australian third and Queensland last. Asked if he thought this an injustice to the colony's horses, Gordon replied, 'Certainly ours are the worst class of horses in Australia', though in explaining the poor quality of the horses sent to Africa, he emphasized the haste with which the consignments had been put together. Many came from the coastal regions where lime was often deficient, resulting in poor bone development, and were rejects left behind by the Indian buyers.[21]

Witnesses heard by the committee were unanimous as to the deterioration of the colony's horses and attributed it to the use of inferior stallions, especially in the more settled areas, the poverty of the mares, which some saw as resulting from the number exported, and the influence of horse racing in the emergence of weedy Thorough-breds. But the prime cause, the committee decided, was the facility with which horses could be bred by anyone who had a mind to do so.

> The fact that horses can be left to their own resources and brought up on the natural grasses of the country at little or no expense creates, in the mind of the owner, a condition of irresponsibility and indifference frequently fatal to the exercise of that discrimination in the selection of sire and dam which a breeder would inevitably employ if it cost more to produce horse stock.

Remarkably, the classification given by Lord Downe is confirmed by the figures worked out by Malcolm Kennedy for the trade with India from 1861 to 1931. Victoria had the clear lead over the other colonies both in total numbers (152 742 for the 70 years) and in average prime costs (£21 11s 10d). Queensland was a strong second with a total for the 70 years of 121 519, but came last in terms of prime costs, with an average of £14 6s 10d. (See Appendix 5.)

From the beginning of the twentieth century, Toowoomba on the Darling Downs became the chief horse market of the Commonwealth, attracting buyers from four states who bid for horses drawn from the rich local pastures and from as far away as Roma and Charleville. The local stock firms conducting the sales were Doneley and Rogers, T. G. Robinson and Company, and Neil McPhie and Company, the last mentioned becoming the most important in the final years of the Indian trade.

Toowoomba's lead owed much to its natural advantages as a market town for a rich agricultural region but its access by rail to the newly deepened port of Pinkenba on the Brisbane river was crucial. A report in the *Queenslander* of 5 November 1904 described the loading of 412 horses on the British India steamer *Islanda*, 296 owned by R. J. Hunter, who had been one of the first to ship Queensland horses to India, 96 by R. O. Tullock and 20 by Tom Naples. It was not a fast journey, as the route to Bombay took in further stops at Newcastle, Melbourne and Adelaide to take on more horses, including possibly a further 100 for Naples, who shared with Bob Gove, the South Australian shipper, in a cargo of 124 horses intended for Bombay in the *Fultala*. Prices of from £15 to £20 were reported, probably reflecting the competition from Japanese buyers stocking up for the war against Russia and from Americans buying for their army in the Philippines. Though the Pinkenba facilities were praised, the shippers were angered by the hefty charges for wharfage and harbour dues. They had the further inconvenience of needing to spray or dip the horses, at the insistence of the Indian government, to prevent the introduction of Queensland ticks.[22]

Thomas C. Naples, formerly a farmer and shire councillor of Creswick in Victoria, had begun his career as a shipper taking remounts and private horses to Java in about 1893. By 1904, probably earlier, he had graduated to the Indian trade and was able to write from Buculla to his sister Marion that he had been the most successful of the

Bombay shippers for the season and expected to receive the largest commission for the following year. He had recovered from an acute attack of renal colic with the help of morphia injections but was left feeling weak and terribly homesick. The mood was heightened by hearing someone in the adjoining bungalow playing familiar airs on a piano, taking him back to 'bygone days'. His marriage had failed not long before, perhaps a casualty of his frequent absences from home, and he sighed, 'Oh for the days that are past & gone'. The life of a married horse shipper was subject to much pressure; one of those who survived was Steve Margrett, whose solution was to take his wife on most of his trips to Calcutta.[23]

Improvements in Queensland's port facilities, coinciding with a vastly increased military demand for horses in southern Africa and East Asia after 1899, imparted to the trade a new significance in the eyes of the colonial government. When the trade was beginning to pick up, some reversal occurred owing to the effect on the colony's horse population of the protracted Australia-wide drought of 1899–1900. It pulled the numbers down from a maximum of 480 469 in 1898 to 456 788 on 1 January 1900 and exposed the survivors to a number of lean seasons that greatly affected the quality of young stock. Nevertheless, the export figures for 1900 and 1901 showed a trend that horse breeders and governments could not fail to notice, with a doubling of volume under the influence of the Boer War demand, from 6686 to 13 659.[24]

For the prospects held out by these export figures to be fully realized, it seemed essential to the Queenslanders involved in the trade that the state's reputation for horseflesh should be rescued from the damage caused by poor showing of its consignments to southern Africa. The select committee of 1903 headed by Joshua Bell was a first step towards that goal: it recommended a reform that was soon to be introduced in Victoria, a tax on stallions and registration of approved sires to drive the unsound ones out of service. The proceeds were to be spent on buying state-owned stallions that would stand for low fees. But the bill incorporating the idea was lost on the second reading in August 1905. One positive move was the appointment of Frederick Jones as the Trade Commissioner for Queensland in the Far East: in one early report of February 1904 he drew attention to the progress made in that arena by New South Wales exporters as a result of the promotional work of J. B. Suttor. On the evidence of Queensland's share in the Japanese demand for horses in 1904–05, and in the Philippines' importations in 1907–09, he justified his appointment. By 1910, when a thousand Queensland horses had been sent to the Philippines, the United States Adjutant-General was able to give a favourable report on their performance, in spite of initial doubts.[25]

Another governmental initiative from which the horse trade benefited was the conclusion of a new agreement with the British India Steam Navigation Company which gave Queensland ports, from the beginning of 1911, a four-weekly inwards and outwards service via Torres Strait, India and Suez, with the United Kingdom.[26] But the great breakthrough, lusted after by horse breeders throughout Australia and pursued energetically by federal and state governments, including Queensland, was not to be achieved. They all remembered as a golden age the two occasions when the Indian government had sent buying missions to Australia comprising remount officers and veterinary surgeons, (that is, in the mid-1840s and at the time of the Mutiny). The hope that the depots set up by these missions would be made permanent, imparting stability and security to the trade and increasing the breeders' share of the profits by virtually eliminating the middleman, was not fulfilled. Replying to the breeders' claim that the deterioration in the quality of Australian horses had been a result of their uncertainties as to the Indian demand, a Horse and Mule Breeding Commission set up by the Indian government in 1900 pointed to the ever increasing purchases of Australian remounts.

Proposals for depots and buying missions were rejected on the following grounds:

1 The experiment had been tried and proved a failure.
2 Exceptional skill would be needed on the part of the buyers, and there was danger of an adverse ring being formed amongst breeders.
3 Heavy expenses in buying land and erecting depots.
4 The difficulty of selecting sound horses on the strength of a purely visual examination, and the likelihood of government buyers being 'stuck' with their mistakes.
5 Complaints of interference with a trade.
6 Money would be better spent in fostering horse breeding in India.

An essential argument was left to the last:

The only reason which can be alleged in favour of the proposal seems to be that the middleman would be got rid of, but as he takes all the risk up to the moment of purchase in India, his elimination would be of doubtful value . . . enough has been said to demonstrate the impracticability of the scheme, which the Commission have no hesitation in advising the Government of India to reject.

In the covering despatch that accompanied this report to the India Office, the powerful point was made that even if three purchasing officers were appointed, they

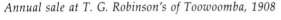

Annual sale at T. G. Robinson's of Toowoomba, 1908

would find it hard to manage efficiently in so extensive a country as Australia, 'so our power of quickly purchasing a large number of horses, in times of emergency, would be more restricted than at present, since in the shippers whom we now employ we have a number of skilled buyers each of whom is prepared to undertake purchases for us at the shortest notice'.[27]

It may be noted, in confirming the Indian government's self-interested wisdom, that the B.I. steamship *Satara* foundered on Seal Rocks in April 1910 after loading at Newcastle, on the way to take on more horses at Gladstone. Long memories would have been aware of the loss of the *Hydrabad* in 1845 with a cargo of remounts newly bought by an Indian mission and of the *Chesterholme* in 1859 with Tasmanian horses bought by the Robbins mission.[28]

A horse cargo that did not go down in Torres Strait was one that left Gladstone in 1903 with a batch of remounts bred on Grosvenor Downs, one of which was to become the most famous Waler of the Edwardian period. This was Rupert, a black gelding of 15 hands 3½ inches, foaled in about 1897 on a station of 550 square miles which had carried 18 000 head of cattle and 500 breeding mares before the big drought. Situated seventy-five miles north-east of Clermont, inland from Mackay, in well-timbered country famous for the variety of its grasses—including blue grass— Grosvenor Downs was fairly typical of the stations that went in for the remount trade as a major sideline at the turn of the century, with such noted sires, later on, as Nonette, My Man and Sir Volette. Alexander Bonar McDonald bought the property

Jack Sign with Myrtle, Grosvenor Downs, c. 1924

from William Forlong in 1872, and it was he who bred Rupert, though he sold the station in 1909 and it passed in 1910 into the hands of J. H. Clark, who gave it to his daughter, Mrs C. P. Gordon.

Rupert became the mount of Arthur Octavian Boyd, a Royal Horse Artillery sub-altern stationed in Bangalore when the city was visited by the Prince of Wales at the time of the 1906 Durbar. The Prince, one of the keenest sportsmen of his generation, confided to his diary for 7 February 1906, 'After breakfast, I tried a horse belonging to Lt. Boyd . . . he is a Whaler [*sic*] & good looking, beautifully broken, 9 years old, black & 15.3 hands. I think I shall buy him for £250 for a charger'.

Boyd, who was returning to England to be married, accompanied the horse on the voyage to Southampton. Rupert remained for many years a favourite mount and lived in the Royal Mews, whence the Prince regularly took him to Hyde Park for early morning exercise. When King Edward VII died in May 1910 it was Rupert that carried the new King George V in the funeral procession to Westminster Hall. A photograph of the King riding beside the German Kaiser Wilhelm was published with remarkable despatch in the *Queenslander* of 2 July 1910, with the brand of Grosvenor Downs, 2GD/20, distinctly visible on the near shoulder of the handsome black gelding. 'Jessie,' we can hear little Alexander McDonald saying to his sister, 'the King is riding one of father's horses'.

Rupert continued as the King's mount for at least six more years, and the famous and all too visible brand was recognized by two McDonald nephews when they were in camp on Salisbury Plain in 1916 and the King rode Rupert in a review of the Australian troops commanded by General Monash.[29]

The story of Rupert from Grosvenor Downs takes us naturally into the life of a

Rupert, the King's horse bred on Grosvenor Downs, in the Royal Mews

King George V on Rupert, his favourite charger, c. 1911

man, long associated with that station, who dominated the Queensland remount trade until his death on the steamer *Changte* at Jetty Wharf, Townsville, after a game of deck quoits, on 28 November 1933. James Simpson Love was born in Scotland seventy years earlier and in 1879 sailed for Queensland to join an expedition to Cape York led by his stepfather, Robert Logan Jack. After a short period of station employment, he operated a livery stable at Townsville and in the 1890s moved into the remount trade, exporting not only to India but also to southern Africa and later Egypt. During the 1920s, when the military demand for horses in India settled down to an average of about 2000 a year from a total importation from Australia of about 3500, Love supplied, according to historian Anne Allingham, up to 700. Cosmo Gordon, however, who sailed with several Love consignments in the late 1920s put the figure at from 1200 to 1800, which seems excessive. By this time, Love had a stake in many pastoral properties, including two which acted as depots for his Indian purchases: Butcher's Hill in the Cooktown district and the more important Egera Station near Charters Towers. Cosmo Gordon remembers especially the B.I. steamer *Janus*, designed for the horse trade with big steel doors just above the water-line where the horses were conveniently loaded. Except in rough weather, the doors were kept open to cool and ventilate the animals and the trip might take no more than sixteen to eighteen days. From Townsville they sailed south to take advantage of the passage through the Barrier Reef at Gladstone and from there they used the outer route until Torres Strait was reached.[30]

In buying his remounts, Love used the services of Alfred Lee and his nephew Ian Macpherson but some stations, like Grosvenor Downs, he visited personally, staying for several days in the big, veranda-enclosed homestead which Alexander McDonald had built. Cosmo Gordon recalls how the big man arrived in his immaculately kept black Bentley. He was a six-footer with huge shoulders, remembered for the bout he had fought years before at Mackay with Frank Armstrong, husband of Dame Nellie Melba. Changed in due course into khaki working clothes tailored for him in Calcutta, Love would be driven for miles around by Gordon, looking at horses on neighbouring properties and having first refusal of the best on Grosvenor Downs itself. His selections, especially if intended for field artillery, had been bred largely by putting fine big Thoroughbreds over dams that were the results of crosses with Suffolk Punch or Clydesdale stallions. Amongst the photographs in the Cosmo Gordon Collection, now held at James Cook University, is one of a handsome Clydesdale named Young Kentyre imported from New Zealand in 1929 at a cost of £2000.

Love also bred his own remounts on Egera Station, using imported stallions such as Chantenmerle and Olympian, and also imported mares such as Palette. Some of the progeny he raced with the Townsville Turf Club, of which he was secretary from 1894 to 1924 and president till his death. Cosmo Gordon often stayed with him in his suite at Queens Hotel, near the waterfront in Townsville. From here Love superintended his pastoral, exporting and business interests throughout Australia, India, Southeast Asia and England that brought his estate to a declared value of £207 166, enabling him to maintain himself in style.

Anne Allingham writes: 'Of seemingly complex character, Love was described as a man of energy, enterprise and great personal charm, as a firm friend and unforgiving enemy; elsewhere as an autocrat, an iron disciplinarian, and by Indian workers as a fearsome bully'. Harry Creen was an employee of Love's at his office in Townsville from 1921 till the end of 1933 and was in Calcutta supervising remount sales when the news came of the boss's death. In fourteen years, Creen had not once seen Love smile or heard him laugh. Life was a serious enterprise for Love and there was no room for suffering fools gladly. Workers at railway crossings, when they sighted the big Bentley, made sure of being well clear, for Love knew only one speed—flat out. He was a hard man, with a dour sense of humour. Creen recalled on returning from India with soft hands being ordered out to to dig post holes. It was a joke, of course, but the sort that only went in one direction. No one ever chaffed J. S. Love, and when he threatened, as he often did, to throw someone through an upstairs window, the assumption was made that the man was serious.

J. S. Love's life and death illustrate the rise and fall of Waler exporting, since the trade for which he was best known was in a state of irreversible decline in the years preceding his death in 1933. The numbers of horses exported from Australia to all destinations fell from 6331 in 1928–29 to a mere 3407 in 1932–33, and from 1934 to 1938 the value of horse imports exceeded that of exports in three out of four years. So far as Love personally was concerned, this was conveyed by a terse paragraph in a letter of 28 March 1936, written by his executors to the Registrar of the Supreme Court, 'For the two years prior to Mr Love's death Indian Remounts Ltd. incurred a loss on trading, and the horse business carried on at Egera was not remunerative over a long period of years'.[31]

Previous chapters examined the early history of the Waler trade, its origins in New South Wales and its development both there and in Victoria. What now follows is a broad discussion of the special contributions made to the trade by New South Wales, Victoria and South Australia, backed up by statistical summaries in the Appendix which draw largely on the work of Malcolm Kennedy.

Victoria's special advantage in horse breeding during the last thirty years of the nineteenth century, compared especially with Queensland, lay in the possession of wealthy urban communities that offered a ready sale for good hacks. Breeding took

Walers on Grosvenor Downs

place in pastures that stretched from the Upper Murray through Gippsland to the rich Western District. H. F. Watson of Tintaldra was an important breeder of Walers, as were J. F. H. Mitchell of Khancoban and H. and C. Douglass of Bringenbrong, who though situated in New South Wales took their horses to the big sales conducted at Wodonga by Adamson, Strettle & Co. of Melbourne and C. L. Griffith & Co. of Albury. The *Australasian* of 24 March 1900 described the sale there over a three day period of 1030 horses, many of them Indian remounts from Khancoban which fetched up to £35. Prices were influenced by the southern African demand, as represented by shipper Charlie Gidney. The report made the point that many purchases were on account of city clients in Melbourne, whither, of course, the bulk of the horses were taken by rail, some for despatch to India. Amongst the Wodonga contingents, at almost every sale, were horses bred by E. and R. M'Illree of Stony-park Albury, who described themselves in a letter to the *Argus* of 26 February 1908 as having been 'among Victoria's largest breeders of Indian horses for the last fifty years'.

Marnie Bassett's superb history of *The Hentys* shows that, with the exportation of Walers by Charles Lethbridge, manager of Merino Downs, the pioneering family achieved 'a realization of one of Thomas Henty's earliest dreams'. A few years earlier the Melbourne *Argus* of 9 July 1869 had explained that the growing difficulty in securing well-bred horses was a result of the drain to India. 'The *Andromeda* sails today for Madras with 40 thoroughbred Touchstones, selected from Mr Lyall's stud; several of the Snowdon and Prince William stock, bred by Mr Mitchell of Table Top, and some few thoroughbreds from Mr M'Leod's of Gipps Land'. Many of them were expected to perform in the Christmas and New Year meetings in Madras.[32]

Wodonga's importance in the Waler trade came with the completion of the rail link with Melbourne in 1873 and the growth of that marvellous metropolis. Horses were brought to the sales from as far away as Queensland and most of the stock from the Riverina were sold there, which helps explain why the Waler exports from New South Wales fell so sharply at this time while Victoria's expanded. An Australian record total of £13 500 was taken at a Wodonga sale in May 1900, when 1436 horses changed hands.[33]

All of this tended to consolidate Melbourne's position as the principal port for the Indian trade in the 1870s. This had been made possible by the city's financial dominance as a result of the income from gold and the hectic growth of the colony's population. Good trucking and shipping facilities were built there a decade ahead of New South Wales, and the technological progress of Port Melbourne, so vital for the horse trade, was not matched in the north until walk-on facilities were provided at Newcastle in 1892. Not till then were the breeders of the Upper Hunter able to realize their potential in relation to India.

The beginning of a new era for Newcastle was described by a *Sydney Morning Herald* report of 17 September 1892. The SS *Woolloomooloo* had been loading the first draft of 252 horses, largely from the runs of Clift Bros. and James White of Denman, which had been brought to the wharf in a special train of twenty-three trucks, arranged by the Newcastle shippers Warren and Tulloch. An enclosed platform with an easy incline was laid down from the vessel to the truck, a quiet horse was haltered and led up the incline, followed by his companions 'as sheep do a wether', and then down matting-covered inclines and passages until they were placed and secured in

Patrick Osborne weighing in at the Bong Bong picnic races, 1902

their narrow 2 foot 6 inch berths. The ship was expected to load a total of 550 horses, chiefly remounts intended for Bombay.

From statistics published in *Knagg's Nautical Almanac* it is clear that the *Woolloo-mooloo*'s cargo was of exceptional quality, since it had an average value of £25. Both numbers and average values fell in 1893 and fluctuated until 1897, when 1144 horses were sent to India from Newcastle at an average value of £15 10s. The port shared largely in the enhanced demand stimulated by warfare in southern Africa and East Asia at the turn of the century, with a total horse export of 3306 in 1900 and 1473 in 1901. An even larger bonanza occurred for the Hunter River breeders during the First World War. Chamber of Commerce reports show that 3763 were shipped from Newcastle in 1914, 14 436 in 1915, and 3999 in 1916. Most of them went to India and Egypt as remounts, with a large proportion of the 1915 exports being destined for the Australian Light Horse.

From 1921 to 1930 horse exports from Newcastle fell to an annual average of 398 and the decline continued in the 1930s, reflecting a general trend away from horse transport to the motor car in Australia's traditional markets. Nowhere was this more acutely felt than amongst the breeders and shippers who had supplied Indian remounts.

South Australia, though regarded since the the 1850s as the granary of Australia, lacked the extensive pastures that were needed to support remount breeding on the scale that had become necessary to success in the later stages of the trade. According to the *Official Yearbook of the Commonwealth*, South Australia ranked fourth amongst the states in terms of horse numbers in 1901.[34] Because of its strength in wheat farming, a large proportion of the state's equine population was composed of draught horses, which were not part of the Waler trade.

I have been unable to find records of South Australian horse exports until the year 1888, when the *Statistical Register of South Australia* began publication. Ceylon received 126 horses from the colony in that year valued at £6000. Through the 1890s cargoes were sent chiefly to India but there was a sprinkling of horse exports to Java, Mauritius and Singapore. The same source reveals the disappointing outcome of the long held hopes for direct Waler exports from Darwin to India. In fact, none were sent there during the 1890s, though a total of 47 went to Manila, 10 to Singapore and 12 to Java.

Malcolm Kennedy shows a total export from South Australia in the 1890s of 1664 that we may consider as Walers. But when Sidney Kidman came to Kapunda, starting what soon became the largest and most famous horse sales in the country, the South Australian share in the Indian trade grew rapidly. In the decade 1901–10, 3465 horses valued at £73 992 were sent to India, and in 1911–20, the numbers rose to 12 485 valued at £263 394 as a result of the wartime demand. Very few of these horses, however, had been bred in South Australia. The boom was created by Kidman himself, overlanding huge numbers of horses for sale at Kapunda from his stations in the Northern Territory, western Queensland, New South Wales and South Australia.

Other writers have told the astonishing story of the strapping thirteen-year-old who rode off into the sunset on a one-eyed horse in 1870, and who by the time of his death in 1935 owned or controlled 68 stations covering about 100 000 square miles. He had the wit to make friends with an Aboriginal boy named Billy and learned from him the bush skills that contributed to his achievements as a pastoralist. Also critical to this success was his concept of buying two chains of stations 'stretching in nearly continuous lines from the well-watered tropical country round the Gulf of Carpentaria, south through western Queensland to Broken Hill, and across the border into South Australia within easy droving distance of Adelaide'.[35]

The annual horse sales at Kapunda, a sleepy town 40 kilometres north of Adelaide, began in October 1900 with the auctioning of 350 horses at the rear of the North Kapunda Hotel. Numbers rose quickly and from 1903 till the end of the First World War it is unlikely that fewer than 1000 head were yarded in any year. The horses came from Kidman's own stations and they were driven, over country that had ideally enjoyed the flush of spring growth, to the week-long sales at Kapunda in late September or early October. Coles and Thomas of Kapunda conducted the auctions, which attracted hundreds of buyers from the whole of eastern Australia and always a strong contingent of Indian shippers, partly because of the quality of the horses and also because the sales were made without reserve prices. Proceedings were carried on with an air of rough levity and good humour, led all too often by the dapper little Steve Margrett, known universally as the 'Colonel', who was not above dropping firecrackers in places where they caused embarrassment and dismay. The Indian

Main buyers at Sidney Kidman's Kapunda horse sales, 1905

shippers despatched their animals to holding paddocks, most of them near Melbourne, and prepared them for the trip to Calcutta or Bombay. As we have seen, Kidman followed the horses to India for the occasion of the durbar of 1911 and took pleasure in recognizing his brands wherever he travelled in India.

Interviewed by the Melbourne *Argus* on 22 February 1908 at a time when the remount industry had been thrown into disarray by some radical proposals of Colonel H. S. Goad, Kidman explained why horse breeding in the 'corner country' and the Macdonnell Ranges was so successful:

> Out there we get country on lease at 1/- to 5/- per square mile per annum, and we can raise horses 25 to 30 per cent cheaper than in the settled districts. The country is open, dry and stony, and the young stock thrive like goats, and are very hardy. They fatten quickly, retain their condition, and travel well.

These horses were not scrubbers, but well-bred animals; the Adelaide *Advertiser*, reporting the sale of 22 August 1904, said that 210 horses had been sold that day at an average price of £12 15s. Confirming this impression, and showing also the contribution that a man like Kidman made to equine quality in Australia, is a letter written by Bryan Colquhoun of Kim Kim, who in the 1930s and 1940s worked as a stockman on Nockatunga in far south-west Queensland. While there he regularly attended musters on the neighbouring Kidman–Reid property of Bulloo Downs, which with the adjoining lease of Norley was used to breed extensively for the Indian market. Together they comprised 4000 square miles and carried 20 000 head of cattle and 6000 horses, from which 1000 foals a year were branded. Colquhoun adds:

> Many high quality thoroughbred stallions were used on Norley and Bulloo Downs at the time, one of them being Sir Simon, a son of the great St. Simon, who was nine years leading sire in England, and had never been beaten as a racehorse. One of Sir Simon's progeny bred at Norley was Bullawarra, who won the [Australian] Grand National Steeplechase, and was bought by Edward Prince of Wales when he was visiting Australia in the early 20's, and taken to England. Other stallions used included sons of Passing By, an extremely high quality horse imported from England by Sir Sidney Kidman.[36]

A friend of Colquhoun's, 'Red Jack' Easton, told of an occasion when he had taken 900 unbroken horses from Bulloo Downs to Adelaide for immediate shipment to India. They were about a month on the track, eating the spring grass, and then loaded onto a ship, 300 to each deck, presumably after being accustomed to dry feed for a week or two.

Kidman was not alone in the remount business in South Australia. Janet Callen reveals the large share held in the trade by Barker Brothers of the John Bull Bazaar in Adelaide.[37] In August and September 1917 they handled 1850 horses, chiefly from central Australia, with 3000 the following year, largely remounts. Alex Robb of J. E. Robb and Sons tells of journeys he took with his father throughout the state and the Northern Territory buying horses for shipment to India, spending thousands of pounds every year without any more than 'a shake of hands and a word of honour'. They were on the track from April to July and trucked their purchases to a depot at Dry Creek, about nine miles north of Adelaide. Here the horses were handled—so as to make them amenable to leading and tying up—and turned out into grazing paddocks until time for shipment in early November. Then they were mustered and given a 'refresher handling', while at the same time they were accustomed to dry feed. Manes and forelocks were clipped off close, 'tails brushed out and squared off 4 inches below hock level, and hooves trimmed neatly'. Finally they were loaded onto rail trucks at Dry Creek and delivered to the wharf beside the ship, ready to be walked aboard.[38] Callen makes the point that the horse shippers were highly skilled and experienced men, who needed courage as well as horse sense to survive the vicissitudes of the trade. In doing so, they made significant contributions to a classic and distinctive Australian industry. (Appendix 6 shows the shares taken by each of the colonies in the export of Walers to various destinations, including India.)

10

The Waler at War

W ITH THE DESPATCH OF the New South Wales contingent to the Sudan in 1885, Australian horses had their first experience of warfare as mounts for Australian soldiers, drawing the six nine-pounders that were used in action by a battery of the colony's gunners. This small, initial effort has been little remembered by Australians, as is conveyed by the title of the centenary publication edited by Peter Stanley in 1985: *But Little Glory*.

It was a very different story with the contingents of mounted infantry that went with their mounts to fight in the Boer War of 1899–1902. A new military body was formed, the Australian Light Horse, whose performances on the veld established a tradition that was central to the national myth making which accompanied the federation of the Australian colonies in 1901. Although the men themselves achieved much credit, there was controversy about the performances of the horses, some 37 245 of them, which accompanied or followed the contingents to southern Africa. Significantly, while the Waler remounts were being criticized by Kitchener and Downe, those that had come to Durban as seasoned mounts belonging to Indian cavalry regiments justified the reputation that had made them indispensable on the subcontinent.

Before, during and after this military adventure there was a large though fluctuating demand for Walers in China during the Boxer Rebellion and for the Japanese army during the Russo–Japanese War of 1904–05. At about the same time the Dutch in the Indies were buying military cobs and civilian hacks and carriage pairs, and a little later the United States forces in the Philippines began importing Queensland horses as cavalry remounts.

Throughout the first two decades of the twentieth century the Indian demand for Walers remained keen and it was only satisfied because of the improved supply from

168

Queensland. The level of that Indian military demand was largely a result of the despatch of Indian cavalry units overseas, to serve in China, then in southern Africa and also in the Middle East and France. During the First World War, trouble broke out in Afghanistan and the north-west border regions, which stretched India's military and administrative capacities beyond a safe limit, bringing to an end, for example, the old *silladari* system of the irregular cavalry units. For Australian breeders and shippers, however, that twenty years must have appeared as a golden age; at the end of it Steve Margrett, the premier Victorian shipper, bought a house in Toorak to confirm his family's newly won position.

The ancient deserts of Palestine served as the great proving ground for the Australian Light Horse in a campaign that reached a climax with the action at Beersheba on 31 October 1917, involving the 4th and 12th Regiments of Light Horse. Arguably the last great horse-borne charge in military history, it showed Australian riders and horses were capable of dramatic and decisive action. Both men and horses were products of the open and adventurous life of the Australian bush, accustomed to surviving in droughty land and well prepared for the heat of Sinai. Their efforts were made possible by the breeders and shippers who organized the movement of perhaps 120 000 Waler remounts to serve Australian, Indian and British units. The

E. R. White of Denman

achievements of these horses, contrasting with the disappointments of the generation that went to southern Africa, had much to do with the treatment they received, above all, in being allowed to acclimatize before being called on for a supreme effort.

Sydneysiders learned of the death of General Charles Gordon at Khartoum on 11 February 1885. Next day the Acting Premier of New South Wales called a special cabinet meeting which empowered him to cable an offer to the British government of two batteries of artillery 'properly horsed' and a battalion of infantry, to serve in the Sudan in the imperial force. In fact, only one battery was required, though not its guns, and the contingent sailed from Sydney on 3 March 1885 amongst scenes of intense enthusiasm, with a complement of 800 men and 224 horses.

Introducing the recent booklet commemorating the event, Peter Stanley points out that the importance of the contingent lay not only in its being 'Australia's first formal involvement in an overseas war', but also in setting the pattern for much of what followed in the Boer War and the First World War. There was a remarkable impulsiveness in the offer, which took little account of how useful the force might be, or how much it would cost. In one of those ironies that Australian history produces, the telegram from the secretary of state accepting the offer of the contingent was received by the acting premier when he was being entertained by the Hon. John Nagle Ryan, M.L.C., son of the Ned Ryan who had been transported in 1814 for his part in an affray against British troops.

So precipitate was the departure of the contingent that the selection of the horses had to be made in Sydney, largely in the stables of the Tramway and Omnibus Company, who did very nicely by selling the animals at an average price of £39. Five were lost on the voyage to Sawakin, on the Red Sea, but the battery saw virtually no action and there were few casualties from fighting apart from injuries suffered by a *Sydney Morning Herald* correspondent who was ambushed by a party of Dervishes.

Two further patterns were set for the future by this adventure: Australian troops had their first experience of fighting alongside an Indian cavalry regiment that was mounted on Walers, as they did later in southern Africa and Palestine; and not for the last time, the horses were not brought home. They were exchanged, in what proved a brilliant bargain for Britain, with the six nearly obsolete nine-pounder guns that were supplied to the battery on arrival.[1]

L. M. Field's well-balanced study, *The Forgotten War. Australian Involvement in the South African Conflict of 1899–1902* has shown that, contrary to the popular tradition, the governments and people of Australia had little enthusiasm for the Boer War, either at the very beginning or in its latter stages. To some extent the offer by the Dickson government in Brisbane of what became the Queensland Mounted Infantry pushed New South Wales and Victoria, rather against their initial inclinations, into offering contingents, which were accepted by the British government.

By 1900 the big, decisive battles had all been fought and the war developed on the British side into a highly mobile effort to find and destroy the Boer Commandos,

Lieutenant Alfred Ebsworth and the Belltrees contingent to the Boer War

while at the same time neutralizing their sources of material support by burning Boer farms and putting their families into camps. Small wonder that the men in the field, not least the contingents of Australian volunteers, became disenchanted with the grim reality of the war and pressed to be returned to their homes. Yet because of the changed character of the campaigning and the new reliance on mounted infantry, there were repeated calls for further Australian detachments, since it was widely recognized that they were better fitted by experience of bush life for the work that had to be done.

Field shows that a total of eight Australian contingents sailed off to the war, most of them accompanied by horses. They disembarked not only at Durban and Cape Town, but also at Beira in Portuguese East Africa (now Mozambique), where a force of Citizens' Bushmen was used to frustrate a possible Boer attempt to trek into Rhodesia (Zimbabwe). The contingents, which included a party of New South Wales Lancers who disembarked at Cape Town on their way home from a visit to London, so becoming the first in the field, made up a total of 16 378 officers and men. Casualties were surprisingly low: a total of 1400, including 251 killed, 267 who died of disease, and 735 wounded, an overall rate of 8.55 per cent.[2]

Australians, who had come together as a federation a little more than a year after the war began, could afford to feel some pleasure at the low casualty figures and the high proportion of decorations won by the men, a total of 524, including five Victoria Crosses. Our prime concern is with the horses that went from Australia with the contingents and subsequently as remounts that were broadly applied to the needs of the British forces. These were, with the exception of the small number in the Sudan contingent, the first Walers to serve overseas with an Australian military force. So, how many were involved and what were they like? How did they compare with the scores of thousands that had established the Waler's reputation in India? How did they perform, and how were they perceived in southern Africa? What casualties did they suffer and what effect did the experience have on the horse trade after the war?

Barry Bridges, who devoted a chapter of his doctoral thesis to a study of the Australian remounts for southern Africa, gives rounded numbers of 25 000 horses for the remount service and a further 15 000 accompanying the mounted or horsed formations. This seems to include New Zealand horses (which incidentally won a much higher reputation), for the detailed list of remount sailings in the Truman Report shows a total of 22 245, indicating a grand total of 37 245. As at the Sudan, not one of the horses is known to have returned to Australia.[3]

We do not know how many Walers died of disease or injury but the total loss in the war was 326 000 horses, at a rate of about 67.3 per cent. St John Brodrick told Lord Kitchener in a private letter 'you will go down to history as the largest horse killer of your or any other age'. If Walers shared the general rate, some 25 000 will have perished, mostly of hunger, disease and aggravated maltreatment, but the likelihood is that they suffered far more than other imports because of their special difficulty in becoming acclimatized. When sick, the majority of the seasoned campaigners were recklessly destroyed and often replaced by inexperienced Argentinian remounts. A few survivors were offered for sale by the Remount Department, some being bought by Indian Army officers going back to the subcontinent with their regiments. There is no doubt that these Walers had a miserable experience of war.[4]

The Walers had an extremely high survival rate on the voyage to southern Africa, compared especially with that on the journey to India. The Truman Report records twenty-six shipments of remounts that had been paid for in Australia by Colonel Hunt and his fellow buyers, with a total of 14 876 embarked and 634 lost at sea, a casualty rate of only 4.3 per cent. In addition to these 'free on board' horses, there were fourteen shipments on a carriage insurance freight basis, comprising 7369 embarked and only 96 lost at sea, making a loss of only 1.3 per cent. These horses were speculative cargoes arranged by professional shippers, like Krcrouse and Madden of Melbourne, whose returns depended on what they could sell horses for in Cape Town or Durban. They were far more experienced than the army shippers, and their managers and grooms would have been given the best possible incentives for care on the voyage. (The overall remount loss rate was 3.3 per cent; I do not have figures for the horses accompanying the contingents.)[5]

One of the intrinsic problems for the Walers in southern Africa was that they were grass-fed horses, accustomed to open range tucker, and needed a good deal of time to adjust to a regime of hand feeding with corn or mealies. In India, after some years of instructive experience, the military and civil importers of Australian horses learned to treat them gently for six months or so until they had got over their shipboard travails and adjusted to a new diet. Significantly the Walers that went to Natal with Lumsden's Regiment—including English Lord—won nothing but praise. One of the real tragedies of the war was that from beginning to end the remounting and veterinary services were placed under intolerable pressures that resulted largely from poor planning and, as a consequence, the horses arriving in Cape Town or Durban were not given any time for acclimatization but despatched immediately in cattle trucks for the front. There they endured service that would have stretched the capacities of the fittest animals.

The fittest animal for service in south Africa was undoubtedly the Cape horse itself, bred from a mixture of Arab and Thoroughbred stock, inured by generations of hard living to the very special pastures and climate of the veld. One of the merits of Sir Frederick Smith's magisterial *Veterinary History of the War in South Africa 1899– 1902* is his success in evoking the landscape and climate of the country and the contribution it made to the problems of horse management. Shortages of water, scantiness of grass in most seasons, extremes of temperature and the absence of trees for shade and firewood, long familiar to the well mounted and powerfully armed Boers, required careful adjustment by their imperial antagonists. In fact, neither man nor horse was given that sort of breathing space.

Shipping horses for southern Africa, Pyrmont Wharf, Sydney, 1900

Though war between Boer and Briton may have seemed inevitable from the time of the abortive raid into the Transvaal led by Dr Jameson in 1896, the English leaders, as long as they were able to cling to hopes of a peaceful settlement, deferred actions that might have looked like mobilization. As the event proved, nothing could have been more important to them than the possession of an adequate supply of horses, mules and oxen. Ideally, local horses would have been accumulated and imported animals brought in early enough to season them to a strange environment. Initially only British and Australian remounts were available and the latter were neither trained nor long accustomed to hand feeding. As the Truman Report makes clear, this failure gave rise 'to the most serious inconvenience, to enormous expenditure, and to waste of horseflesh'.[6]

Throughout the war the need for horses remained so pressing that on disembarkation remounts were promptly trucked to the front lines, often going for days without food. Worse still, they were placed by the first commander-in-chief, General Sir Redvers Buller, on what was effectively a starvation ration that was persevered with despite protests from commanding officers. Then they were put into action carrying a total of twenty stone against tough Boer ponies whose riders carried the minimum of gear, and in the event of sickness faced a hopelessly deficient supply of veterinary officers and medicines. None of the imported remounts stood up to this strain, no matter what their quality and the average mounted soldier went through seven remounts during the course of the war.[7]

In his Foreword to Smith's book, Evelyn Wood described it as a 'severe though just indictment of a Nation which prides itself on its love of horses'. Painful as he found the admission, he thought the facts of the history showed that 'as a race we are not good horsemasters'. The same criticism was widely made of the Australians in southern Africa who, though daring and skilful riders, failed often in the basic tasks of the horsemaster, possibly because they came from a land where horses were so cheap.[8]

Even allowing for the slowness with which the Waler acclimatized there is good reason to believe that those sent to south Africa were all too often poor specimens. Several senior officers who had experience of the carefully bought, acclimatized Waler in India were surprised at what they saw of them in southern Africa. Colonel C. T. Deane, former Director of the Indian Army Remount Department thought them 'very bad indeed'. Major-General Elliott, commanding the Mobile Division, made a detailed contribution to a 'Report on Australian Horses', commenting, like several colleagues, on their being too large and coarse bred. These factors were aggravated by their being unbroken and unconditioned; in the time available it was impossible to rectify those faults and since the majority of the recipients were poor horsemen they simply could not tackle them.[9]

Elliott recalled that in India the Waler was given at least six months settling in and training before being put to hard work: 'if you can give them the time, I consider the Australian one of the best horses in the world . . . quite as good if not better than the best class of English remounts issued under similar conditions [having] . . . as a rule, harder legs and better feet'.

Perhaps the most revealing comments were made by two officers who found the Walers awkward and clumsy in broken country and rough ground and therefore susceptible to strains and broken legs. Their evidence underlines the untypicality of the Walers sent to southern Africa, or at least the massive damage they sustained from their treatment there, for they were universally admired in India for their sure-footedness in bad terrain.[10]

On 5 March 1902 the *Sydney Morning Herald* startled its readers by publishing criticisms that had been made of the Walers in southern Africa by Lord Kitchener, who on seeing those landed from the *Norfolk* had said that many were quite unfit for purchase. Colonel Brodrick, Inspector of Remounts at Cape Town, had been badly disappointed by Waler imports and had remarked that the draught types 'were a positive scandal', though the smaller horses such as cobs and nuggets he classed in a range from good to excellent.

Coming from no less a personage than the commander-in-chief, these strictures caused some dismay in Australia, though the ground had been prepared for many years by the warnings of old horsemen that the breed was deteriorating in Australia. The *Herald* rushed to the defence of a great national institution by publishing a series of articles by A. B. ('Banjo') Paterson, who had been employed at the front as a

Captain A. B. ('Banjo') Paterson inspecting a tired horse

correspondent. In the first article, on 7 March 1902, he made the absolutely un-answerable point that the British remount buyers in Australia had got exactly what they paid for, cheap horses. Quoting prices from memory, he said—with only slight exaggeration—that the Waler had cost much less than those from any other country except Argentina, and less than half the prices given for Canadian and British horses. He went on:

> It is manifestly unfair to our horses, and to the officers selecting them, to insist on getting the cheapest possible animals, and then contrast them with horses which cost more than twice as much. If the English officers who bought here had been allowed to give the same price as was given for American horses, we would have sent over very much superior animals.

Paterson's recollections can be verified by reference to the Truman Report; its comparative list of prices is given in Appendix 7.

Even before Lord Kitchener's criticisms had been published, they had been sent by the War Office to Edmund Barton, the Australian Prime Minister. Already there had been much unease and disappointment in Australia at the small share the country had been given of the lucrative remount market. The low prices, as Barry Bridges argues, had been set by the War Office largely in consequence of advice given shortly before the war by Major-General G. A. French, and confirmed by Lord Brassey, that 'horses suitable for mounted riflemen could be obtained here in myriads for nominal prices'.[11]

The prime minister, aware of the implications of all this for the future of the Australian remount trade, wrote in late February and March to a number of leading breeders asking, in effect, if the British criticisms had done justice to Australian horses and if the supply of good animals had in fact been exhausted. One of the points that emerged from the replies was that the British prices, once set, had been held to in spite of the way the market had moved in response to buying from a number of quarters. A German mission seeking horses for China paid 30 to 40 per cent more than the British figure, keeping pace with the market's rise by the end of 1900 under pressure from the export demand.[12]

One of the most revealing replies to the prime minister's circular was from A. A. Dangar of Baroona, a noted breeder for the local and Indian markets. While stressing the decline in quality that had resulted from 'this terrible drought' and more broadly from the influence of sprint racing, he thought a limited number of better and stouter horses would have been obtained if current Australian prices had been offered. More significantly, he passed on a comment made by another breeder who deeply resented the proceedures used locally for remount purchasing:

> when they were in this district, if you had a horse he had first to be sold to the Agent who resold him to the Remount Agent, consequently the horses were bought at from £9 to £12, and resold to the Imperial people at from £15 to £20. I don't know the exact amounts but it is public property that three agents in this district cleared £8,000, £10,000 & £12,000 each whilst the breeder got no more than perhaps the second rate horse was worth. We sent four horses for inspection but they were pronounced as too good and we only asked £20 each for them.[13]

Sir Rupert Clarke, one of the long established breeders of the Western District of Victoria, who had gone into the Indian market in the mid-1890s, ascribed the poor quality of the horses landed in southern Africa 'entirely to bad buying', a view strongly supported by Dangar's story. It must be remembered that the small British remount mission in Australia had very large orders to fill and they could only do so by using sub-agents, for they could not hope to compete against experienced local buyers in sales that saw a horse knocked down every sixty seconds.[14]

Again and again, it came back to prices and economics. James C. Campbell, principal of a big firm of stock buyers, wrote contrasting the price given by remount buyers of £13 10s to £15 10s per head with his firm's recent sales at Wodonga, where private shippers to Africa had given from £16 to £23 10s. George Rouse of Mudgee, member of one of the oldest horse breeding families in New South Wales confirmed this, while E. R. White of Denman similarly saw the evil as having flowed from the fixing of an absurdly low price. He offered to find 300 horses suitable for any cavalry in the world on three estates in the Upper Hunter, Martindale, Turanville and Bando, if the price were lifted to £18 to £25.[15]

As to economics, Thomas H. Goodwin of Booloocooroo, Curlewis, made a point that has been noticed in relation to the shift of the emphasis in remount breeding from the older states to Queensland. In his part of New South Wales the supply of suitable horses was practically exhausted, because the price of land had become too high to justify a continuance in horse breeding. 'And when we know sheep gives a much higher return per acre per annum, it is not a matter for surprise that the land holders have given their attention to sheep, & neglected horses—excepting a few for their own use.' It was for this reason that the Macarthur stud, one of the pioneers of the Indian trade, had been broken up forty years earlier.[16]

The adverse publicity given to Australian horses as a result of their showing in southern Africa elicited for a year or so a good deal of action—private, governmental and diplomatic. The columns of the newspapers and of journals aimed at the rural community fairly bristled with demands for change and reform. It was not simply a rude question of the survival of an export industry—the oldest relating to live cargoes from Australia—but potentially a matter of national security. Horses played, after all, a vital role as draught animals for artillery and as vehicles for mounted infantry in the First World War.

So, the newspaper files and government archives of 1902–03 contain reports of conferences of horse breeders, seeking legislative action by the states to improve breeding standards by placing taxes on stallions to eliminate the second rate and unsound, and to use the proceeds to finance a system of state stallions. Except in Victoria, where the breeding of draught horses had become a major interest, little was done to carry out the urgings of the reformers.[17]

Australians remembering the deeds of their soldiers in the First World War have fastened their imaginations on two events, the landing at Gallipoli on 25 April 1915 and the charge of two regiments of the 4th Light Horse Brigade at Beersheba on 31 October 1917, described by Bill Gammage as perhaps 'the last great successful mounted charge in history'. Lieutenant Guy Haydon, descendant of an old pastoral family on the Upper Hunter, whose gallant mare Midnight had been shot when they reached the line of Turkish trenches wrote from a hospital bed in Cairo a few days after the charge:

The 12th Australian Light Horse Regiment

At 4 p.m. orders came to mount and we marched along to within 3 miles of the tower until we could go no further without being in full view ... Then followed a few moments later the order 'The 12th and 14th [*sic*] L.H. Regiments will charge Beersheba on Horseback, the town is to be taken at all costs,' and five minutes later we were on the way. We trotted for the first two miles, then the Turks opened fire on us from a line of redoubts about half a mile out from the town and we could hardly hear anything for the noise of their rifles and machine guns. As soon as their fire started we galloped and you never heard such awful war yells as our boys let out. They never hesitated or faltered for a moment. It was grand. Every now and again a rider would roll off or a horse fall shot, but the line swept on. As we neared their trenches our men were falling thicker and thicker and the pace became faster. Thirty yards from their trenches were some old rifle pits and as soon as my eye lit on them I wheeled my horse round and yelled to the nearest men to jump off, let their horses go and get into the pits and open fire. Just previously I had seen Major Fetherstonhaugh's horse go down killed, the Major got up and ran for cover only to fall again shot through both legs. A few seconds afterwards a Bullet hit me high up in the left buttock, just under the belt, lifting me clear off my horse and dropping me sprawling on a heap of dirt that had been thrown out of a rifle pit, and I rolled down into the pit and into safety. But all this time, really only a few seconds the charge went on men raced their horses through and over the trenches and while some of us were still engaged in hand to hand fighting in the trenches, the remainder had charged through the town and went on to the high ground a mile beyond. The town was ours.[18]

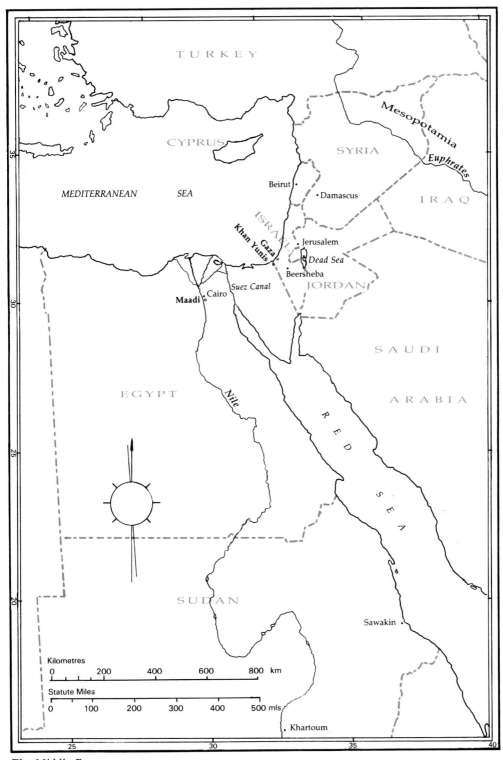

TURKEY

CYPRUS

SYRIA

Mesopotamia

Euphrates

IRAQ

MEDITERRANEAN   SEA

Beirut •

• Damascus

ISRAEL

Gaza

Khan Yunis

• Jerusalem

Dead Sea

• Beersheba

JORDAN

Suez Canal

Maadi • Cairo

SAUDI

ARABIA

EGYPT

Nile

R E D

S E A

SUDAN

Sawakin •

Kilometres

| 0 | 200 | 400 | 600 | 800 km |

Statute Miles

| 0 | 100 | 200 | 300 | 400 | 500 mls |

• Khartoum

The Middle East

The success of this charge, pressed by two Australian regiments containing 800 men against a well entrenched and capable enemy, with over 1000 rifles, nine machine-guns, three batteries of artillery, and having the support of two aircraft armed with machine-guns and bombs, was one of the most astonishing exploits in the history of war. As military historian Ian Jones argues, 'the exercise was impossible' and it was this very consideration which imparted the element of overwhelming surprise that helped carry the day for the men of the Light Horse.[19]

Beersheba was to prove a crucial battle in a campaign that sought initially to defend the Suez Canal, and all that it implied for the British war effort, from the very real danger of seizure by the Turkish army. In the response to that threat the Desert Mounted Corps under Lieutenant-General Sir Harry Chauvel put together a massive horse-borne force which combined with British infantry divisions in a march to the north-east that sought to destroy the basis of Turkish power. Gaza, a strongly defended town on the coast, had held up the British advance and the attack on Beersheba, some sixty kilometres inland, not only offered an alternative route north but also a source of water, peculiarly necessary in a desert campaign.

Chauvel's essential aim in the charge was to secure the seventeen wells of Beersheba before they were blown up by the enemy, a prospect that seemed very likely if the town were taken instead from the west by the British infantry. The horses had not been watered in the preceding twenty-six hours, some, in forty-eight hours, and one of the legends about the day is that the smell of water in the wells and troughs gave them extra speed. To carry through the element of surprise, Jones estimates, the two regiments covered the final two kilometres before the trenches at a gallop in about two and a half minutes. The ground was uneven and covered with a mass of large stones and shingle, broken by little wadis and washaways, yet in spite of this, and the enemy's fire, the lines of the attackers maintained almost perfect order. Those that galloped over the trenches were in the streets of Beersheba within ten minutes of the charge starting, in time to save all but two of the wells.

One of the points to make about all this is that Beersheba really was a classic cavalry charge rather than an action by mounted infantry, though the description by Lieutenant Haydon savoured more of the latter. The message of Beersheba is simple and striking. Clearly, this great charge, the high point of a long and distinguished campaign, entirely vindicated the reputation of a horse that had been maligned sixteen years earlier.

David Kent of the University of New England wrote an article about the Australian Remount Unit in Egypt, in which he explains what might have appeared to be the surprising success of the Waler in Palestine. He attributes it to the Waler's long period of acclimatization, for it was getting used to the the diet, the sand and the climate from its arrival in Egypt in December 1914 until the Light Horsemen returned from Gallipoli in 1916.[20]

A total of 14 873 horses had sailed to Egypt in 1914 to form the establishment of artillery, infantry and three brigades of Light Horse that comprised the initial Australian Imperial Force. This may be seen as the nucleus but it was dwarfed by the purchases subsequently made by the Remount Branch of the Australian Military Forces, which had been established in 1911. The branch's direct purchases for the Australian forces came to a total of 42 926 before buying was halted in January 1917, and its indirect purchases in conjunction with British and Indian missions in

Australian Remount Unit rough-riders

Australia made a further 93 000. The grand total of 135 926 horses, all of them Walers, were shipped to Egypt, India, Britain and France, for service in the cause of the British Empire, at an average first cost of £20 a head. As David Kent points out, this was way below the figure of £42 given by the British commissions in Canada and the United States, though perhaps the margin had been lessened since the Boer War. But the essential difference from that previous campaign was in the treatment the Waler experienced.[21]

The increased longevity and effectiveness of the Waler in the Near East was largely due, as David Kent makes clear, to the work of the Australian Remount Unit, operating from convenient bases west of Suez, first at Maadi and eventually at Moascar. Here the incoming remounts, often virtually wild horses from remote parts of Queensland, were held and trained until they were ready for issue to the troops. They were then despatched to the front by the newly built railway which was as indispensable to the campaign as the water pipes that ran alongside it. Among the hundred rough-riders were some of the outstanding horsemen of colonial times, including Sergeant-Major Jack Dempsey. Captain A. B. Paterson was one of the two company commanders of a unit that was famous for the unconventionality of its rig and for its efforts in keeping up the flow of well-prepared horses. How different from southern Africa! Some lessons had in fact been well learned.

Another element in the success of Australian troopers and their mounts was the generalship shown by Chauvel in commanding first the Australian Mounted Division and later the Desert Mounted Corps, a composite force of regiments from Australia, New Zealand, Britain and India. Harry Chauvel, grandson of a retired Indian army officer who had settled at Tabulam on the Clarence River, had grown up among horses and ridden many winners as an amateur at country race meetings. It was in southern Africa that he had learned how to handle a mixed command of

Guy Haydon on Midnight

colonial and British horsemen, and in the course of the desert campaign he built up a great *esprit de corps*, combining an effective discipline with a respect for individuality that brought out the special talents of his men. The Australian's gift for improvisation in handling the problems of desert life is well exemplified by Lieutenant-Colonel Wilson's introduction of the 'spearpoint' pump of Queensland which revolutionized the mode of water supply for the horses.[22]

Henry Gullet tells the story of Major Robertson and his regiment of Western Australians surprising a Turkish column whose leader insisted that he would only surrender his sword to the officer in charge. 'Somewhat embarrassed, Robertson said that he was the leader. He was as dusty and disreputable-looking as his men, and the Turk handed over his weapon with the air of a man resigned to a violent death at the hands of savages.'[23]

A. J. Hill, Chauvel's biographer, saw the general's care for the horses in his command as a significant factor in its achievments. The view is supported by David Kent, who remarks on the Australians' use of a fast walk as the normal pace for desert travel, in contrast with the British preference for the trot. Guy Haydon, whose letter from Cairo after Beersheba opened this section, took pride in writing to his father at Murrurundi, contrasting the 70 per cent incidence of sore backs among the mounts used by a neighbouring squadron of London Yeomanry with the rarity of the problem in his own troop. His letters reveal a tenderness for the mare, Midnight, which had been bred on his father's property. Hardly a letter passes without news of the horse, of its victories in the regimental sports and its enjoyment of regular swims in the canal.[24]

What is remarkable, on reading Haydon's letters, is the continuity they reveal with the spirit expressed by the grandfather who had founded the Bloomfield property. Thomas Haydon's letter of 31 July 1847 to his brother Luke in Ireland exulted in the

Loading Walers for despatch to the front, Egypt

presence in the district of 'some of the finest Horses in the world . . . from the Arabian and English blood . . . I have some very good ones of the finest blood in the colony'.

During the second battle for Gaza, Midnight remained continuously under saddle for seven days and Guy himself averaged three hours sleep a day, but he was able to tell his father on 24 April 1917 that his old mare was going well and after some soreness on going from the sand to hard ground was again 'in real good condition'. He added:

> We have a fine lot of horses in the LH over here. I didn't think that there were so many good sorts of light horses in Australia, the majority of them are Queensland bred & about 50% of them have O'Donnell's brand on them. [O'Donnell was a Maitland buyer.] They must have handled thousands of horses since the war started & made pots of money.

The speed and desert hardiness of the Walers made them invaluable for reconnaissance and sometimes put them in places where they were least expected. On one occasion a Turkish divisional commander was on his way to take over the command of the Gaza garrison, accompanied by a small mounted patrol and believing the nearest British forces were somewhere about Khan Yunis:

> As he sat back in his gharry,[a horsed vehicle resembling a bathing machine] enjoying the keen morning air, he was startled by a wild whoop and the noise of galloping hoofs, and in a moment was surrounded by a body of grinning, unkempt Australians on their great steaming horses . . . three or four of the light horsemen sat on their horses and, moved by the comedy of the situation, laughed aloud at the little Turkish general. Greatly flustered, the Turk . . . nervously produced a gold cigarette-case and offered a smoke to the troopers. Not to be outdone in courtesy, an impudent, harum-scarum New South Wales boy produced from his breeches-pocket a half-smoked 'fag', and solemnly handed it to the general.[25]

On 1 October 1918 the long desert march that had begun at the Suez Canal two and a half years earlier ended with the penetration of Damascus by the 3rd Light Horse Brigade, who were the first Allied troops to enter the city. Chauvel made a ceremonial entry at the head of of a force representing every element of the Desert Mounted Corps: 'the Australians and New Zealanders on their big walers, the English Yeomanry and Indian Lancers, the French Spahis in their steel helmets, the armoured cars and the guns of the Horse Artillery'.[26]

One of the questions that now arose was how to deal with the thousands of Walers that had survived the campaign. Both Chauvel and his men objected to their being sold to the Syrians and Palestinians, since they had been appalled by what they saw of the treatment of animals in the region. A. J. Hill sums it up:

> So the old and sick horses were shot; the rest were handed over to British units. It was a time of great sadness. A memorial to the 'gallant horses' of the Desert Mounted Corps was unveiled by Lady Chauvel in Sydney on Anzac Day 1950. The inscription includes these words: 'They suffered wounds, thirst, hunger and weariness almost beyond endurance but never failed. They did not come home. We will never forget them.'[27]

The End of the Indian Remount Trade

A BOOK THAT WELL EXPRESSES in its title the sentiments of cavalry officers in India, and perhaps the world over, at the prospect of mechanization was published by E. G. French in 1951. It was called *Good-Bye to Boot and Saddle, or the Tragic Passing of British Cavalry*.

What may seem astonishing about French's book is that more than a decade after the blitzkriegs of the Second World War, a military writer should have so urgently deplored the sweeping away of the horsed soldier and his replacement by tanks and other mechanized units. Less surprising was the campaign fought during the 1920s by Lieutenant-General Sir Harry Chauvel, the hero of the Desert Mounted Corps, for the retention of horsed units in the Australian army, partly on the basis of their superiority in reconnaissance. Chauvel's warnings about the decline in the quality of our horses were given years before Hitler had come to power and even longer before the British army had been committed to mechanization.

French's views explain in a nutshell the extreme reluctance of the British authorities, at home and in India, to adjust their military thinking to the realities of modern transport. Brian Bond's *British Military Policy betweeen the Two World Wars* accounts for the slow pace of change largely in terms of the conservatism and immense prestige of the class from which the British cavalryman derived. Not the least of the influences opposing recognition of the machine age was the delight of the officer, and more specifically the cavalry caste, in the pleasures of hunting. Yet in 1931 when an experimental tank battalion was formed, the country was 'the leading pioneer in mechanization'. But that lead was allowed to slip so far away that by the outbreak of war in 1939 Britain was virtually without armoured forces.[1]

Our study of the Waler's use in Indian sport makes it easy to accept Bond's

Detail from The Central India Horse: The Last Mounted Parade — October, 1939, *oil painting by Lionel Edwards*

conclusion that, 'If possible the part played by games and hunting in Army service in India was even greater than at home'. Young M. C. A. Henniker on joining his regiment at Roorkee in 1929 found that not a single officer possessed a motor car, and that their minds were claimed by three interests: soldiering, polo and shooting, of which the second was almost obligatory.[2] The pleasures of equine sports, so important to young unmarried British officers in India, contributed to their readiness to accept the additional tardiness with which the Indian army converted its cavalry and field artillery to the machine age. This, despite what the military historian, Captain Basil Liddel Hart, described as the 'remarkable success' enjoyed by the early light tanks when they were tried on the north-west frontier of India in 1933. A company

had done a hundred miles a day for three days without exhausting its crews and during the dangerous rising of the Mohmand tribes in 1935 they had won much praise. 'Their rapidity and invulnerability to rifle fire came as an unnerving surprise to the tribesmen, who christened them "the snakes that spit." '[3]

Confirming the tendency of the Indian army to drift and fall behind competitors in such an area as modernization were three special factors, relating to politics, finance and terrain. The progress of the nationalist movement and the increasing representation of Indians in the legislatures made it very difficult for the government to contemplate the substantial capital costs that would have been involved in any mechanization programme. By the 1930s it was clear that such changes would depend on capital grants from Britain, where financial stringency operated for most of the decade, most particulary in the least popular of the armed services. Finally, in spite of the experience on the north-west frontier, it was felt that the poor state of Indian roads and the difficult terrain of the frontier, on which strategic thought was concentrated, made likely the continuing use of horses and draught animals.

The Indian government deferred a decision to embark on a long range programme of mechanization till 1937, when the commander-in-chief agreed to discontinue horse purchases from Australia for at least three years, and perhaps for ever. Intimation of the cessation of government orders was given to that now small and precious band of official shippers, numbering six firms trading to Calcutta and two to Bombay, in December 1937. As the Report of the Army Remount Department for 1937–38 expressed it, 'The news came as a great blow to them, especially as they had received no previous notice . . . They immediately demanded compensation in lieu of notice and their application in this respect is at present under consideration at Army Headquarters'.

In that final year of remount buying from Australia, the six Calcutta shippers, who shared orders for a total of 783 horses, were: Gilder & Macpherson; Lyon & Davis; Margrett & Murray-Smith; McKenna & Son; Glasscock Bros.; and J. E. Robb & Sons. Two firms shipped to Bombay, with orders amounting to 388: R. G. Baldock & Son and T. D. Gove. So there was a total for 1937 of 1171 government orders, which compared with the 1929 total of 2768 shared among twelve shippers. Looking at it another way, the average remount order per shipper had fallen in eight years from 230 to 146 and there must have been real doubts as to the continuing profitability of the trade. For those firms that remembered the boom of the First World War, when the Indian government bought an average of 21 620 Walers a year, most of them for training and shipment to Mesopotamia or Egypt, the fall in profits was nothing less than a calamity.[4]

The war of 1914–18 was not only a swan-song for mounted services in the great armies of the world; it also created a legacy that proved embarrassing for the British and Indian governments and costly for the Australian shippers. In the last year of the war the Ministry of Reconstruction began to look at the problem of what was to be done with the vast numbers of animals that would become redundant when hostilities ceased. An estimate made on 1 January 1918 for the eastern theatre including Egypt and Mesopotamia gave a total of 89 000 horses and 74 000 mules. Shipping would simply be unavailable to send them back to Australia or on to Britain, and in the back of many minds was the question that had been asked by Colonel Lockwood in the House of Commons on 12 October 1916 about the government's plans for horses cast from units serving in the Near East.

> We pride ourselves on being—and I hope we are—the most humane nation on the earth. We have numerous societies, perhaps twenty or more, concerned with the care of animals . . . I come to the sale of horses on the Eastern Front, and I honestly say that my blood boils at the idea of what occurs, for there is no greater devil on earth as master of a horse than the Eastern master of a horse . . . There is no torture that those fellows do not inflict on their horses, in driving them, starving them, and overworking them. It is to these people you quietly allow English troopers to be sold.[5]

In spite of assurances given during and after the war by Lloyd George and

Churchill that cast horses would either be destroyed or sold at prices and under conditions that would ensure careful treatment, gross abuses of old troop horses were found to have occurred, especially in Egypt. As late as the 1930s a fund was established to buy old war horses and to destroy them humanely. No doubt the victims included a number of old Walers, although great care had been used in disposing of them to potentially humane masters, or otherwise destroying them. So far as I am aware, only one Waler made it back to Australia, and he was 'Sandy', General Bridges's charger.[6]

The problem of absorbing fit troop horses from the eastern theatre inevitably raised questions for the Indian government, because it maintained cavalry units there after 1918 and because its relative proximity reduced the likely cost of transportation. On 14 December 1918 the Viceroy cabled the Secretary of State in response to the latter's suggestion that his government create a demand for the surplus horses by suspending imports from Australia for two years. His view was that such a stoppage would not materially affect the huge numbers involved. He went on:

> Total prohibition of import of army horses from Australia [is] moreover, undesirable, as this step would drive out of the horse supply business, men whom it has taken years to educate up to our requirements and would practically involve a breach of faith with them, whose knowledge and experience have helped us so greatly during the war. The Commonwealth Government would probably raise strong protests against prohibition, as Indian requirements are practically the backbone of the Australian horse breeding industry, maintenance of which, is moreover, of great importance at present to the army in India.[7]

Several months earlier the Indian government had shown a sensitiveness to the needs of the Australian shippers, and a concern to conserve its relationship with such well established and trusted suppliers, in considering a request by the New Zealand government for a share in the remount market. The Prime Minister, Mr Massey, had drawn attention to the contribution made by his country to the empire's horse needs —a figure of 12 000 horses was mentioned—and it wished to have the opportunity of supplying 2000 of the cavalry horses needed by India for the 1918 winter season. The Viceroy had cabled the Secretary of State on 15 September 1918 advising his intention to reject the offer. New Zealand horses required a longer sea voyage and would probably cost more. In any case such a decision would operate 'hardly on old Australian importers'.[8]

Nevertheless, in spite of this good will on the part of the Indian government, the accumulation of surplus war horses had a most depressing effect on the Australian trade until the season of 1922. It was only then that the remount demand returned to something like normality, though this was soon muted by the heavy use of blue pencil by the Retrenchment Committee under Lord Inchcape.

For much of the period between the wars the Indian army in its defensive role was caught in a dilemma. The war had revealed massive deficiencies in the organization of the army when it was used as an element in the global responsibilities of the British Empire, supplying battalions for service in France and the Near East. One change that had to be made immediately was to scrap the *silladari* system on which the Indian cavalry had been based, so that the state henceforth assumed the full costs.

During and after the war, it was found necessary for wages to be dramatically increased for all ranks, and at the same time new services were established, including the Air Force.[9]

The Indian army had two broad tasks, the protection of the country's frontiers and preservation of internal security. The second had been made vastly more difficult by the growth of the nationalist movement and the accompanying elevation of communal violence. Ten cavalry regiments were included in the forces that had this responsibility. Simultaneously, the north-west frontier went through two decades of almost continuous unrest and warfare which began with the Third Afghan War. As a strategic assessment expressed the point in 1921:

> We must face the unpleasant fact squarely that the Amir, quite apart from his power to declare a holy war, is able to stir up our frontier tribes almost at will, and by the expenditure of a few hundred rupees and a few thousand rounds of ammunition among them to land us in an expenditure of crores . . . local disorder, unless suppressed in its initial stages, will spread with amazing rapidity. It is for this reason that we lay such stress on retaining the power to deal with local disturbances in their initial stages . . . This postulates the power to strike, both hard and quickly, and is provided for by the location of mobile columns at convenient centres.[10]

This continuing need for remounts to serve the needs of cavalry used both for internal security and frontier defence resulted during the 1920s in the deputation to Australia on two occasions of the director of the Army Remount Department, largely because of a growing anxiety as to the country's capacity to perform its traditional function as a large-scale remount farm.

Yet there were massive pressures for reductions in military expenditure, both from the demands of Indian members in the legislatures and the prescriptions of the Retrenchment Committee presided over by Lord Inchcape in 1922. The result, so far as it concerned the Australian horse trade, was a reduction in the size of the cavalry establishment and the replacement of several British cavalry units with Indian. What this latter change made possible was an increasing dependence on Indian country-bred horses and a corresponding diminution in Waler imports. Though the news given to the shippers in December 1937 had indeed come as a shock, the people involved had been forced for two decades to adjust to a slow process of attrition.[11]

What of the other elements in the horse trade, the animals that were sold to the Princely States, and also the private market for hacks, carriage pairs, racehorses, and polo ponies? The broad answer is that this market declined between the wars even more calamitously, under the influence of a general trend on the part of the well-to-do to replace the horse with the motor car. There is some evidence of a new activity by the agents who bought remounts for the armies of the Native States, and Charlie Pascoe of Eidsvold often sold as many as sixty horses a year on his own account to the Princely States of Bikanir and Gwalior. Polo ponies continued to be a good thing for Curtis Skene and his son Bob, soon to become the highest rated player in the world. But overall, the story was one of decline.

Expert impressions of the state of the remount breeding industry in Australia during this period are supplied by the reports made to the Remount Department by senior officers after visits to Australia in the 1920s. Major R. S. Scott made a point in his 1922 report that reiterated a concern expressed in 1908 by Colonel Goad, and anticipated that of Brigadier Anderson in 1929. It was, indeed, a complaint perennially made by Australian breeders of light horses from the late 1860s, that it simply did not pay them to produce animals suitable for the Indian remount market. Scott described the trend away from horse breeding in the more closely settled parts of Australia as land became more valuable and the transfer was made to sheep and cattle, which were more profitable and less risky. He illustrated the latter point by quoting the forceful example given by one of the largest horse breeders in the country: 'Bullocks may be blind of an eye, spavined, lame and blemished, but given weight and condition they are equally saleable with their sounder brethren. A horse gets a blow in the eye from a twig, from which date he is unsaleable'.[12]

Sir Rupert Clarke, one of the best known pastoralists in Victoria, who had bred remounts for the Calcutta market in the 1890s, told Scott he had never cleared more than 5 per cent on his investment, though he had bred and shipped his own horses. After a few years experience, 'satisfied that the profits were not commensurate with the risks undergone', he retired from the business.[13]

The claim that breeding for the Indian market was unprofitable had a long pedigree. A typical exposition of the case was made in the *Australasian* of 19 January 1867 by a correspondent who had been in the trade for some years. 'The fact is, sending horses to India is a bad spec. The animals that would really pay are very scarce in this country, and command nearly as high a price here as they would do at Hunter and Co.'s, Calcutta'. Ernest Baynes, a leading Queensland authority, was quoted in the *Australian Pastoralists' Review* of 16 April 1918 on the need for a more remunerative price for breeders as a condition for the survival of a high quality industry. Again,

Grosvenor Downs Clydesdales pull a Model T Ford out of the Isaacs River crossing

when Brigadier W. H. Anderson reported to the Remount Department after his extensive visit in 1929, he told the same story, of a loss of profitablility for both breeders and shippers and a need for better prices—despite a natural inclination for a buyer to look with a jaundiced eye on the complaints of producers and sellers.[14]

Scott showed that though the prices paid by the Remount Department for British Service cavalry horses had risen from £45 in 1914 to £52 10s in 1922, freights had gone up from £7 10s to £14 and higher labour costs, interest rates, feed, insurance and other incidentals had absorbed all of the price increase. He made the interesting point that before the war, none of the Australian shippers were making more than a bare living out of the business. And the profits made during the war depended not only on the increased scale of operations but also on the rise in the value of the rupee. This view was confirmed for me by Stephen Murray-Smith's account of the activities of his grandfather, Steve Margrett, who had done very well on the side by currency speculations on his wartime trips to India, adding 20 per cent to his profits.[15]

Some slight compensation for the decline in the Indian demand came from regular purchases made by remount buyers acting for the Dutch authorities in the East Indies. Major Scott commented on it in his 1922 report, and it was still going strong in 1934. The *Sydney Morning Herald* of 8 December 1934 reported the arrival in the *Nieuw Holland* of a party of nine soldiers who were to take charge of a batch of 105 horses that were to be shipped on the decks of the liner from Melbourne and Brisbane.

By the time of Brigadier Anderson's visit to Australia in 1929 the tale of decline was more marked. The great Kapunda sales which Sidney Kidman had begun a quarter of a century earlier had come to an end. In Queensland itself, the last stronghold of the remount breeding industry, the advantage of cheap land was no longer sufficient to keep pastoralists in the business and many cut down their programmes so as to breed only for their own needs. Even J. S. Love, by far the largest breeder and remount shipper in Australia, was suffering losses from the trade in the few years before his death in 1934.

A striking illustration of the impending collapse of the trade was given by Anderson in his story of a visit to horse sales in Warwick, where, from 250 horses offered, he saw only two that came up to Indian army specifications. Of those one was too old and the other unsound! Reinforcing the impression from this piece of evidence was the difficulty experienced by the Remount Department in three previous years in buying sufficient horses to meet the agreed target. The shortfalls had been 83 in 1924, 73 in 1925 and 195 in 1926. Anderson had to spend a good deal of his energy in contradicting the impression, which he found throughout Australia, that the Indian government would require no more horses after 1930. This, he had been assured, would come as a result of mechanization and the increased reliance on country-bred horses. It had not been easy to refute what he described as this 'mischievous and misleading information'.[16]

The anxieties and doubts of the Australian breeders had probably begun to germinate in the years from 1918 to 1922, when the remount trade had been almost suspended. Their basic pessimism was fully justified, though their timing of the final axe was premature. With the decision on mechanization, the Defence Department of the Government of India was faced with much the same problem as the British War Office in 1918–19, of disposing of a huge number of cast horses. A letter of

27 September 1939 described the safeguards that had been framed to prevent troop horses from falling into the hands of people who could not be trusted to look after them. Polo playing officers enjoyed a brief bonanza in being able to buy ponies of quality at Rs 100 each, but for the most part they now had sterner things to occupy their minds.[17]

Mechanization could not be accomplished overnight. Walers continued to be used in cavalry units employed in internal security for several years, and they had a major place still on the frontier, as in the Waziristan Campaign of 1940–41. But the decision announced to the shippers in the winter of 1937 implied the end of a trade that had lasted almost continuously from July 1834, when Collins had sent that first cargo of remounts from Sydney to Madras.

What had the horse trade meant to the two countries principally involved? It was aptly symbolic that the word 'Waler', which stuck to Australian horses abroad for so many years and in such widely diverse uses, should have been coined in India to describe horses imported from New South Wales.

The Waler's value to the Indian army was well attested by its dominance of remount purchases for the last sixty years before mechanization. Admittedly, there was a degree of cynicism in the army's long sustained insistence on letting the shippers assume the risks of the trade until the point of purchase. Exceptions were made only at times of crisis, during the mid-1840s, the Indian Mutiny and the First World War. Yet there was a sympathy for the interests of the Australian shippers and a respect for their judgement that reflected their indirect contribution to the internal security and defence of India. As shown by the durbar of 1911, that apogee of the British Raj, the horse and the mounted soldier were potent expressions of the nature of the empire in India.

The Waler's role as a sporting horse and hack in India must have been for many owners only slightly less significant than its military function. For many Britishers who came to India in our period the great attraction, so well evoked by Churchill's *My Early Life*, was that of polo and other equine sports.

To Australian horse breeders the Waler trade had a significance that exceeded any simple financial measure of total receipts and profitablility. Horse exports had begun even before Collins; they were the first of Australia's live cargoes. In the 1840s they were seized on by desperate pastoralists as relief from one of Australia's worst depressions. For much of the century that followed, the demand for strong, active, well-bred horses in India represented a consistent stimulus to quality control and a spur to the importation of Thoroughbred and Arab sires and dams. The examples of the Macarthurs, the A.A. Company and the Scotts in the early period, and of the Whites, the Dangars, Sidney Kidman and J. S. Love later on, make the point of what the market leaders were doing. The presence of Indian buyers at the horse sales, from Kapunda to Wodonga, from Maitland to Toowoomba, injected a grand taste of ready money, sometimes into flagging markets. Major Scott told the story of a sale he attended in 1922:

A useful type of Indian Cavalry horse came into the ring and was purchased by an Indian shipper for £18. This horse was found, on inspection, to be 7 years old, and consequently too old for shipment. He was therefore resubmitted for sale the following morning, and with no shippers bidding, was knocked down at £6.[18]

Beyond the value of the horses themselves was the stimulus offered by the trade to shipowners like Robert Towns at a time when any outward cargoes were eagerly welcomed. The shippers themselves created an export industry that generated a powerful demand for skills, services and materials. Consider, for example, the fodder required by the 200 000 Walers taken to southern Africa and Egypt. While at sea they ate 9000 tons of oats and bran and 18 000 tons of hay; 350 ships were used in transporting them, with a total capacity of half a million tons.

An image that sums up the Waler trade concerns Thomas Haydon of Bloomfield at Murrurundi. There was a special thrill for the British who were transplanted to Australia in the possession and breeding of fine horses and in 1843 he had bought from the Scotts of Glendon the great Thoroughbred stallion, Dover, from which many of the Bloomfield lines still trace. On 31 July 1847 he wrote to his brother Luke in Ireland. In the midst of a general letter about family and pastoral affairs he used words that speak for many of the men and women who bred horses then and now in Australia, 'I feel a greater pleasure in horses than any other kind of stock'.

Epilogue

ALTHOUGH THE ORIGINAL and central reason for the Waler's existence came to an end with the mechanization of the Indian army, exportations of Australian horses of the Waler type have continued intermittently on a small scale since the Second World War. They are almost without exception sporting horses, that is, racehorses and polo ponies, though a veterinarian, Grahame Taylor, of Harden drew my attention to a cargo of horses which he helped to certify in July 1987. It was a batch of 112 mares described in a newspaper report as the 'thoroughbred type', intended for the Thai army, bred on properties in Victoria, New South Wales and South Australia, which travelled on a special 747 charter flight from Melbourne.[1]

One of the most consistent of the Asian markets is the Hong Kong Jockey Club, which was supplied largely by the Toowoomba dealer, F. A. Woods, in association with W. A. Jones of Melbourne. Jones was one of the old established shippers who had begun taking racehorses to the race clubs of Shanghai and Hong Kong by the late 1930s. The trade continued to be sea-borne in the 1950s but it is now carried by air.

Polo ponies have been shipped from Fremantle since 1965 by Leonard Hamersley of Walkaway, Western Australia, who is possibly the only person now sending cargoes by sea. His contact is with the Sultan of Johore, who maintains a magnificent string of ponies and pays top prices. Hamersley is a keen polo player and has accompanied the horses himself. In 1986 his daughter Marnie took six ponies to Singapore for the Sultan's stables on the cattle ship *Buffalo Express* and they made the trip in eight days, landing the horses, as Marnie put it, in 'fantastic' condition with shiny coats and neatly brushed tails. It was a far cry from the Fremantle cargoes a century earlier which ran into calms that might last for a fortnight, causing disastrous losses.[2]

Lindsay Jameson of the Suffolk Vale Pastoral Company, who like Leonard Hamersley plays sometimes in the Royal Pahang Tournament, assembled a team of quality polo horses and took them to Malaysia in September 1989. They were played before being offered for sale. As he points out, the ponies for this market need to be a little smaller with a lighter mouth than those commonly used in Australia because of the slighter stature of the players. From him I received a copy of the *Australian Stock Horse Journal* for October 1988, which described the efforts of John Halliwell of Dandenong, Victoria, to export registered Stock Horses for use in Malaysia and Singapore as polo ponies. The first consignment left in November 1974 and is reported to have given satisfaction to the buyers. Clearly, the huge costs of taking horses by air will restrict the scale of this trade to a fraction of the pre-war traffic in Walers. Since the Australian Stock Horse, as defined by the Society formed in Tamworth in June 1971, is essentially the same style of horse as the old Waler, the tradition is being kept alive.

Let me conclude by quoting from Brigadier John Paley's account of a reunion he attended in November 1986 of Skinners's Horse, the oldest and perhaps most famous of the *silladari* regiments. The group of six retired officers, which included a direct descendant of Colonel James Skinner, had visited St James Church in Old Delhi to mark the 150th anniversary of its construction by the colonel as a thanks offering for his recovery from severe wounds incurred in battle. Leading the party was Lieutenant-Colonel Douglas Gray, a former commanding officer of the regiment, who had won the Kadir Cup in 1934 on a Waler known as Granite.

While in Delhi the party watched from the Polo Club Pavilion as the President's Bodyguard went through its mounted training, practising dummy thrusting with swords and tent-pegging with lances. Two hundred men were involved, Rajputs, Sikhs and Jats, and as the old officers watched they were joined by twenty or so members of the diplomatic community.

Suddenly from the left we saw someone approaching at full gallop with lowered lance, going for the tent pegs, opposite the Polo Club . . . As he got closer we recognised with alarm that the rider was Duggie Gray in a white polo helmet. He narrowly missed the peg in this first attempt. Round he went again and without slowing up in the slightest and this time shouting the Regimental Motto, 'Himat-i-Mardan. Madad-i-Khuda.' (The bravery of man, is with the help of God) A loose translation.

This time he drew the peg clean out of the ground. A spontaneous cheer went up from soldiers and spectators alike. Round he went again and this time he twirled his lance, as well as shouting the motto, but on this occasion he hit the peg, but did not manage to pull it out of the ground.

This was a man approaching 77 years of age, who had not tent pegged since just before the WW II. He was the leader of our group and we were proud of him. He remains for me the epitome of a Bengal Lancer, and the short but true story given above represents the finest example of the Cavalry Spirit, which inspired the British as well as the Indian Cavalry, and in my opinion certainly included the Light Horse Regiments of Australia & N.Z.[3]

Appendix 1

Anticipated Costs of Horse Shipments to India

	£	s	d
First cost of the horse on an average	23	0	0
Freight & water	10	0	0
£44 ... Per Torres Straits insurance £6 per cent against sea risk only	2	8	0
Hay ⅓ ton at £6 per ton = £2. Corn & bran £2	4	0	0
Grooming etc.	1	0	0
Casualties on voyage, valuing each horse at £44	4	4	0
Total	44	12	0

Source: Captain Collins to McLeay, 12 February 1834, NSW Archs 4/2237.1

Appendix 2

Horse Exports to India by Colony 1861–1900

Colony	1861–70		1871–80		1881–90		1891–1900	
	No.	*£*	*No.*	*£*	*No.*	*£*	*No.*	*£*
NSW	1 081	19 689	230	3 543	2 916	45 266	11 448	169 760
Vic	7 292	141 953	24 178	449 613	33 659	772 571	30 336	543 187
Qld	48	784	70	920	267	2 770	7 619	72 719
SA	?	?	245	2 868	818	16 370	1 309	11 132
WA	2 126	43 498	1 419	18 395	999	12 613	2	20
Tas	—	—	2	40	—	—	—	—
Total	10 547	205 924	26 144	475 379	38 659	849 590	50 714	796 818

These figures are adapted from Kennedy's Statistical Appendix K.

Appendix 3

Western Australian Horse Exports to Market Zones 1861–1901

Market Zones	1861–70		1871–80		1881–90		1891–1901	
	No.	*£*	*No.*	*£*	*No.*	*£*	*No.*	*£*
Indian	2 126	43 498	1 419	18 395	999	12 613	2	20
African	104	2 246	997	12 662	1 572	19 433	525	7 485
S.E. Asian	864	19 252	3 109	40 513	2 607	32 440	389	4 143
East Asian	6	135	240	3 077	1 105	13 792	—	—

These figures are adapted from Kennedy's Statistical Appendix J. The Indian market zone in his terms includes Ceylon, Burma and India; African includes Mauritius and Reunion; Southeast Asian includes Indonesia, Indo-China, Straits Settlements and Thailand; East Asian includes China, Japan and the Philippines.

Appendix 4

Participation in the Indian Horse Trade: The Market Leaders

| | 1891–1900 | | 1901–1910 | | 1911–1920 | | 1921–1930 | |
	No.	Av. £	No.	Av. £	No.	Av. £	No.	Av. £
NSW	11 448	14.8	12 792	21.5	19 744	20.8	4 073	25.3
Vic	30 336	19.9	25 700	25.7	21 202	24.3	10 375	20.8
Qld	7 619	9.5	34 186	11.3	58 936	15.6	23 093	15.5
SA	1 309	8.5	3 465	21.4	12 485	21.1	4 345	17.7

These figures are adapted from Kennedy's Statistical Appendix K. The prices are those paid in Australia before shipment. The prices paid by the remount buyers in India ranged from £45 to £55.

Appendix 5

Total Australian Shares in the Indian Horse Market 1861–1931

	Total number	Total first costs £	Average first costs £
NSW	52 284	1 026 690	19.63
Vic	152 742	3 297 726	21.59
Qld	121 519	1 742 585	14.34
SA	22 667	444 540	19.61
WA	4 723	77 701	16.45
Tas	2	40	20.00
Total	353 937	6 589 282	18.61

These figures are adapted from Kennedy's Statistical Appendix J.

Appendix 6

Distribution of Waler Exports to Market Zones 1861–1931

	Indian No.	£	*African* No.	£	*S.E. Asian* No.	£	*E. Asian* No.	£
NSW	52 284	1 026 690	19 791	310 831	10 919	331 012	8 216	258 948
Vic	152 742	3 297 726	22 108	409 295	16 636	340 182	2 400	55 566
Qld	121 519	1 742 585	21 432	198 084	4 045	68 208	10 733	140 486
SA	22 667	444 540	908	13 706	513	10 011	90	2 033
WA	4 723	77 701	5 697	84 436	7 248	115 164	1 357	17 094
Tas	2	40	282	5 060	—	—	—	—
Total	354 937	6 589 282	70 218	1 021 412	39 361	86 457	22 796	474 127

These figures are adapted from Kennedy's Appendix J. The Indian market zone includes Calcutta, Madras, Bombay, Ceylon and Burma; African includes Cape Colony, Natal (Union of South Africa), Portuguese East Africa, German West Africa, Sudan, Mauritius and Reunion; Southeast Asian includes Dutch East Indies, Indo-China, Straits Settlements and Thailand; East Asian includes China, Japan, Hong Kong, Guam and the Philippines.

Appendix 7

South African Remounts: A Comparison of Prices Paid and Numbers

	Cavalry			Artillery			Cobs			Numbers
	£	s	d	£	s	d	£	s	d	
Home (U.K.)	42	10	0	39	0	0	30	0	0	56 984
Australia	15	0	0	20	0	0	12	0	0	23 028
New Zealand	22	0	0		—		18	15	0	(incl. in Aus.)
Argentina		—			—		8	0	0	26 544
Canada	28	0	0	30	0	0	25	0	0	14 621
Hungary	30	0	0	35	0	0	20	0	0	?
U.S.A.	20	3	3		—		15	0	0	106 658
Russia		—			—		26	10	0	?

Taken from the Truman Report, which at this point included the New Zealand remounts, numbering 1683, in an Australasian total.

Glossary

assamee	The *assamee* or circle system, originally adopted at the Pusa Stud, involved the loan to farmers, or *assamees*, of government mares that were covered by government stallions.
bursati	A skin eruption spread by flies, commonly occurring among horses in India.
cast horse	A horse dispensed with because of age or infirmity.
chukker	Each of the periods of play in polo.
crore	A hundred lakhs, or Rs 10 000 000.
dafadar	A non-commissioned officer with the rank of corporal.
Dervish	A Muslim friar who has taken vows of poverty and austerity.
gram	A horse food widely used in India, from Portuguese *grao*, for grain, and Hindi *chana*, for chick peas.
jheel	Low-spots of standing, stagnant water.
kaboobs	An Anglicized spelling of kebab, a meat dish cooked on a skewer.
Kadir	The grassy verge of the Ganges, haunt of wild pigs.
kumri	A condition marked by weakness in the loins and backs of horses.
masullah boats	Craft used at Madras for conveying goods and passengers through the surf from ship to shore, of light, pliable construction.
nala	Sometimes spelt 'nullah'; a deep fissure in the ground.
Native States	Sometimes referred to as 'Princely States'; semi-autonomous states, ruled by indigenous princes.
north-about	The route to India via the Queensland coast and Torres Strait.
nugget	An Australian term used for a small, compact horse.
seer	A measure equivalent to a kilogram.

sepoy	An Indian private soldier.
silladar	An irregular trooper, similar to the English yeomanry.
south-about	The route to India via the Great Australian Bight and Cape Leeuwin.
sowar	An Indian trooper.
span of horses	A pair of horses harnessed and driven together.
syce	An Indian groom.
wadi	An Arabic term for a ravine which becomes a watercourse after rain.
zamindar	Literally, a landholder.
Zilladar	More commonly, *silladar*, an irregular trooper.

Abbreviations

AACo	Australian Agricultural Company
A.D.B.	*Australian Dictionary of Biography*
App.	Appendix
Arch(s)	Archive(s)
Aust.	Australia
B.I.S.N.	British India Steam Navigation
Colln	Collection
Consns	Consultations
Corresp.	Correspondence
Def. Dept	Defence Department
Desp(s)	Despatch(es)
Dirs	Directors
H. of C., *P.P.*	House of Commons, *Parliamentary Papers*
H.R.A.	*Historical Records of Australia*
I.O.	India Office, London
I.O.L.	India Office Library, London
J.R.A.H.S.	*Journal of the Royal Australian Historical Society*
Mil.	Military
M.L.	Mitchell Library, Sydney
N.A.M.	National Army Museum, London
Nat. Mar. Mus.	National Maritime Museum, Greenwich
P.R.O.	Public Record Office, London
Q., *P.P.*	Queensland, *Parliamentary Papers*
Q.S.A.	Queensland State Archives
Q., *V & P*	Queensland, *Votes and Proceedings*
S.A., *P.P.*	South Australia, *Parliamentary Papers*
S.M.H.	*Sydney Morning Herald*
uncat.	uncatalogued

Notes

1 Walers at the Coronation Durbar

1 Bowen, *Kidman*, pp. 147-57, 183-4.
2 Hardinge, *My Indian Years*, p. 46.
3 Fortescue, *Narrative of the Visit to India*, pp. 119-23.
4 'The Durbar Ceremonials', in Waddy (ed.), *T.K.S. at the Delhi Durbar*, pp. 22-4.
5 Ibid., pp. 24-6, 72-5; Fortescue, *Narrative of the Visit to India*, pp. 164-5.
6 *Narrative of the Visit to India*, p. 122.
7 Wurgraft, *The Imperial Imagination*, pp. xviii, 7, 54-5.
8 Nicolson, *King George the Fifth*, pp. 86-8.
9 *T.K.S. at the Delhi Durbar*, p. 75.
10 *Narrative of the Visit to India*, pp. 165-6, 163 & note.
11 Hardinge, *My Indian Years*, pp. 47-8, 79-81.
12 *Burke's Landed Gentry*; Maxwell, *I am ready*, p. 56.
13 N.A.M., Maxwell Diaries, summaries for 1903, 1904.
14 *I am ready*, p. 92.
15 *T.K.S. at the Delhi Durbar*, p. 88.
16 Letter from Peter Yeend, Archivist, The King's School, 1 December 1988.

2 Origins: India and Australia

1 *S.M.H.*, 7 March 1902.
2 *The A.I.F. in Sinai and Palestine*, p. 34.
3 Ibid., p. 39. If New Zealand had been included in our study of horse exports (which it is not, because for our purposes that country is essentially part of the domestic market), we should have had the opportunity of noticing what was probably the first export of a horse from New South Wales. I refer to the supply by the Rev. Samuel Marsden of several horses and cattle, at his own expense, to the missionary party whom he planted in the Bay of Islands in December 1814.
4 The Role and Significance of Bullocks and Horses, vol. 1, p. 35.
5 Ibid., p. 166; *H.R.A.*, series 1, vol. 18 , p. 650.
6 Quoted in W. Gilbey, *Small Horses in Warfare*, London, 1900, p. 45.
7 *Varieties of Vice-Regal Life*, vol. 2, p. 324.
8 *Queensland Agricultural Journal*, 1904-05, vol. 15, pp. 889-91.

[9] Anglesey, *History of the British Cavalry*, vol. 1, pp. 216-22.
[10] Farwell, *Queen Victoria's Little Wars*, p. 90.
[11] Anglesey, *History of the British Cavalry*, vol. 1, pp. 63-4.
[12] *A Matter of Honour*, p. 138.
[13] Ibid., pp. 138-40, 173.
[14] *History of the British Cavalry*, vol. 1, p. 182.
[15] Ibid., pp. 75, 107; Mason, *A Matter of Honour*, pp. 140-1.
[16] Mason, *A Matter of Honour*, p. 143.
[17] Ibid., p. 144.
[18] *History of the British Cavalry*, vol. 1, p. 106.
[19] Ibid., pp. 106-7.
[20] Jackson, *India's Army*, p. 473; Anglesey, *History of British Cavalry*, vol. 1, pp. 100-11, vol. 3, pp. 142, 156.
[21] Anglesey, *History of the British Cavalry*, vol. 1, p. 109.
[22] Tylden, *Horses and Saddlery*, p. 50.
[23] 'Remounting of the Madras Cavalry', p. 582.
[24] Ibid., but see Madras Desps, I.O.L., E/4/906.
[25] Armstrong, *Port of Madras*, n.p., n.d., pp. 214-15.
[26] B. Hall, *Travels in India*, London, 1931, pp. 142-5.
[27] Tylden, *Horses and Saddlery*, pp. 51-2.
[28] Addington, 'Remounting of the Madras Cavalry', p. 587.
[29] *Standard Encyclopedia of South Africa*, p. 592.
[30] *Early History of the Thoroughbred*, pp. 159, 169, 177.
[31] Ibid., p. 173.
[32] Ibid., p. 152.
[33] Millar, *Plantaganet in South Africa*, pp. 70-1, 102, 152.
[34] *Records of Cape Colony*, xxiii, 182, 241-3, 273-5, 488-91.

3   A Great Trade Begins

[1] Kennedy, Bullocks and Horses, pp. 268-9.
[2] *Sydney Gazette*, 3 May 1817.
[3] *A.D.B.*, vol. 2, pp. 379-82.
[4] Piper Papers, M.L. A254, pp. 475-80.
[5] Macarthur Papers, M.L., vol. 4, pp. 79b-f.
[6] Bassett, *The Hentys*, pp. 29, 122 & note.
[7] *A.D.B.*, vol. 2, p. 158; AACo Corresp. A78/9/1, 1 December 1827, pp. 356-77; July 1829, pp. 348-50; B78/9/2, 26 May 1828, p. 852.
[8] *A.D.B.*, vol. 1, p. 334.
[9] AACo Desps, 78/1/17, p. 183.
[10] Alder, *Beyond Bokhara*, p. 92.
[11] Ibid., p. 95.
[12] Ibid., pp. 95-7.
[13] Ibid., p. 184.
[14] Ibid., p. 114.
[15] Ibid., p. 118.
[16] Ibid., p. 181.
[17] I.O.L., Madras Draft Desps, E/4/941.
[18] I.O.L., Madras Mil. Consns, 11-21 June 1833, pp. 6605-21.
[19] I.O.L., Madras Mil. Consns, 6-20 August 1833, no. 46, p. 874.
[20] *H.R.A.*, series 1, vol. 18, p. 650.
[21] NSW Archs, 4/2237.1, 23 August 1833.
[22] *H.R.A.*, series 1, vol. 18, p. 651, letter of 19 September 1833.
[23] NSW Archs, 4/2237.1.
[24] NSW Archs, 4/2237.1, replies to circular of 23 May 1834.
[25] AACo Desps, 78/1/14, Parry to Court, 19 May 1834, p. 50; 78/1/15, Dumaresq to Court, 24 September 1834, p. 8.
[26] *Sydney Herald*, 7 July 1834.
[27] *Sydney Herald*, 5 January 1835, 13 June 1835.
[28] *H.R.A.*, series 1, vol. 18, p. 655, 2 January 1837.
[29] AACo Desps, 78/1/15, p. 115.

30 Ibid., p. 11.
31 Atchison, Port Stephens and Goonoo Goonoo, p. 115.
32 AACo Desps, 78/1/15.
33 I.O.L., Madras Mil. Desps, F/4/1584, report dated Arcot, 9 September 1835; see for example reports continued in F/4/700, by Major Hill and Brigadier Showers of 10 March 1837, 2 April 1836.
34 I.O.L., Madras Mil. Desps, F/4/700; E/4/947.
35 AACo Desps, 78/1/17, p. 184.
36 I.O.L., Madras Mil. Desps, E/4/955, 24 April 1840, 13 April 1841.

4 Depression, War and Trade 1843–1850

1 M.L. B825, Diary of John Betts, pp. 164-6.
2 S. H. Roberts, *The Squatting Age in Australia*, Melbourne, 1935, p. 193; C. M. H. Clark, *A History of Australia*, Melbourne, 1973, vol. III, pp. 293-4.
3 Clark, op. cit., p. 293.
4 N.A.M., 8303-105-1191, Ellenborough to Gough, 28 May 1844.
5 I.O.L., F/4/2109, Major Thomas to I.O., 15 January 1845.
6 I.O.L., Bengal Commercial Reports 1841-44.
7 *S.M.H.*, 13, 14 April 1843; Scott Papers, M.L. 38/18X, p. 39.
8 *A.D.B.*, vol. 2, p. 428.
9 I.O.L., Board's Collection, F/4/2109.
10 *History of British Cavalry*, vol. 1, p. 95.
11 Ibid., pp. 232-3.
12 Ibid., pp. 234-5.
13 N.A.M., 8303-105-1191.
14 I.O.L., F/4/2109.
15 N.A.M., 8303-105-1203; 8303-105-1208; 8303-105-1223; *Shipping Gazette*, 10 April 1846, 30 January 1847.
16 I.O.L., F/4/2109, 19 July 1844. This file deals with the NSW mission.
17 I.O.L., Bengal Desps, E/4/780, 4 September 1844.
18 I.O.L., Military Board letters 28 May, 1 June 1844.
19 Bullocks and Horses, vol. 1, pp. 278-88.
20 Leslie Letters, Oxley Library, 10 May 1847.
21 Leslie Letters, March 1847; *J.R.A.H.S.*, vol. 16, part 7, p. 485.
22 I.O.L., India and Bengal Desps, F/4/98912.
23 Macarthur Papers, M.L. A2993, vol. 37, p. 101.
24 C. Bateson, *Australian Shipwrecks*, Sydney, 1972, vol. 1, p. 183; for the 13 cargoes see files of *Shipping Gazette*, 1845-47; for Van Diemen's Land see *Hobart Town Courier*, 10, 22 April 1845.
25 Scott Papers, M.L. 38/18X, Mackillop Stewart & Co Calcutta, 9 October 1844; Blundell details in Macarthur Papers, M.L. A2963, vol. 67 and A4240; Plaistowe's report in *Shipping Gazette*, 15 March 1845, pp. 75-6.
26 Towns uncat. MSS, set 307, Towns to Brooks 12 August 1847.
27 Towns uncat. MSS, set 307, Towns to Throsby, 31 July 1846.
28 Towns uncat. MSS, set 307, Towns to Mackay & Co., 22 June 1846.
29 *Shipping Gazette*, 23 January 1847, p. 358; Wyndham, Early History of the Thoroughbred, pp. 159, 169, 177.
30 *Shipping Gazette*, 11 September 1847, p. 600.
31 AACo Desps, 78/1/17, King to Dirs, 26 December 1844, p. 1119; 16 December 1845, pp. 517-18; 22 June 1846, pp. 684-9; 78/1/20, Blane to Dirs, 25 June 1851, pp. 183-4.
32 AACo Desps, 78/1/20, Blane to Dirs, 26 September 1851, p. 246.
33 AACo Desps, Blane to Dirs, 14 November 1851.
34 AACo Desps, 7 August 1852 & encls, pp. 614-16.
35 AACo Desps, Report of Committee of Consn, pp. 4-5, 63-9; 36th Report, p. 10.
36 Towns uncat. MSS, set 307, Towns to Mackay, 22 May 1849, p. 36; 7 January 1851. p. 212; other letters, pp. 198-215.

5 India and the Great Remount Debate 1846–1873

1 Anglesey, *History of British Cavalry*, vol. 1, p. 183.
2 Charles Trench, *The Frontier Scouts*, London, 1985, p. 2.
3 Lumsden and Elsmie, *Lumsden of the Guides*, pp. 58-9.
4 Ibid., p. 66.

⁵ Elliott, *The Frontier*, pp. 151, 156.
⁶ Lumsden and Elsmie, *Lumsden of the Guides*, pp. 79-80.
⁷ Ibid., p. 302.
⁸ *History of British Cavalry*, vol. 2, p. 125.
⁹ Lumsden and Elsmie, *Lumsden of the Guides*, p. 302.
¹⁰ Anglesey, *History of British Cavalry*, vol. 2, pp. 242-5.
¹¹ Ibid., pp. 101-2.
¹² I.O.L., Board's Colln, F/4/2441.
¹³ I.O.L., Board's Colln, F/4/2441, enclosed in Grant's report 29 July 1847.
¹⁴ I.O.L., F/4/2441, letters of 23 February, 26 March 1847.
¹⁵ I.O.L., F/4/2441, 10 February 1847.
¹⁶ I.O.L., F/4/2241, Wheatley, 1 May 1847.
¹⁷ I.O.L., F/4/2241, Hurford, 1 May 1847.
¹⁸ I.O.L., L/Mil/7/9626, Report of the Stud Commission of 1851, Appendix.
¹⁹ Kennedy, Bullocks and Horses, vol. 2, note 24, p. 65.
²⁰ I.O.L., F/4/2241, Grant to Gilbert, 25 July 1845.
²¹ I.O.L., F/4/2441, Gough to Gilbert, 8 July 1846.
²² Bullocks and Horses, vol. 1, p. 327 and vol. 2, note 25, p. 65.
²³ I.O.L., F/4/2241, Angelo to Mil. Sec., 3 August 1846.
²⁴ I.O.L., F/4/2241, P. Grant's letter of 14 April 1847. See also Madras Desps, E/4/968.
²⁵ I.O.L., L/Mil/7/9626, Appendix, Report of C. A. Browne, 15 August 1851 to Gilbert; Draft Mil. Madras, E/4/976.
²⁶ I.O.L., Draft Mil. India, E/4/849.
²⁷ Gilbert's letter gave the annual allocation of 1200 remounts used by the Bengal army as follows: 200 to the 13 troops of horse artillery, 100 to the 12 troops of field batteries, 150 to the 3 regiments of dragoons, and 750 to the 10 regiments of light cavalry.
²⁸ I.O.L., L/Mil/7/9626, pp. 13-49.

6 The Waler's Fortunes 1851–1900

¹ I.O.L., Madras Draft Desps, E/4/982.
² I.O.L., L/Mil/7/11236.
³ I.O.L., Draft Mil. Desp., E/4/855.
⁴ I.O.L., L/Mil/7/11236.
⁵ I.O.L., L/Mil/7/11236, desp. of 18 October 1860.
⁶ I.O.L., L/Mil/7/11236, Appendix.
⁷ I.O.L., Draft Mil. Desps, E/4/855.
⁸ I.O.L., L/Mil/7/11236; R. Therry, *Reminiscences*, Sydney, 1974 edn, pp. 402-3.
⁹ *S.M.H.*, 16, 24 September 1857, 25 January 1859; Argus, 10 March 1858, quoting Empire.
¹⁰ Summed up in E. Perry's 'Memorandum on the Govt Studs of India', 5 March 1873, in H. of C., *P.P.*, 1874, vol. 48, paper 69.
¹¹ I.O.L., L/Mil/7/9627.
¹² The Perry Memorandum included the following table

Establishment of Horses in India

	British Troops	Native Troops	Total
Bengal	6 380	9 564	15 944
Madras	2 082	794	2 876
Bombay	1 537	3 541	5 078
Total	9 999	13 899	23 898

¹³ I.O.L., L/Mil/7/9627, Part VI and appendix F of Report.
¹⁴ Perry memorandum, op. cit.
¹⁵ I.O.L., L/Mil/7/9627, Part VI.
¹⁶ I.O.L., L/Mil/7/9627; Argus, 16 October 1869; S.A., *P.P.*, 8 October 1869.
¹⁷ Copy of Thacker Report in S.A., *P.P.*, Paper 25, 1875.
¹⁸ For the effect of the new prosperity, see Hallen's memo of 22 March 1888 in L/Mil/7/9641, p. 4.
¹⁹ *Bell's Life in Sydney*, 26 June, 18 September 1858.
²⁰ I.O.L., L/Mil/7/9627.
²¹ I.O.L., L/Mil/7/9673.
²² I.O.L., L/Mil/7/9641, Desp. to I.O., 1 January 1889; F. Smith, *History of the Royal Army Veterinary Corps*, London, 1927, p. 194.
²³ I.O.L., L/Mil/7/9673, Minute by E. H. Collen, p. 6.

24 Ibid., pp. 6-7.
25 I.O.L., L/Mil/17/S/1687-4, pp. 1194-7.
26 Ibid., p. 1204.
27 I.O.L., L/Mil/7/9641, Hallen's memo of 22 March 1888, pp. 3, 4.
28 I.O.L., L/Mil/7/11268, Watson to Undersec., 7 April 1896.

7 Ships, Shippers and Shipping

1 *S.M.H.*, 9 November 1850.
2 Vanrenen Collection, La Trobe Library, Adrian to Henry, 15 May 1885, encl. biographical notes; de la Ferte, *A Notable Record*, Preface.
3 *A.D.B.*, vol. 3, pp. 509-10; Blake, *B.I. Centenary*, pp. 117-18.
4 Blake, *B.I. Centenary*, ch. 6; Jones, *Two Centuries of Overseas Trading*, ch. 5; B.I.S.N. Archives, Nat. Mar. Mus., BIS/7/57, 1892-93 file on competition for Australian trade.
5 Vanrenen Collection, Chamberlain to Vanrenen, 31 August, 29 September 1873, Henry's replies, 16, 30 September 1873.
6 Vanrenen Collection, Martin to Vanrenen, 4 December 1873.
7 Ibid., letters by Adrian of 20 November 1874, Andrew Martin, 5 November 1874; *Colonial Clippers*, pp. 256-7.
8 'Veterinary Notes on a Horse Ship Bound for India', *c.* 1895, p. 523.
9 I.O.L., L/Mil/7/11268.
10 'Veterinary Notes', p. 531.
11 Aust. Arch., CP 624/1, Bundle 13.
12 'Veterinary Notes', p. 538.
13 *Among Men and Horses*, pp. 43, 193-5.
14 William Hegarty, unpublished autobiography, courtesy Mrs Joan Burch, pp. 1-12, 101, 124.
15 Ibid., pp. 128-9.
16 Ibid., pp. 32-53.
17 Ibid., p. 53.

8 Walers in India at Work and Play

1 *Indian Memories*, pp. 30-1.
2 *New South Wales Sporting Magazine*, 1848, pp. 18, 29, 78-9; for Scott, see *A.D.B.*, vol. 2, pp. 428-9.
3 *Sporting Magazine*, p. 20.
4 Ibid., pp. 24, 73-6; *Shipping Gazette*, 1 July 1848, p. 159.
5 *Sporting Magazine*, pp. 64-5.
6 Wyndham, *Early History of the Thoroughbred*, p. 159; *Shipping Gazette*, 22 March 1845, p. 83.
7 *Early History of the Thoroughbred*, pp. 177-8.
8 Ibid., p. 177; Gene Makim, 'The Waler Lives On', *Land Magazine*, 1 September 1988, p. 9.
9 Wyndham, *Early History of the Thoroughbred*, pp. 173-8; Hayes, *Among Men and Horses*, p. 231.
10 J. C. Galstaun, *Racing Reminiscences*, Calcutta, 1942, pp. 20-1.
11 Hayes, *Indian Racing Reminiscences*, pp. 196-9.
12 Hayes, *Guide to Training*, pp. 3-6; Khan, *Racing Reminiscences*, p. 92.
13 Hayes, *Guide to Training*, 5th edn, p. 138.
14 *Among Men and Horses*, pp. 196, 199.
15 Ibid., p. 198.
16 Ibid., p. 199.
17 *My Early Life*, pp. 117, 120.
18 Ibid., p. 134.
19 Curzon, *Leaves from a Viceroy's Note-book*, quoted in NSW Polo Association, *Countess of Dudley Cup Tournament*, pp. 4-6.
20 Stanley Reed, *The India I Knew 1897-1947*, London, 1952, pp. 18-19, 141.
21 *Memoirs*, p. 4.
22 Ibid., p. 12.
23 Interview with Bob Skene, 15 May 1984; NSW Polo Association, op. cit., pp. 12, 34.
24 *Indian Memories*, p. 34.
25 *My Indian Journal*, Edinburgh, 1864, p. 326.
26 Ibid., p. 327.
27 Letter, Gray to author, 22 June 1989; *Oriental Sporting Magazine*, December 1874; Cornish, *Letters and Sketches*, pp. 378-80, 384, 411-13.

[28] Letter, Edward-Collins to author, 6 October 1988.

[29] Letter, Alexander to author, 28 December 1988.

[30] Ibid.

[31] Massey's notes, enclosed in letter, Gray to author, 5 November 1988.

[32] Letter, Glover to author, 20 October 1988, enclosing letter from Gray, 17 October 1988.

[33] Ibid.

[34] 'From Sunset to Sunrise', vol. 29, 1939, pp. 245-60, courtesy Keith Adam.

[35] Ardern Beaman, 'A Cavalry Officer's Experiences on the Indian Frontier during the War,' *Cavalry Journal*, vol. 28, 1938, pp. 298-341.

[36] Ibid., pp. 335-6.

[37] Letter, Walker to author, 27 June 1984.

9   Waler Exports

[1] Rica Erickson, *Old Toodyay and Newcastle*, Toodyay, W.A., 1974, pp. 75-6.

[2] Kennedy, Bullocks and Horses, vol. 2, App. H.; de Burgh, *The Old North Road*, pp. 29-33.

[3] de Burgh, loc. cit.

[4] Kennedy, loc. cit.

[5] *Inquirer*, 10 March, 3 November 1858; Arrivals and Departures, Fremantle, Battye Library.

[6] Kennedy, Bullocks and Horses, vol. 2, App. J; *Inquirer*, 4 July 1862.

[7] Perth *Herald*, 26 October 1872; *Inquirer*, 19 March 1873.

[8] Prinsep Diaries, Battye Library, 1869-70; Rica Erickson, (ed.) *Bicentennial Dictionary of Western Australia*, vol. III, Nedlands, W.A., 1988, p. 2537.

[9] New Norcia Arch, letters from Calcutta 28 February, 28 March, 17 April, 23 May 1877.

[10] New Norcia Arch, Cingalese file, 1878-79.

[11] See also E. J. Underwood, *Trace Elements in Human and Animal Nutrition*, New York, 1971; de Burgh, *The Old North Road*, p. 33.

[12] Kennedy, Bullocks and Horses, vol. 2, note 161, p. 72; *W.A. Govt Gazette*, 8 November 1881, p. 348.

[13] *Wanderings in Western Australia*, p. 125.

[14] See App. 3; R. T. Appleyard, 'Economic and demographic growth', in C. T. Stannage, (ed.) *A New History of Western Australia*, pp. 218-19. Aust. Arch. (Vic) Def. Dept, (1) Accession No. B168 File 1902/795; Circular 10 March 1902 and reply.

[15] McInnes, 'The Two Companions, "Sapphire" and "Marina"', pp. 27-33; Mr McInnes kindly lent a copy of the British Parliamentary Paper, 'Papers relative to the affairs of Queensland', 1861, dealing with the wrecks.

[16] Glen Lewis, *A History of the Ports of Queensland*, St Lucia, 1973, pp. 44-5, chs 4-6.

[17] Vanrenen Collection, Henry's letters of 1903-04; Lewis, op. cit., p. 156.

[18] Kennedy, Bullocks and Horses, vol. 2, App. K.

[19] For Murray-Prior see *A.D.B.*, vol. 5, p. 323; *Australasian Pastoralists' Review*, 15 November 1892, p. 844, 15 December 1892, p. 962; Rouse in M.L. Pamphlets 042, p. 85.

[20] *A.D.B.*, vol. 5, pp. 436-7; Q., *P.P.*, 1903, pp. 21-2.

[21] Q., *P.P.*, 1903, pp. 1-3.

[22] *Queenslander*, 29 October, 5 November 1904.

[23] Naples letters from Java in 1895, from Bombay 26 April, 12 May 1905, courtesy J. Anderson of Geelong.

[24] Q., *V & P*, 1901, vol. 4; 1902, vol. 3.

[25] *Queenslander*, 26 August 1905; Q.S.A., AGS/N57; Q., *V. & P.*, Reports on Agriculture & Stock, 1904-10, giving statistics and commentary; Q.S.A., AGS/N334 for corresp. with Manila.

[26] *Queenslander*, 24 December 1910.

[27] Q.S.A., AGS/N 334, incl. the 1900 Report and corresp. with Governor Chelmsford.

[28] *Queenslander*, 30 April 1910.

[29] Brisbane *Sunday Mail*, 8 January 1939; H. J. Fox, *History of Queensland*, Brisbane, n.d., vol. 2, pp. 782-5; Yarwood, 'From Sheep Station to State Stable', pp. 302-3, referring to the King George V diaries with kind permission of Her Majesty the Queen.

[30] Anne Allingham's MS. for *A.D.B.*; obituaries in *S.M.H.*, 30 November 1933, *Queenslander*, 7 December 1933; his will, courtesy Qld Trustees, Townsville; interviews with Cosmo Gordon and Jack McLean in Mackay, and in Townsville with Harry Creen, Jim Burnett, Perry Hardy and John Brabon, in June and July 1986.

[31] Statistics from *Commonwealth Year Books*, 1934, 1939.

[32] *The Hentys*, p. 535.

[33] A. J. Dunlop, *Wodonga: over river and plain*, Melbourne, 1976, pp. 68-9.

[34] The distribution of the 1 620 420 horses in Australia in 1901 was:

NSW	Qld	Vic	SA	WA	Tas
486 716	462 119	387 277	178 199	73 710	32 399

[35] *A.D.B.*, vol. 9, pp. 583-5; Bowen, *Kidman*.

[36] Letter, Colquhoun to author, 5 July 1984.

[37] *Heritage*, Spring 1987.

[38] *Australian Stock Horse Journal*, April-May 1988, p. 8.

10 The Waler at War

[1] P. Stanley (ed.), *But Little Glory*, Canberra, 1985; NSW Arch., 4/853; M. Barrett, *King of Galong Castle*, Sydney, 1978.

[2] L. M. Field, *The Forgotten War*, Melbourne, 1979, Apps c, d; R. L. Wallace, *The Australians at the Boer War*, Canberra, 1976, p. 237.

[3] Bridges, New South Wales and the Anglo-Boer War, p. 744; W. R. Truman, Report on the work of the Remount Dept, 30 March 1903, P.R.O. War Office, 33/271, App. G.

[4] F. Smith, *A Veterinary History of the War in South Africa 1899–1902*, London, 1912, p. vii.

[5] Truman, Report on Remount Department, App. G.

[6] Ibid., p. 9.

[7] Smith, *Veterinary History*, pp. 14, vii; Col. Bayley, quoted in *Sydney Stock and Station Journal*, 21 February 1902.

[8] General French, quoted in Field, *The Forgotten War*, p. 116.

[9] Deane, quoted in Bridges, New South Wales and the Anglo-Boer War, ch. 3, note 14; Elliott, 'Report on Australian Horses', P.R.O. War Office, 33/242, 75057, p. 13.

[10] Evidence of Gen. Knox, Col. Rawlinson in 'Report on Australian Horses', P.R.O., War Office, 33/242, 75057, pp. 13-14.

[11] Bridges, New South Wales and the Anglo-Boer War, p. 744.

[12] Aust. Arch. (Vic) Def. Dept, (1) Accession No. B168 File 1902/795; Circular 10 March 1902, and abstract of replies; Bridges, New South Wales and the Anglo-Boer War, p. 751.

[13] Replies to circular, 10 March 1902, Dangar to Barton, 17 March 1902, encl. extract dated 19 March.

[14] Replies to circular, Clarke to Barton, 26 March 1902.

[15] Replies to circular, Rouse to Barton, 5 April 1902; White in *Sydney Stock and Station Journal*, 14 March 1902.

[16] Replies to circular, Goodwin to Barton, 14 March 1902.

[17] First conference of horse breeders, *Agricultural Gazette of New South Wales*, vol. XII, November 1901, pp. 1426-33.

[18] Copy in author's possession, courtesy of the late F. B. Haydon of Bloomfield, Murrurundi. The letter incorrectly refers to the 12th and 14th regiments; the 12th and 4th regiments carried out the charge.

[19] 'Beersheba. The light horse charge and the making of myths', *Journal of the Australian War Memorial*, no. 3, October 1983, pp. 26-37.

[20] 'The Australian Remount Unit in Egypt', p. 14.

[21] Aust. Arch. (ACT) CRS A2 Item 14/4179; Kent, 'The Australian Remount Unit in Egypt', p. 10.

[22] Gullett, *The A.I.F. in Sinai and Palestine*, pp. 60-1, 104.

[23] Ibid., p. 222.

[24] Hill, *Chauvel of the Light Horse*, p. 84; Haydon Corresp., 21 September 1916, 2, 14 January 1917.

[25] Gullett, *The A.I.F. in Sinai and Palestine*, pp. 268-9.

[26] Hill, *Chauvel of the Light Horse*, pp. 178-81.

[27] Ibid., note p. 195.

11 The End of the Indian Remount Trade

[1] Bond, *British Military Policy*, pp. 63-71, 160, 174.

[2] Ibid., p. 66.

[3] *The Memoirs of Captain Liddel Hart*, p. 244.

[4] I.O.L., Indian Army Remount Department Reports for 1929-30, 1937-38; the wartime figures are given in the 1925-26 Report.

[5] I.O.L., L/Mil/7/9706, Ministry of Reconstruction to I.O., 13 February 1918, quoting question and Lloyd George's reply.

[6] Brooke, *Good Company*, pp. 221-3; Kent, 'The Australian Remount Unit in Egypt', p. 14; 'The Tragedy of the Old War Horse in Egypt', pamphlet in L/Mil/7/9691.

[7] I.O.L., L/Mil/7/9706.

[8] I.O.L., L/Mil/7/9705.

[9] I.O.L., Remount Dept Report for 1925-26, pp. 2-3; L/Mil/17/S/1793, An assessment of military needs and capabilities, *c*. 1930, pp. 3-4.

[10] An assessment of military needs and capabilities, pp. 6, 11.

[11] Ibid., pp. 7, 6.

[12] Aust. Arch. (ACT) A1194, Scott Report, Item GB 499/1/560, p. 2.

[13] Ibid., p. 9.

[14] Anderson, Report by Director of Remounts, India 1930, pp. 22-3.

[15] Scott Report, op. cit., pp. 11-12; Murray-Smith interview, tape in author's possession.

[16] Anderson Report, op. cit., pp. 41, 7-8, 38, 46, 17-18.

[17] I.O.L., L/Mil/7/9691.

[18] Scott Report, op. cit, p. 4.

Epilogue

[1] *Sun-Herald* (Sydney), 26 July 1987.

[2] Journal kept by Marnie Hamersley, 18-26 April 1986.

[3] Letter, Brigadier John Paley to author, 20 February 1989.

Bibliography

This select bibliography comprises those sources of which substantial use was made in the research for this book. Its arrangement is as follows:
  Archival Sources
  Manuscript Collections, Public and Private
  Published Primary Sources
  Private Journals
  Newspapers and Periodicals
  Books and Journal Articles
  Theses and Unpublished Manuscripts

Archival Sources

Archives of Business and Labour (Australian National University)
Australian Archives (Canberra and Melbourne)
India Office Library (London)
National Army Museum (London)
New Norcia Archives (Benedictine Mission, Western Australia)
New South Wales State Archives
Queensland State Archives
Royal Library, Windsor Castle

Bibliography

Manuscript Collections

Public Libraries

At the Mitchell Library, Sydney, I used the Berry, Betts, Bettington, Macarthur, Scott, and Towns papers.
La Trobe Library, the Vanrenen Collection
Oxley Library, Leslie Letters
Battye Library, Prinsep Papers

Private Libraries

C. V. de Falbe Papers (U.K.)
F. B. Haydon Papers, Bloomfield, Murrurundi
J. S. Love Papers, Queensland Trustees, Townsville
White Papers, Belltrees, Scone

Published Primary Sources

Historical Records of Australia
House of Commons, *Parliamentary Papers*
Queensland, *Votes and Proceedings*
South Australia, *Parliamentary Papers*
Agricultural Gazette of New South Wales
Queensland Agricultural Journal

Private Journals

Marnie Hamersley, journey on *Buffalo Express* to Singapore, 1986
Henry Prinsep, journey to Calcutta in 1870
Henry Polman Vanrenen, journey in the *Udston* to Calcutta, 1874

Newspapers and Periodicals

Argus (scattered references, 1855–1901)
Australasian (scattered references, 1870s–1890s)
Australasian Pastoralists' Review (1892–1929)
Australasian Sketcher (scattered references, 1870–84)
Bell's Life in Sydney (1850–60)
Herald, Perth (1872)
Illustrated Australian News (scattered references, 1880s)
Inquirer, Perth (1845–75)
Kapunda Herald (1904–07)
New South Wales Shipping Gazette (1840–50)
Perth Gazette (1872)
Queenslander (scattered references, 1899–1912)
Sydney Morning Herald (scattered references, 1832–1940)
Sydney Stock and Station Journal (1900–04)
Town and Country Journal, Sydney (1873–80)

Books and Journal Articles

Addington, R. A. 'Remounting of the Madras Cavalry in the days of the Company Bahadur', *Cavalry Journal*, vol. 19, 1929, pp. 580–8.

Alder, Garry. *Beyond Bokhara. The Life of William Moorcroft Asian Explorer and Pioneer Veterinary Surgeon 1767–1825*. London, 1985.

Anglesey, Marquess of. *A History of the British Cavalry*. 4 vols. London, 1972–85.

Australian Dictionary of Biography. 11 vols. Melbourne, 1966–.

Bach, John. *A Maritime History of Australia*. Melbourne, 1976.

Baden-Powell, Robert. *Indian Memories. Recollections of Soldiering, Sport etc.* London, 1915.

Barlow, Glyn. *The Story of Madras*. London, 1921.

Barrie, Douglas M. *The Australian Bloodhorse*. Sydney, 1956.

Bassett, Marnie. *The Hentys*. London, 1954.

Blake, George. *B.I. Centenary 1856–1956*. London, 1956.

Bond, Brian. *British Military Policy between the Two World Wars*. Oxford, 1980.

Bowen, Jill. *Kidman. The Forgotten King*. Sydney, 1987.

Brooke, Geoffrey. *Good Company*. London, 1954.

Bruce, Alex. 'Our Saddle Horses: what they were; what they are now; what brought about the deterioration; and how their superiority can be restored', *Agricultural Gazette of New South Wales*, vol. XII, December 1901.

Calcutta Port Trust. *A Brief History of Fifty Years' Work*. Calcutta, 1920.

Calcutta 200 Years. A Tollygunge Club Perspective. Calcutta, 1981.

Churchill, Winston S. *My Early Life A Roving Commission*. London, 1930.

Cornish, Francis T. Warre. *Letters and Sketches 1884–1901*. Eton, 1902.

Curr, E. M. *Pure Saddle-Horses, and How to Breed Them in Australia*. Melbourne, 1863.

de Burgh, W. J. *The Old North Road*. Perth, 1986.

de la Ferte, E. Joubert. *A Notable record. Some account of the many families descended . . . from Daniel Van Reenen*. London, 1926.

Denison, William. *Varieties of Vice-Regal Life*. 2 vols. London, 1870.

Elliott, J. G. *The Frontier 1839–1947. The Story of the North-West Frontier of India*. London, 1968.

Farwell, Bryon. *Queen Victoria's Little Wars*. London, 1973.

Fortescue, John. *Narrative of the Visit to India of their majesties King George V and Queen Mary and of the Coronation Durbar held at Delhi 12th December 1911*. London, 1912.

French, E. G. *Good-bye to Boot and Saddle or the Tragic Passing of British Cavalry*. London, 1951.

Galvayne, J. C. *Racing Reminiscences*. Calcutta, 1942.

Gilbey, Walter. *Horse-breeding in England and India and Army Horses Abroad*. London, 1901.

Graham, R. B. *Military Report on the Arrangements for the Coronation Durbar held at Delhi in December 1911*, Calcutta. 1913.

Grimshaw, Anne. *The Horse: a bibliography of British books 1851–1976*. London, 1982.

Gullett, Henry S. *The Australian Imperial Force in Sinai and Palestine, 1914–18*. St Lucia, Qld, 1984.

Gutsche, Thelma. *There was a Man. The Life and Times of Sir Arnold Theiler KCMG of Onderstepoort*. Cape Town, 1979.

Hardinge, Viscount. *My Indian Years 1910–1916*. London, 1948.

Hart, Basil. *The Memoirs of Captain Liddel Hart*. 2 vols. London, 1965.

Hayes, M. Horace. *Among Men and Horses*. London, 1894.

——. *A Guide to Training & Horse Management in India*. Calcutta, 1875.

——. *Indian Racing Reminiscences*. Calcutta, 1883.

Hill, A. J. *Chauvel of the Light Horse. A Biography of General Sir Harry Chauvel, G.C.M.G., K.C.B.* Melbourne, 1978.

Hodson, George (ed.). *Hodson of Hodson's Horse*. London, 1889.

Ismay, General the Lord. *Memoirs*. London, 1960.

Jackson, Donovan. *India's Army*. London, 1940.

Jones, Stephanie. *Two Centuries of Overseas Trading. The Origins and Growth of the Inchcape Group*. London, 1986.

Kent, David. 'The Australian Remount Unit in Egypt, 1915–19', *Journal of the Australian War Memorial*, no. 1, October 1982, pp. 9–15.

Khan, Jaffer. *Racing Reminiscences and Hints on Training*. Calcutta, 1897.

Lubbock, Basil. *The Colonial Clippers*. Glasgow, 1921.

Lumsden, Peter and Elsmie, George. *Lumsden of the Guides*. London, 1900.

McInnes, Allan. 'The two companions, "Sapphire" and "Marina"', *Royal Historical Society of Queensland Journal*, vol. 10, 1977, pp. 27–33.

——. 'Dangers and difficulties of the Torres Strait and Inner Route', *Royal Historical Society of Queensland Journal*, vol. 10, 1979, pp. 47–73.

Mason, Philip. *A Matter of Honour*. London, 1974.

Maxwell, Charlotte (ed.). *Frank Maxwell, Brigadier General, V.C., C.S.I., D.S.O. A Memoir and some letters*. London, 1921.

——. *I am ready*. London, 1955.

Millar, Anthony Kendall. *Plantaganet in South Africa. Lord Charles Somerset*. Cape Town, 1965.

[Mole, Edwin]. *A King's Hussar, being the military memoirs of twenty-five years of a troop-sergeant-major of the 14th (King's) Hussars, collected and condensed by Herbert Compton*. London, 1893.

Moorhouse, Geoffrey. *India Britannica*. London, 1983.

Nicolson, Harold. *King George the Fifth. His Life and Reign*. London, 1952.

Nolan, L. E. *Cavalry; its history and tactics*. London, 1853.

Paterson, A. B. 'Special article on horses in warfare', in J. C. Ridpath and E. S. Ellis. *The Story of South Africa*. 2 vols. Sydney, 1899.

Pilcher, T. D. *Some lessons from the Boer War*. London, 1903.

Rogers, H. C. B. *The Mounted Troops of the British Army*. London, 1946.

Sandhu, G. S. *The Indian Cavalry*. New Delhi, 1981.

Shadbolt, Sydney H. *The Afghan Campaigns of 1878–80*. London, 1882.

Shadwell, L. H. *North-west Frontier Warfare*. Calcutta, 1902.

Shakespear, Henry. *The Wild Sports of India*. London, 1860.

Taunton, Henry. *Wanderings in Western Australia and the Malay East*. London, 1903.

Temple, Richard. *India in 1880*. London, 1881.

Thompson, J. L. 'Horses for Indian and European Markets', *Agricultural Gazette of New South Wales*, vol. 5, October 1894.

Tylden, G. *Horses and Saddlery. An Account of the animals used by the British and Commonwealth Armies from the Seventeenth Century to the Present Day with a description of their Equipment*. London, 1980.

Waddy, Stacy (ed.). *T.K.S. at the Delhi Durbar 1911. Being the impressions of the Headmaster and a party of fourteen boys of The King's School, Parramatta, who had the good fortune to be present*. Parramatta, 1912.

Wurgraft, Lewis D. *The Imperial Imagination. Magic and Myth in Kipling's India*. Middletown, 1983.

Wyndham, H. A. *The Early History of the Thoroughbred Horse in South Africa*. London, 1924.

Yarwood, A. T. 'From Sheep Station to State Stable', *Country Life*, 24 July 1986, pp. 302–3.

———. 'The "Indian Business": The Origins of Horse Exports from Australia to India 1834–47', *Journal of the Royal Australian Historical Society*, vol. 73, June 1987, pp. 41–57.

Theses and Unpublished Manuscripts

Atchison, John. Port Stephens and Goonoo Goonoo. Ph.D. thesis, Australian National University, 1976.

Bridges, Barry. New South Wales and the Anglo-Boer War 1899–1902. D.Litt. & Phil. thesis, University of South Africa, 1981.

Hegarty, William. Unpublished autobiography, dealing with forty years in the horse trade, courtesy of his daughter, Mrs Joan Burch.

Hutton, E. T. H. 'Mounted Infantry and its action in Modern Warfare'. Paper given by Colonel Hutton, in National Army Museum.

Kennedy, Malcolm J. The Role and Significance of Bullocks and Horses in the Development of Eastern Australia. Ph.D. thesis, University of Melbourne, 1986.

Maxwell, Francis Aylmer. Diaries 1897–1917, National Army Museum, London.

Index

Text set in 10½ point Palatino
Of this edition 1250 copies have been printed